VOICES OF AMERICA

Ozark Pioneers

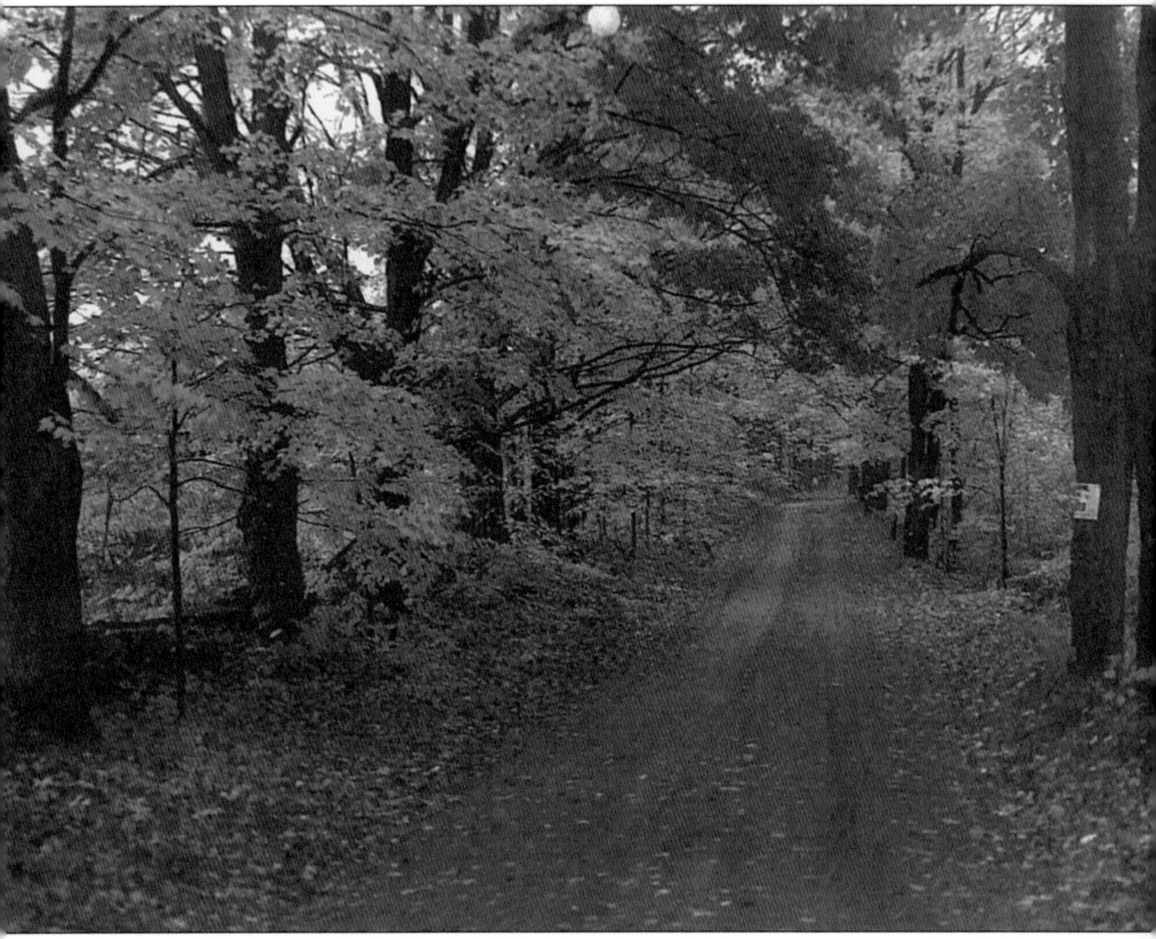

VOICES OF AMERICA

Ozark Pioneers

Compiled by
Vickie Layton Cobb

ARCADIA
PUBLISHING

ISBN 978-0-7385-1858-9

Published by Arcadia Publishing
Charleston, South Carolina

Printed in the United States of America

Library of Congress Catalog Card Number: 2001087677

For all general information contact Arcadia Publishing at:
Telephone 843-853-2070
Fax 843-853-0044
E-mail sales@arcadiapublishing.com
For customer service and orders:
Toll-Free 1-888-313-2665

Visit us on the Internet at www.arcadiapublishing.com

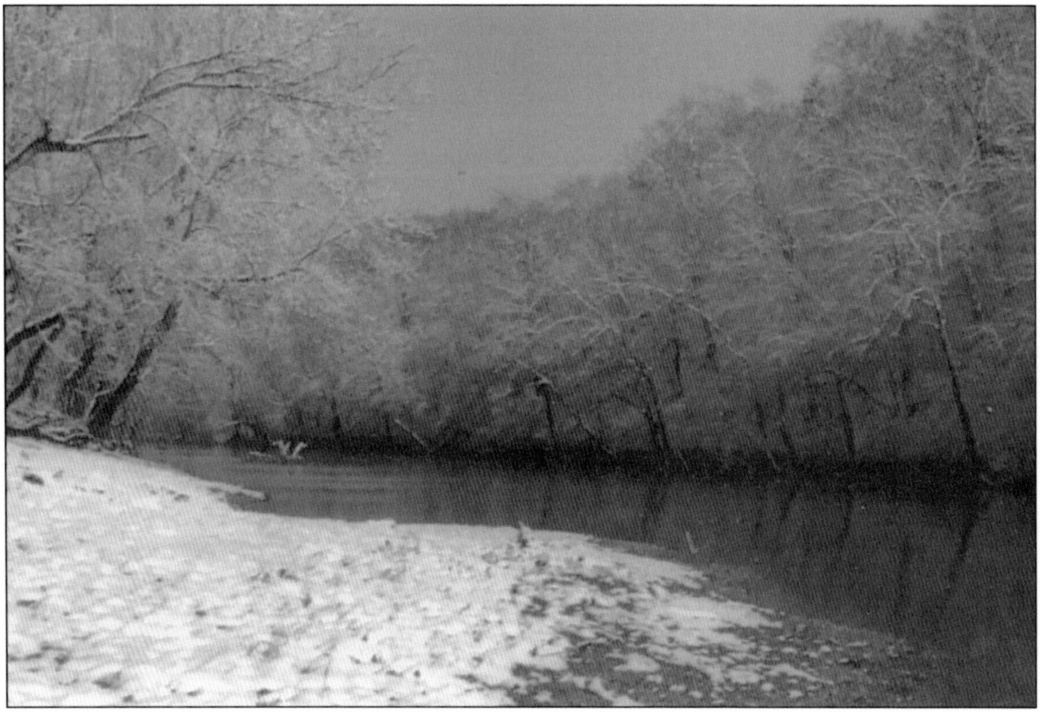

This is The Butler Hole, on James River, in Galena, Missouri.

CONTENTS

Meet the Author

I was born 1955 in Klamath Falls, Oregon. In 1961 my family moved to a farm in Ozark, Missouri, where I grew up and attended school. Several years after graduating from high school I attended Southwest Missouri State University in Springfield.

I began to write lyric poetry at an early age and was also interested in the "good old days." On Saturday mornings I would sit in Mom's kitchen and churn butter while I listened to May Kennedy McCord's radio program *Hillbilly Heartbeats* on KWTO. Her stories fascinated me. She would end her program with a promise to return next week, "the Lord willing," as she would say.

I was fortunate to have been born into this heritage. My Layton grandparents were born and grew up in Taney County. They both had good memories from their childhood and knew many stories handed down to them through older relatives. Grandpa talked about the old days continually. One day he mentioned that I should record the history they knew, and from then on, I did. My grandma helped me start my collection of old photographs by giving me copies or original ones she had. Then other relatives contributed stories and photographs.

No matter what happened in the early 1800s and on through the years, someone in my ancestry was involved. I love life in this area with its beautiful Ozark hills and other scenic views, especially its intriguing and colorful past. I often visit those places which belonged to my ancestors one hundred years ago. I love to go to the old family cemeteries and touch the stones which have stood for a century.

I've been able to collect various personal items which belonged to some of my ancestors. To hold these treasures in my hands makes the reality of their existence very real. Like the tiny pair of wire-rimmed glasses my great-great-grandma Whorton wore. I can visualize her seated in her rocking chair as she read from the Bible by the light of a kerosene lantern.

I am a charter member of the Ozarks Writers League which organized in the early 1980s. I have worked in factories and restaurants for 15 years. I wrote this book while on a kidney dialysis machine for six years prior to my kidney transplant. I'm thankful to have my writing as a hobby and pastime as I continue to write and photograph in the Ozarks.

I have traveled through 16 different states and lived in California and Indiana. I currently live in the historical community of Galena where the James River flows a quarter of a mile behind my home.

I sincerely hope you enjoy reading *Ozark Pioneers.* To write and publish this has been a dream of mine for ten years. I also wrote a second volume entitled *Fallen Leaves Volume II: A Visit to White River Country*. I regret my Layton grandparents didn't live to see this in print, but at least they sowed the seed, and now is the harvest.

Happy Trails,
Vickie Layton Cobb

INTRODUCTION

THE JOURNEY

The pioneers written about in this book loaded their wagons and left their homes and families in search of a new land of their visions. The journey was to take them into the vast Missouri-Arkansas wilderness.

They knew not of the dangers which lay ahead of them, or of the lives they would have and the hardships they would endure. In time, their faith brought them to the land they sacrificed much for.

Some journeyed thousands, and some traveled hundreds of miles. They faced obstacles which challenged their strength and determination. The natural forces of weather, swollen streams and rivers, unfamiliar mountains and valleys, Indians and outlaws in uncivilized territories, encounters with wild animals, and the uncertainty of sickness and death were frequent visitors.

When they crossed the final horizon, they unloaded their wagons and called it home. They broke soil unacquainted with the plow. They cleared timber which knew not the sound of the axe or cross-cut saw. They drank water from cool, clear, and unspoiled streams. They walked through blue stem grass that grew to the horses' shoulders.

They planted crops of wheat, corn, oats, potatoes, beans, turnips, and more. Neighbors helped each other build cabins and shelter for the farm animals. They encountered summer's heat and winter's cold. They prayed for rain when the streams ran dry. The droughts brought pestilence and their crops were destroyed.

Men were killed by Indians as they fought to protect their families. Children witnessed the death of a parent and sometimes the death of both. Children had to take on many responsibilities with the care and raising of those even younger than they. Many of the boys knew how to plow the fields at the tender age of nine. They became acquainted with hard work and it remained a part of their character throughout their lives.

The Civil War came with its glory and cruelty, touching the lives of all. The once beautiful wheat fields of gold soon ran red with the blood of men who so willingly gave their lives for the cause in which they believed. The fertile valleys, where cattle once grazed, lay full of dead men. Mothers, grandmothers, wives, and daughters walked the floors of their cabin homes night after night, while they anxiously waited for their men to return home.

The women who remained behind continued to work on their land, tending the cattle, hogs, sheep, mules, horses, chickens, and other animals. They had to be careful and aware of the bushwhackers that roamed the land. They would kill, steal, and destroy, taking all they could get their hands on.

Many of these women knew how to hide their meat in their ash hoppers and cover it with ashes. They would shell their corn and take it to the caves nearby where they hid it in barrels. They would go to the cave and retrieve the amount of corn needed at a time to make bread for the family.

They had to keep their money and other valuables hidden. The many caves that existed in the hills were a refuge for these women. Their young boys would hide their guns there. The women would bind together thus strengthening the character of all. No book could ever be written to fully describe the perilous time the Civil War bestowed on the women who fought battles of their own as they struggled to maintain the homesteads.

After the war ended the pioneers sought to rebuild that which had been destroyed. They looked to the God of heaven for strength to continue their journey to the sunset of life. Beyond all the calamities that befell, God sustained them through all their endeavors.

Even after the end of the war the bushwhackers still terrorized many of the pioneers. Then the organization of the Bald Knobber era came, and it too left its scar upon mankind. The pioneers were familiar with the many ways of lawlessness that plagued the land.

Yet through all these hard times, it was those who trusted God that held the land and its people together. It is to their names that honor is entrusted and their memory is kept alive.

They chose to journey to the land at the end of the road beyond the distant mountains.

Many leaves fell along the way. Yet the promise of eternity beckoned them on. So their journey took them on to the land where fallen leaves from God's tree of life rest forever at His throne.

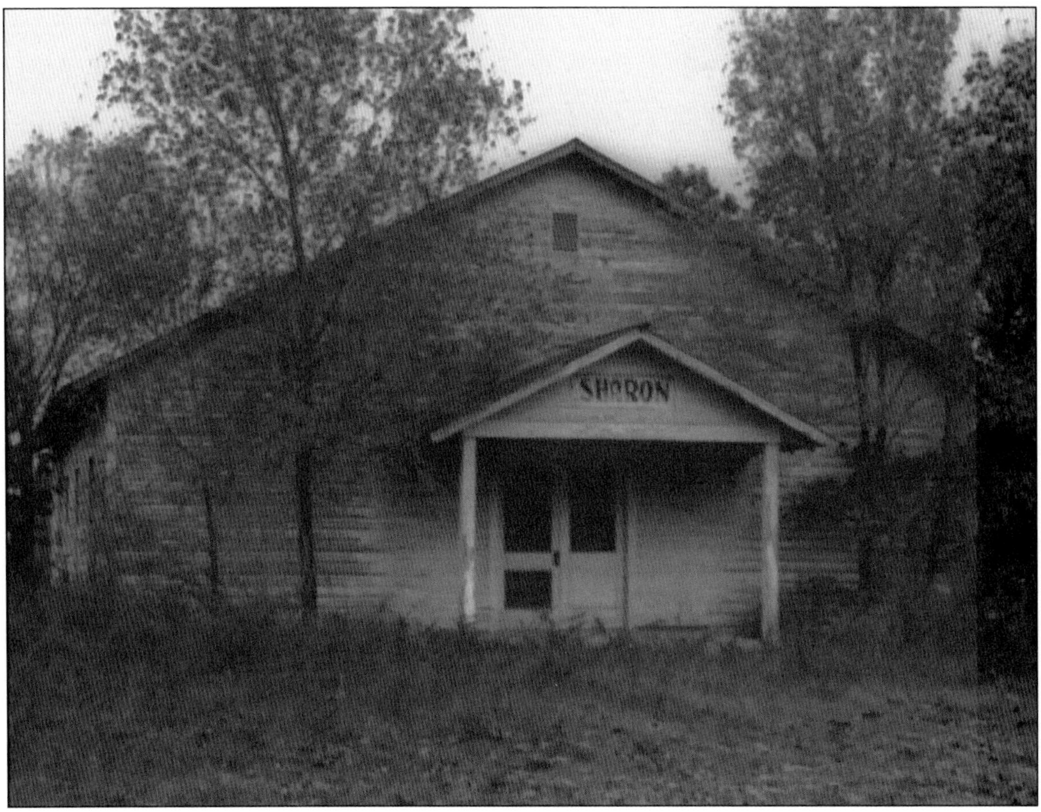

Sharon Church, located near Hunstville, Arkansas.

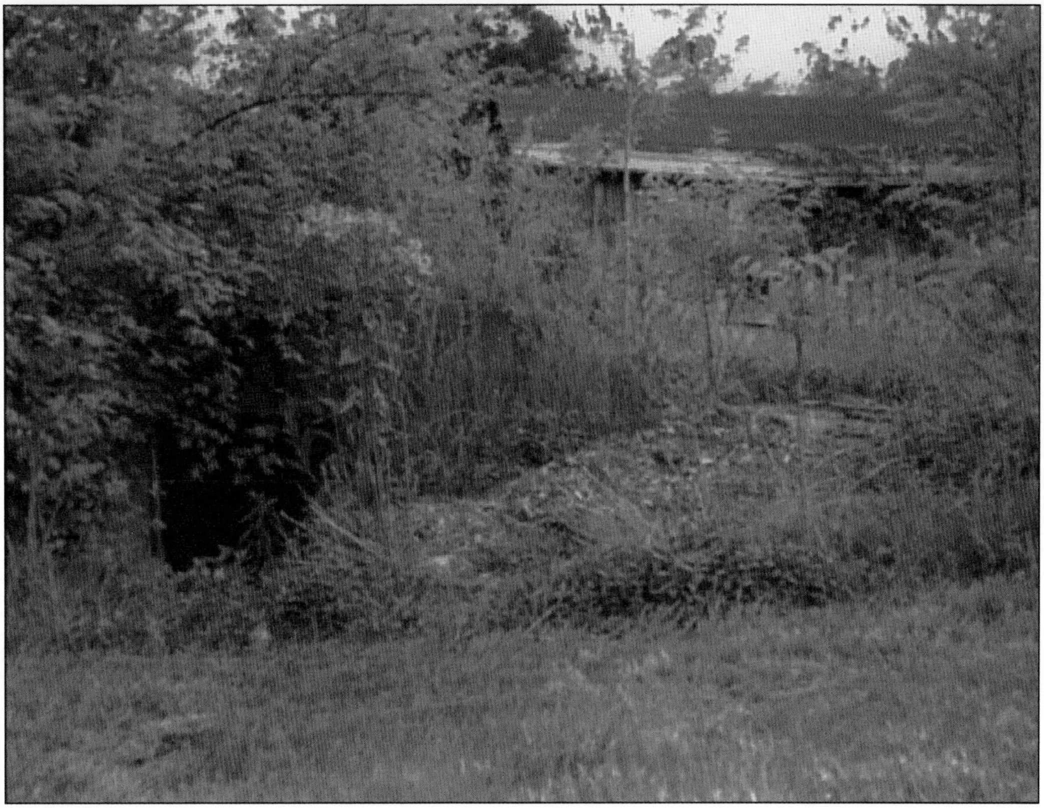

Hazel Layton Cobb's great-grandparents homestead just east of Branson, Missouri, on Highway 76.

Part One

The Allen and Coggburn Family

***Psalms** 78:39 For He remembereth that they were but flesh; a wind that passeth away and cometh not again.*

***Psalms** 89:48 What man is he that liveth, and shall not see death? Shall he deliver his soul from the hand of the grave?*

Samual and Rebecca Allen

In 1842, Samual and Rebecca sold their farm in Monroe County, Kentucky, keeping only a young team of mules, two cows, two mule colts, and various farm implements. Their covered wagon was practically new and Samual had made a new set of harnesses for his team of mules.

He built a 4-foot overjet for the top of the wagon box. Slats were put across this for the bed tick and quilts that Rebecca had made. This made a good comfortable place for their 11-year-old daughter Elizabeth Ann to ride, while Samual and Rebecca rode on the spring seat.

It was February 9 when Samual and Rebecca tied the two cows to the back of the wagon after loading the last of their possessions into place for the long journey to Missouri.

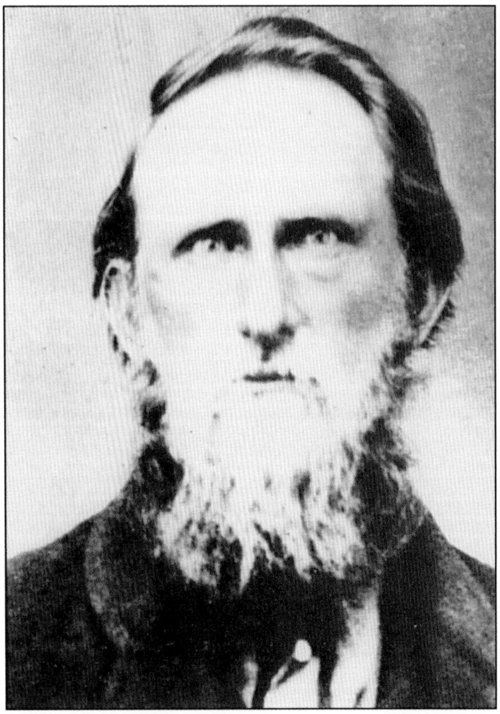

The author's maternal great-great-grandfather Samual Allen, 1802–1867.

Rebecca's wood cookstove was securely packed away within the wagon with the other essential items: food, clothing, tools, cooking utensils, and the old family trunk. Tucked away inside the trunk were items handed down to Rebecca from her parents and grandparents, along with a few yards of calico material, and the family Bible. Sugar was a delicacy for those who lived during their time. It was so precious that she kept it hidden in the trunk to be used only on special occasions.

There were three other families in covered wagons who were also leaving Monroe County to move to Missouri. So bidding farewell to life as they knew it, the band of wagons set forth on a journey to a new home west of the Mississippi.

The first few weeks of the journey went well with only a few minor problems to slow them down such as one broken wagon wheel and the loss of a horse when he stumbled into a ground hog hole and broke his leg. Thus, the horse had to be shot.

One of the families had with them an older woman, who was the grandmother of the man. One night on the trail as they were camped beneath the stars in the chilly night air, the older woman took ill and passed away before daylight.

That morning the men carefully cut down a large tree nearby. They cut a slab off one side and hollowed the trunk as if it were to be a dugout canoe. They placed the elderly woman's body within it, covered her with one of her own quilts, and then carefully laid the slab back and nailed it down. They dug a grave, placed the makeshift casket within, read a few scriptures from the Bible, said a few words of farewell, and prayed. They flattened the grave after they had filled it with dirt and drove back and forth over it with the wagons, so that the Indians wandering in the area wouldn't be able to tell someone was buried there.

After confronting the loss of a loved one the tiny band of travelers once again resumed their journey to the land of "milk and honey." They made their way over mountains where bears and other wild animals were plentiful. Always the excitement and anticipation of homesteading the Missouri frontier lightened their sorrows, and the wagons moved steadily along.

Near the end of April the wagons reached the land of their visions. They split up and went their separate ways as each family had a different area in mind in which they wanted to homestead. Samual and Rebecca headed toward Miller County and arrived about two weeks later.

They chose a beautiful piece of land with lots of timber and a creek flowing nearby. They were soon busy building a small but comfortable one-room log cabin about a quarter of a mile from the stream. When that was finished they began clearing brush from one area to plant spring garden crops, raising their own supply of needed foot items such as potatoes, corn, wheat, tomatoes, and squash. Rebecca had carefully packed seeds for those vegetables before they left Kentucky.

For the Allen family, their new life in Missouri got started and things went very well for them. The crops did well, and the animals stayed fat and healthy. Several other children were born in the years that followed. Other homesteaders soon settled nearby and everyone enjoyed helping their neighbors.

Then one tragic day in 1846 while Rebecca was standing over the fireplace brewing some soup for a sick child, lightning came down the chimney and struck and killed her instantly. The family did mourn their loss. This left Samual with several small children to raise without the help of his wife, but the oldest daughter Elizabeth soon filled the shoes the death of her mother had left vacant. A few years after the death of Rebecca, Samual met and married a woman whose name is not known.

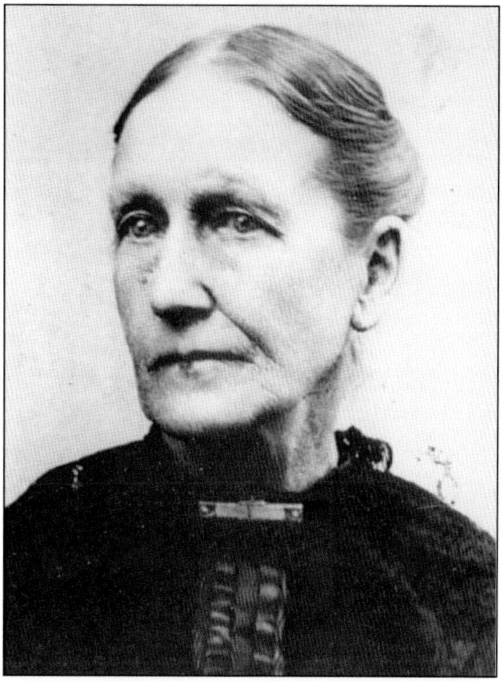

The author's maternal great-great-grandmother, Rebecca Allen, 1805–1846.

Elizabeth Ann Allen Coggburn

Elizabeth Ann Allen was born November 4, 1831, in Monroe County, Kentucky. She came to Missouri with her family when she was 11 years old.

Elizabeth grew up on the homestead in Miller County, Missouri. She married a neighbor boy, John Shell Coggburn, on November 11, 1852, when she was 21 years old. They attended the same school earlier and their family farms joined each other. Shortly after their marriage John and Elizabeth left their family homes to journey to Taney County, Missouri, where they settled 1-mile north of Kirbyville. Today, although there are very few of the "old-timers" left, the land is still referred to as the old Coggburn place, although it is almost within a subdivision of Branson now. John and Elizabeth raised 11 children there.

The Coggburn family was one of the first families to settle in this area and were very well known throughout the community. Elizabeth was known for being a devoted servant to the Lord. It was a common sight to see her rejoicing at local baptisms, walking along the river bank shouting "hallelujah" and "victory in Jesus." She was also good at singing the old time hymns and she held the

Bible and its teachings to be quite sacred.

Elizabeth and John enjoyed attending church services with their children and taking basket lunches with them when baptisms were to be held following services. The beautiful singing of the local people could be heard from afar, and many enjoyed the simplicity of dinner on the grounds by the banks of the White River.

Elizabeth would always wear her best dress for such occasions and dress the children up too. She believed this was part of honoring the Lord on such sacred traditions. She often wore her fine, high-buttoned black shoes and stockings, with a flowered calico dress extending a couple of inches above her ankles. The neck and sleeves of her dress were ruffled and she wore her Sunday bonnet of white with a red rose from her garden pinned on it. She would ride her little gray mare Daisy on the side saddle that her father had given her when she was a young girl. It had a lovely flowered seat of material similar to the texture of carpet.

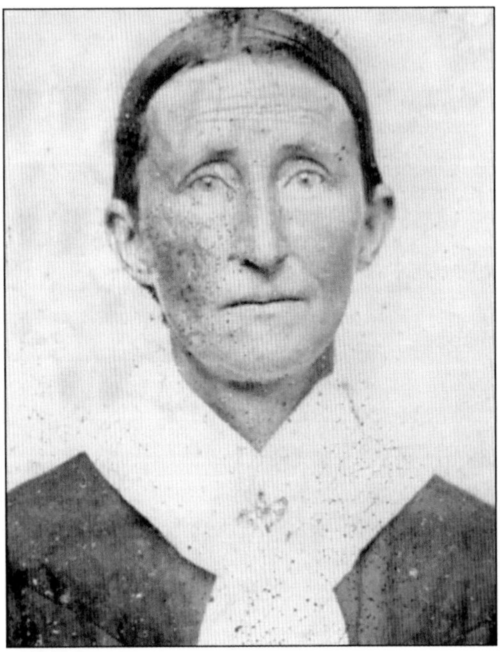

Elizabeth Ann Allen Coggburn, the author's maternal great-great-grandmother, age 20.

And oh, how Elizabeth did enjoy riding Daisy.

Over the years the children grew up and one by one married and began families of their own. The Civil War era began in the 1850s, and like all families in the area, the Coggburns felt the brutal hand of war touch their lives. Two of their elder sons found their young lives entangled within the web of war that separated the northern states from the southern.

After the war had ended and their lives settled once again, John passed away on February 9, 1868, leaving Elizabeth with one son, Thomas Jefferson Coggburn. After John's death Tom never left his mother. His devoted love for her was touching and beautiful. It was a familiar sight to see them on Sundays going to church or going to visit a neighbor. Even at the age of 81 years, Elizabeth would ride a little mare with the grace and smile of a young girl.

Those years passed pleasantly for Elizabeth and Tom. He tended to the livestock and farming while his mother cared for her chickens and made butter that always found a ready sale. Tom made weekly trips to the village of Kirbyville, carrying with him a basket of eggs to trade at the small country store never demurring at loosing time, as some good men are wont to do. Eggs were 6¢ a dozen, and 10¢ would buy Elizabeth enough material to make a new dress. The lace, trimming, and thread were just a few cents more. She would spend the next day or two measuring and cutting a dress to sew by hand. She also made shirts for Tom and bought him ready made overalls.

In Elizabeth's little attacks of sickness, Tom cared for her tenderly, never leaving her side for a moment. But one day there was a tragic accident, which left Tom burned over most of his body. His mind went blank and he poured kerosene on himself, then lit a match. As the flames engulfed him, his mother ran to him, broke the ice from the top of the water barrel, dipped out a bucket of cold water, and threw it on Tom, putting out the flames.

After this terrible experience, there wasn't much one could do for Tom to ease his pain.

But he was surrounded by his family as he lay on his death bed. Then on Sunday morning, March 10, 1912 at 3:00 a.m., Tom drew his last breath.

Thinking of all these things, his honest, upright, useful life, unmarred by the stain of evil, one wonders why he should have been taken in such a manner. Many hearts went out to his bereaved relatives, his heart-broken and aged mother. Yet one had the understanding that "He doeth all things well. And in His own good time, His strange and dark ways shall be revealed unto us." Elizabeth was comforted in knowing that her son was prepared to meet the Lord, and that he left an honorable name. All who knew Tom were proud to remember him as a friend and neighbor. Tom was laid beneath the sod of the Vanzandt Cemetery at Kirbyville.

Following Tom's death, Elizabeth left the old Coggburn place that had been her home for 60 years, and went to live out her remaining days with her daughter, Mary Elizabeth Coggburn Smith, the wife of Tom Smith. She remained with them for 11 years. Elizabeth was confined to her bed for nine weeks before she died on July 22, 1923. She was 91 years, 8 months, and 18 days old. While she lay on her death bed she spoke often about dying, saying she was ready to meet her Savior.

John Shell and Elizabeth Coggburn had 11 children, 49 grandchildren, and 93 great-grandchildren. Elizabeth attended the Presbyterian church for 59 years, living a devoted Christian life to the end. She too was laid to rest in the Vanzandt Cemetery with the Rev. Ivy Brown conducting the funeral service. The following poem was written to her memory by one of her lifelong friends and neighbors:

We miss thee from our home dear one
We miss thee from thy place
A shadow o'er our life is cast
We miss the sunshine of thy face
We miss thy kind and loving hand
Thy fond and earnest care
Our home is dark without thee
We miss thee, everywhere.

In Memory of Thomas Jefferson Coggburn

The tombstone that bears the name Thomas Jefferson Coggburn is the only remembrance of this young man. No photograph of him could be found. Tom was different from most men his age; he was rather quiet, and a home body. He always lived at home with his parents. Then when his father died he took care of his mother until his own tragic death.

During his life he enjoyed working on the family farm, tending to his cattle, the mules, the horses, the pigs, and the land from which he grew crops. He was a loner, minded his own business, kept to himself, and didn't indulge in the things the world had to offer away from home. He was content with the simple things of life, the fruit of his labor was his compensation. He never traveled away from home, never left the land of Taney County, the land on which he was born.

He enjoyed rebuilding old harness equipment he used on the farm and also some of the neighbors'. He was a good hand at anything pertaining to leather. He could raise a beautiful garden of vegetables and made many trips to the local store in Kirbyville with his goods, which sold easily.

Tom was born February 2, 1875, and died March 10, 1912, at the age of 37. He never married. His stone stands quietly in the Vanzandt Cemetery nestled off Highway J near Kirbyville, Missouri, and near the old Coggburn home place that was his home for the duration of his short life.

Kern and Rebecca Ann Coggburn McNalley

Rebecca Ann Coggburn was born May 23, 1854, and died September 20, 1882. Her parents were John and Elizabeth Coggburn. She married Kern McNalley and they left Kirbyville to move closer to the Arkansas line.

They homesteaded a piece of land and

became farmers. They spent many hours working side by side clearing timber and brush from the land to make a field large enough to plant their spring crops to sustain them through the winter months. Kern was a small man but very stout for his stature and he worked hard.

Shortly after the first year of their marriage they had their first child. At this time Kern was working off and on with his brother-in-law, Tom Smith, who managed a freight crew and wagons. So there were times when Kern would be gone from home for a week at a time to make the trip from Kirbyville to Springfield taking a load there and bringing a load back.

Not afraid to be by herself, Rebecca went about her work as she could. Not long after the child had been born she returned to the fields to work in the corn. She carried the baby with her, and laid it on a pallet close to where she worked. Every few minutes she would gaze cautiously at the small bundle lying beneath the shade of the oak tree to make sure it was safe.

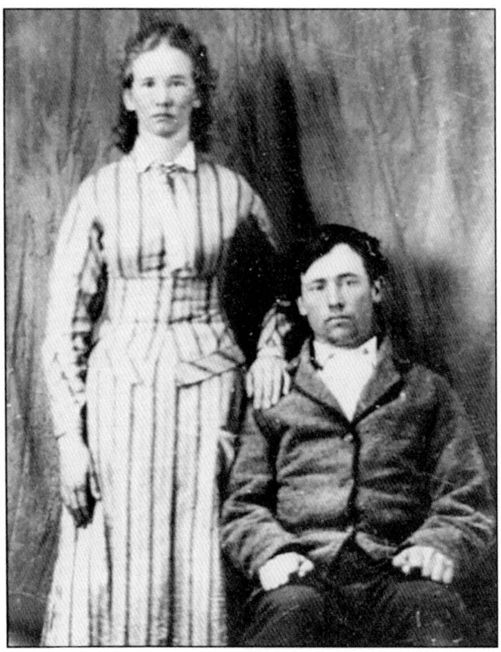

Mary Elizabeth Coggsburn (Smith), age 16 with brother-in-law, Kern McNalley.

One day she wiped the sweat from her brow and stopped long enough from her work to glance at the child. She heard the sound of something slip through the brush nearby. She became leery of the sound and moved the baby closer to her, thinking the animal would become frightened and go away. But it didn't. She caught the glimpse of a panther making its way close to her and the child.

Thinking quickly, she grabbed the sickle she was working with and ran toward the large cat screaming as loud as she could. Luckily, it scared the panther away. She picked up her baby and returned to the cabin, and didn't go back to the field until her husband returned from his trip.

When Kern returned home Rebecca told him what had happened. He took a rifle from above the fireplace and spent the next couple of days teaching her how to use it. She got to be a pretty good shot and from then on she never left the cabin without it.

A short time after that first sighting of the panther it returned to the field while she worked. This time Kern was with her and as he held the baby he let Rebecca use her new rifle skills. As the panther came toward them, screaming its blood-chilling scream, Rebecca quickly took aim and fired! The big cat lay dead.

According to the stone which stands in the Vanzandt Cemetery, Kern was known by the name of Col. McNalley. He was born January 22, 1857, and died May 20, 1883. They both died when they were young adults. According to family history they were killed by bushwhackers who roamed along the Missouri-Arkansas line following the Civil War.

Andrew Coggburn

One of the most active opponents of the Bald Knobbers was young Andrew Coggburn, who lived not far from the Oak Grove church and school house where Nat N. Kinney, known as Captain Kinney, presided over his famous Sunday school class. It seems that young Coggburn had been mercilessly beaten for some trifling offense, and had made wild threats against the night riders.

Coggburn and another young fellow, Sam Snapp, had concealed themselves near a Bald Knobber hideout and had seen some of the secret ritualistic work; later on they exposed those secrets with loud laughter at a crossroads store. Coggburn imitated the "old blue gobbler," a derisive nickname for Captain Kinney. Somebody had sent Kinney a miniature coffin whittled out of cedar, containing a bullet and a threatening note. Kinney believed that Coggburn was responsible. Worst of all, Coggburn had made up some doggerel verses, which he sang to the tune of "My Name is Charles Guiteau." This song is still remembered by a few of the old-timers in Taney County:

Adieu to old Kirbyville, I can no longer stay,
Hard times and Bald Knobbers have driven me away,
Hard times and Bald Knobbers has caused me to roam,
My name is Andrew Coggburn, near Kirbyville's my home.

My friends and relations, it's much against my will
To leave my dear old mother and go from Kirbyville,
But for the sake of dear ones, who wants for me to go,
I'll arm myself with weapons, and I'm off to Mexico.

Bald Knobbers are no gentlemen, they're nothing more than hogs,
They tried to hunt me, down, boys, and treat me like a dog,
With all their guns and horses they tried to hunt me down,
And treat me like the Taylor boys, who now lay in the ground.

There's one big Bald Knobber who is a noted rogue,
He stole from Joseph Bookout some sixteen head of hogs,
Walked boldly in the courthouse and swore they was his own,
He stole them by the droves boys, and horsed them over home.

There is another Bald Knobber who rides a pony blue,
He robbed old Nell MacCully and Mister Tompson too,
He took from them their money, boys, and from them rode away,
And now the highway robbers are the big men of the day.

There is one big black rascal whose name I will expose,
His name is Nat. N. Kinney and he wears his federal clothes,
He tried to boss the people and make them do his will,
There's some that do not fear him, but others mind him still.

To raise a Bald Knobber excitement I made a splendid hand,
I don't fear judge or jury, I don't fear any man,
If the Knobbers want to try me, they've nothing else to do,
I'll take my old Colt's patent and make an opening through.

These Knobbers run the country, but they can't keep it up,
They'll stick their tales between their legs like any other pup,
And there's a day a-coming, boys, when they'll hunt their dens,
And if I'm not mistaken, there's some will find their ends.

The Anti-Bald Knobbers sang this song with glee, and made so much noise that somebody swore out a warrant for young Coggburn's arrest on a charge of "disturbing the peace." Captain Kinney had himself deputized by the sheriff, and the warrant was placed in his hands. Kinney smiled, and said that he would try to arrest Coggburn at the first opportunity. But everybody knew that young Coggburn would never surrender to

Kinney, and that someone would be killed.

One night early in March of 1886, Captain Kinney walked up the path to attend a meeting at the Oak Grove school house. A crowd was already there, and several men were standing in front of the building. Just what happened then is a question, but there is no doubt that Kinney fired one shot, and young Andrew Coggburn lay dying on the ground.

Most of the men present were Bald Knobbers. They carried benches out of the school house, arranged them in a circle around Coggburn's body, and forced the crowd to stand back until the Coroner and the Sheriff arrived. A few hours later there were more than two hundred armed Bald Knobbers on the scene.

When the county officers arrived they found Coggburn dead, with his revolver beside him; some say that it was held in his right hand. Coggburn's friends had left believing that their lives were in danger, which was probably true. The Bald Knobbers swore that Kinney had tried to arrest Coggburn, but Coggburn had drawn his pistol, and Kinney had been forced to kill him in self-defense. Coggburn's friends and relatives assembled in force and were on their way to Oak Grove, but they were persuaded to stay away until after the inquest. The Coroner's jury exonerated Kinney, after which Coggburn's friends were allowed to take the boy's body home for burial.

The Anti-Bald Knobbers raised a great cry about the "cold-blooded murder" of young Coggburn. They claimed that Kinney had shot Coggburn down without warning, and that the cocked revolver had been placed in Coggburn's hand after his death. Sam Snapp, Coggburn's friend, who was with him at the time of the shooting, did not appear at the inquest, and the authorities said that "Snapp could not be found."

The Anti-Bald Knobbers forces alleged that Snapp had been driven away by the Bald Knobbers and threatened with instant death if he attempted to testify before the Coroner's jury.

Even if Kinney did shoot Coggburn down without warning, there can be no doubt that Coggburn was armed, though perhaps the pistol was in his belt instead of his hand, as the Bald Knobbers testified. But Coggburn surely knew that Kinney had a warrant for his arrest, and that Kinney would kill him at the first opportunity. There was, therefore, a certain measure of fair play about the Kinney-Coggburn affair—an element altogether lacking in other killings with which the outlaw leader was credited.

Even the most violent anti-Kinney people had to admit that Coggburn was a grown man and that he carried a pistol. The killing of Coggburn was much less reprehensible than the cowardly murder of the unarmed Taylor boys, or the numerous outrages against women and children for which Kinney and his followers were responsible.

Not long after the Coggburn killing, there was a near-hanging by the Bald Knobbers which the Anti-Bald Knobbers believed was linked to Coggburn's death. They made such a fuss over it that finally a delegation was sent to Jefferson City, asking Governor Marmaduke to send troops to southern Missouri. He said he would look into the matter, but he refused to authorize any action by the militia.

Of all the men who were waiting for a chance to kill Kinney, young Sam Snapp seemed most likely to do the job. Snapp, the friend of Andrew Coggburn, had seen the Coggburn killing, although he wasn't allowed to testify at the inquest.

It appears that the outlaws decided that Snapp had to be eliminated, and Wash Middleton was selected to attend to the matter. On May 9, 1886, Middleton met Snapp in front of the little store in Kirbyville. "Middleton drew his pistol and commenced firing," says the Springfield Newspaper account of the crime. Snapp held up his hand and cried "Don't!"

The first shot broke Snapp's arm, a second bullet entered his left side, and a third one entered his back as he turned. He fell dead immediately. This was described by witnesses as a cold blooded murder. Snapp apparently made no effort to draw a weapon, and some of the by-standers said he was unarmed except for a knife in the pocket of his overalls.

Andrew Coggburn was a cousin to this author's great-grandmother, Mary Elizabeth Coggburn Smith. He had a sister named Sarelda, who married a McClary. The author's grandmother, Ethel Smith Layton told the following concerning young Andrew Coggburn:

"Andrew was a nervous fella, he always seemed restless and had to be on the move doing something. He did have a good sense of humor and could make people laugh to forget their troubles. He liked to handle guns and would practice his marksmanship when by himself, or show off in front of friends. He spent a lot of time running up and down the country roads on horseback, continuously wanting to know what was going on in the community, what people were doing and the like.

"There was a strangeness about him no one ever quite understood. He was a good-hearted boy, but perhaps it was just the ghost of his destiny in life that haunted him. Maybe that was what made him think he could stand up against Capt. Kinney and come out the winner. Little did he know that which he challenged would overpower and destroy him. Perhaps he was running too fast with his life and ended out getting lost within it."

The mystery that surrounds young Andrew Coggburn will never be known. One can only speculate on the reason he challenged a man more powerful than himself. Maybe he had some realization of the role in history he was fulfilling.

Andrew was about 18 years old when he was killed. According to family information he is buried in the Vanzandt Cemetery. However, no marker on his grave could be found.

According to a conversation this author had with Cecil McClary in February 1989, Andrew Coggburn apparently provoked the situation with Kinney which led to his death. Coggburn saw Kinney coming up the road to the Oak Grove church house and walked out towards him and hollered, "Hey Kinney ________," and added some sarcastic remark. So it seems in one sense, Coggburn more or less dared Kinney into the violent confrontation which made him pay such a high price for his foolish actions.

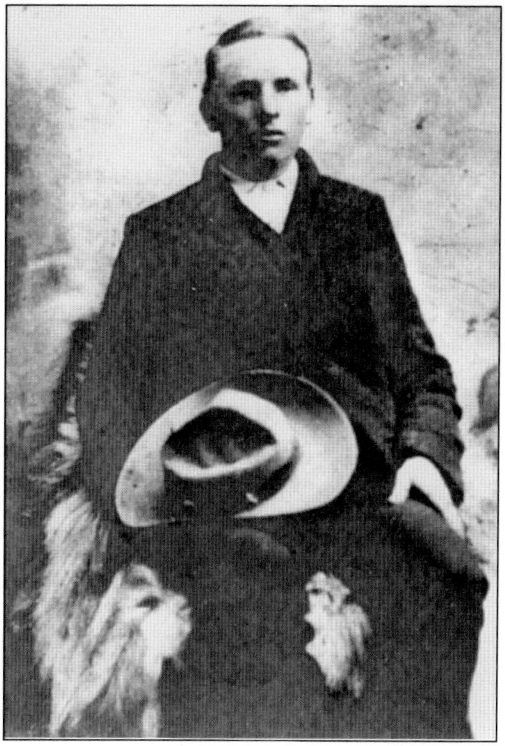

Young Andrew Coggburn is pictured shortly before his death, about 18 years old.

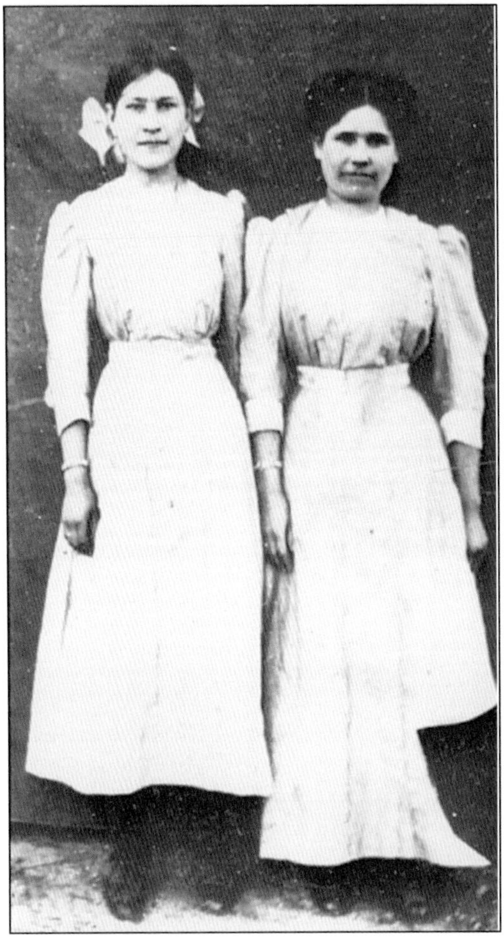

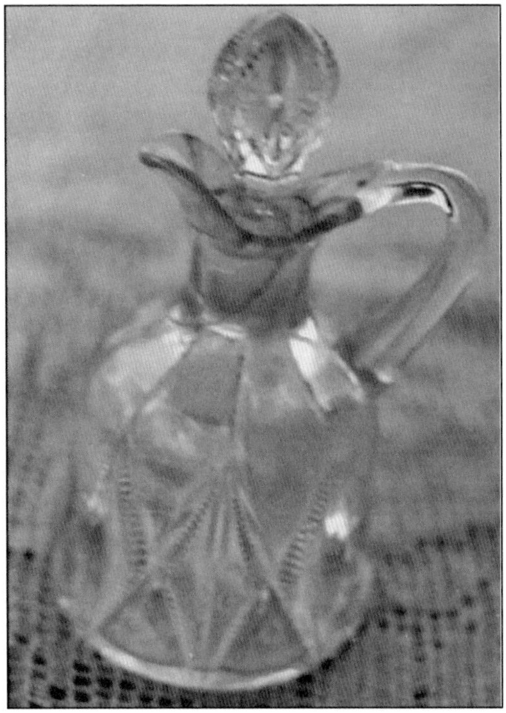

The cast iron skillet, thimble, strand of buttons, and vinegar bottle once belonged to Elizabeth Ann Allen Coggburn. They are over one-hundred years old and have remained in the family. The two girls are Becca and Sally Coggburn. No information is known about them except they were cousins of Andrew Coggburn and Ethel Smith Layton.

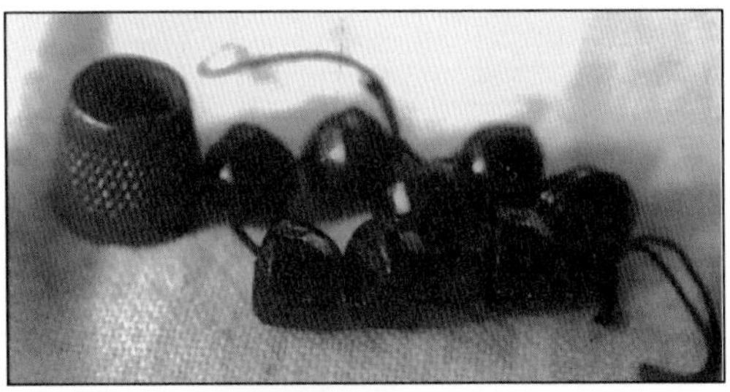

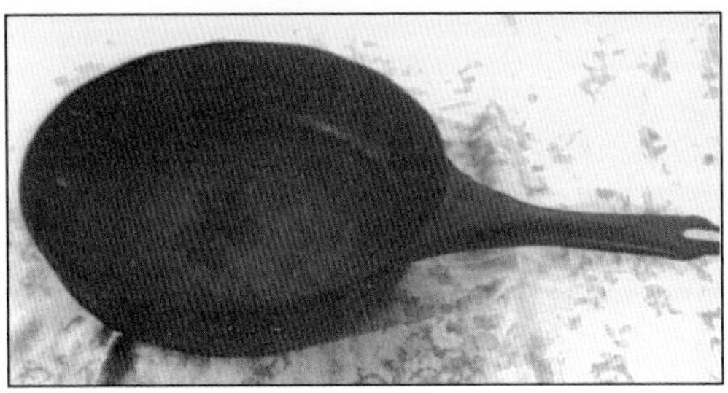

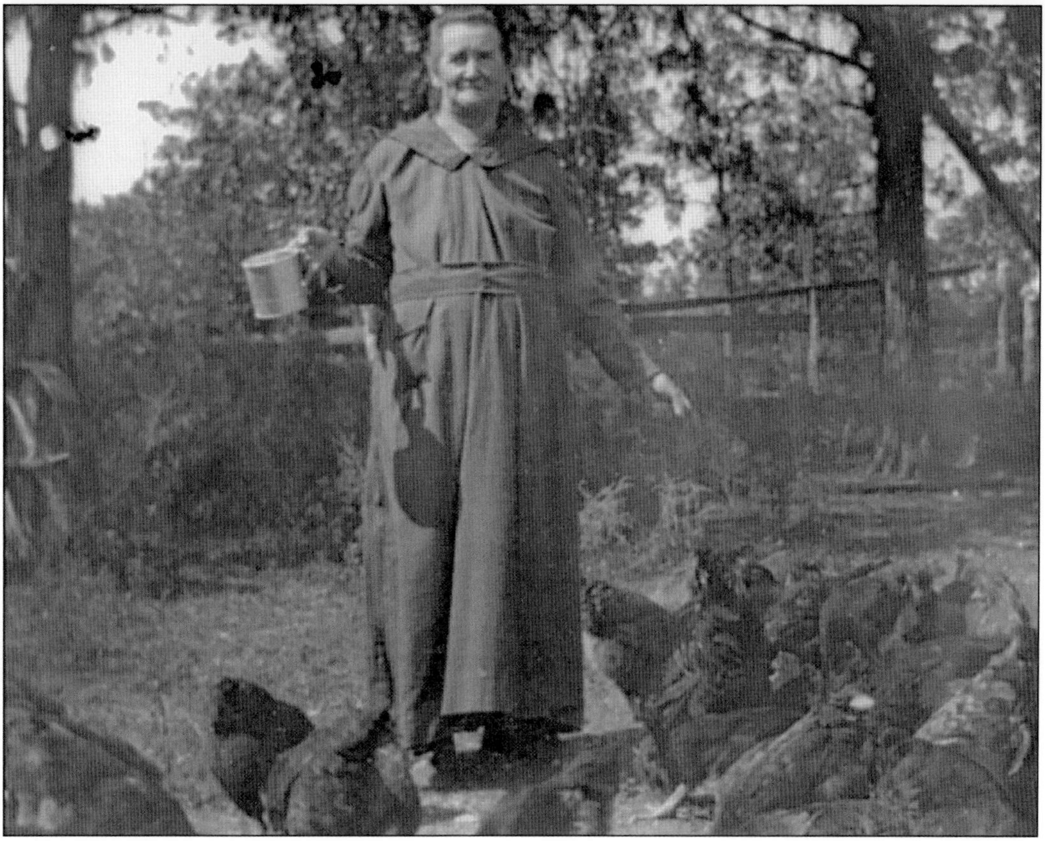

Mary Smith feeding her chickens.

PART TWO

THE SMITH FAMILY

Psalms 103:14-16 *For He knoweth our frame; He remembereth that we are dust; As for man, his days are as grass; as a flower of the field, so he flourisheth. For the wind passeth over it, and it is gone; and the place thereof shall know it no more.*

The Smiths Come to Taney County

Peter and Nancy Smith left their home in Georgia in 1870 to search for new land. They packed their belongings in an ox-drawn wagon and brought a couple of milk cows, horses, and pigs. As they started their journey, the children helped to keep the livestock moving steadily behind the wagon. Their destination was what is now Taney County, Missouri.

After a long and tiresome three month journey they finally reached Kirbyville. They immediately went about the task of building a beautiful log cabin with a huge stone chimney. The spring that flowed nearby soon became known by the "Smith" name.

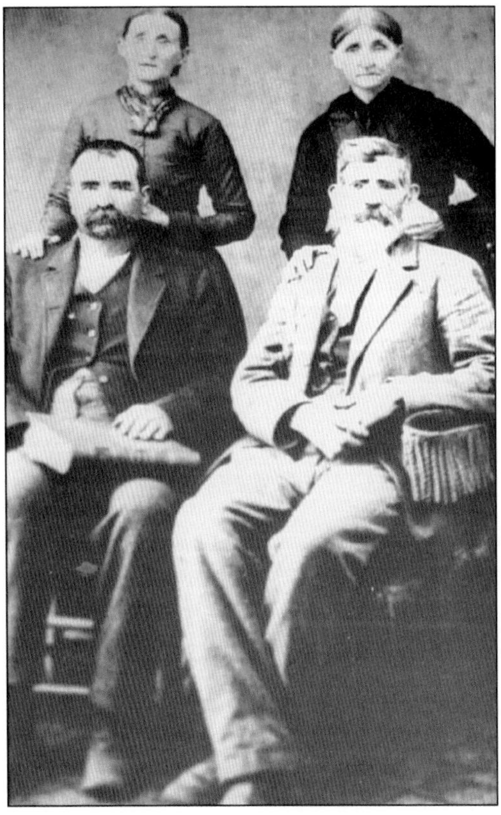

Peter and Nancy Smith with John Shell and Elizabeth Ann Allen Coggburn. John; 1829-February 21, 1901.

Nancy was a full-blooded Cherokee Indian. She was a good hand to sew, piece quilts, and weave baskets from the wild buckbrush that flourished among the timber. Nancy knew many ways to live a self-contained life. She even brought a few hens with her from Georgia, keeping the eggs buried in salt, a layer at a time, in a stone jar. This was the only method she had to keep the eggs fresh.

She also kept a batch of "starter dough" for making light bread which was buried in flour so it wouldn't dry out. The dough was brought back to life by pouring warm potato water over it 24 hours before it was to be used. Flour, salt, sugar, or honey was added to it before the 'kneading process" was done. Nancy would let it rise, knead it down again, then let it rise one more time before she baked it in loaves.

A piece of dough about the size of a cup was always saved for the next time she needed to bake bread. This small piece was buried in the flour tin. Many times a neighbor would come in need of some "starter dough." Nancy would pinch off enough to start a batch for them, but she always kept enough back for her own use.

Peter Smith was a kind and generous man, always ready to help his neighbors in need. He believed in the laws of God and lived it by his willing readiness to help others. His gentle smile was proof of the honest and sincere heart within him. The sparkle in his eyes was a mirror of the peace that overwhelmed him. He cared for his ox-team and the other stock, as he planted in one season and reaped in another consistently from year to year.

Mary Elizabeth Mahnkey of Mincy had known the Smith family for many years as they lived a short distance apart. After the death of Peter, Mary had the following to say about her neighbor whom she admired and respected:

"In the latter years of life, Uncle Peter Smith was almost blind. One of the sweet memories of youth that make the past a book of lovely pages to turn to, was when

Uncle Peter would come to town and our kind Postmaster, Uncle Sol Linzy, would read aloud to him. They sat on the long, cool porch of the little building that housed both the Post Office and the Postmaster's family. The Postmaster had a rich, resonant voice, that sounded musically throughout the quiet little village and some would say, "Uncle Peter has come to town."

Tom and Mary Coggbrun Smith

The Peter and Nancy Smith homestead in Kirbyville joined the "Old Coggburn" homestead of John and Elizabeth. The Coggburn's daughter, Mary Elizabeth, and the Smith's son, Thomas Jefferson, grew up together in the small community. While children, they worked side by side each other in the fields while their parents worked together. Then on December 25, 1886, Tom and Mary were united in marriage. In the years that followed six children were born to them.

Tom Smith was a man who worked hard from daylight to sundown. He had a deep, soft spoken voice and would sing in the evenings when his work was done and the family sat around the fireplace of their home. He had a mustache and always wore a dark colored hat. He didn't indulge in drinking the homemade brew that existed in the hills. But he did like homegrown tobacco.

He was a good father, always trying to teach his children good manners so they would grow up to be respectable citizens. He enjoyed reading the Bible in the evenings by a kerosene lantern as he sat relaxed in his cane-bottom chair. He never failed to give thanks to the Lord for blessing the crops he planted to feed his family and livestock. He was a good hand at carpentry work and as a farmer.

Mary Elizabeth Mahnkey had this to say about Tom Smith: "Thomas Jefferson Smith was one of the last of the old-time 'freighters.' No one knew mules as well as he. No one was more faithful in the care and custody of huge

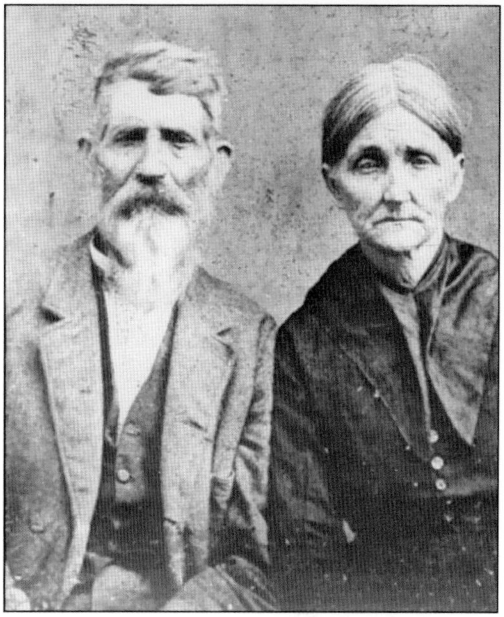

The author's maternal great-great-grand-parents; Peter Smith, June 18, 1830–January 13. 1903. Nancy Cancada Ward Smith, December 25,–1831-July 27, 1912.

loads of valuable merchandise, when it took six days to make a round trip from Kirbyville to Springfield by way of the old Springfield-Harrison road. With a load of produce going up and coming back the average was 2000 pounds. The pay was 50¢ a hundred pound and took in the store!'"

Doug Mahnkey of Kirbyville said this about Tom after his death: "Uncle Tom Smith is dead. I shall miss him very much, for all my life there has been Tom Smith, quiet, hardworking, thrifty, kind, honest, Tom Smith; a pioneer from Georgia, I believe, and I am very sorry to say I did not talk more to him about the old days of Taney County, Missouri."

"One conversation I shall not forget. We were talking of the early days and he told me how, as a boy, he would go with his father, Peter Smith, from the homestead near Kirbyville far across the hills to the old 'Oasis Mill.' It was not known as Oasis then, but as Cedar Valley. They drove oxen and the trip was a long and hard one. They camped two or three nights on the round trip. The hills were covered with luxuriant blue stem grass. At noon the oxen were allowed to graze. The children would pull enough grass to feed them when camp was made.

"I remarked that those must have been mighty hard times to live, and how much better off we are today with fine highways, cars, and trucks. But Uncle Tom Smith shook his white head and said, 'Son, that was the finest time this country ever seen, and I just wish I knew where I could find another country like that. Why! (and his eyes lit up) doggone if I wouldn't start for it in the morning."

That was the true spirit of Uncle Tom Smith. Not afraid of hardships nor dangers, nor long days and rough roads. But meeting the trails in the true American spirit, full of confidence, loving freedom, and the quiet peace that we younger generation have never known, and I fear, never shall.

"Yes, Uncle Tom Smith is dead. I hope St. Peter has a great, wide out-of-doors for him where the hills are covered with blue stem grass; with a great canopy of blue sky over it, for there Uncle Tom Smith will find perfect peace."

Ethel Smith Layton spoke frequently about her dad. One thing she mentioned particularly was every morning without fail when she was a child, he would get up before daylight and build a fire in the wood cookstove. He would take the coffee grinder from its shelf, measure out enough coffee beans for the morning coffee and grind them. He would set the coffee pot on the wood cookstove and before long the house smelled of the fresh brewed coffee.

His wife, Mary Coggburn Smith, doctored their six children and often times a neighbor's child. She used many home remedies handed down to her from her parents. For chest colds she would have Tom kill a skunk, skin it, and she would fry the fat in a skillet. Then she would rub it generously on the children's chest. For coughs she gave them a teaspoon of kerosene and sugar.

Flaxseed poultices were used for infections

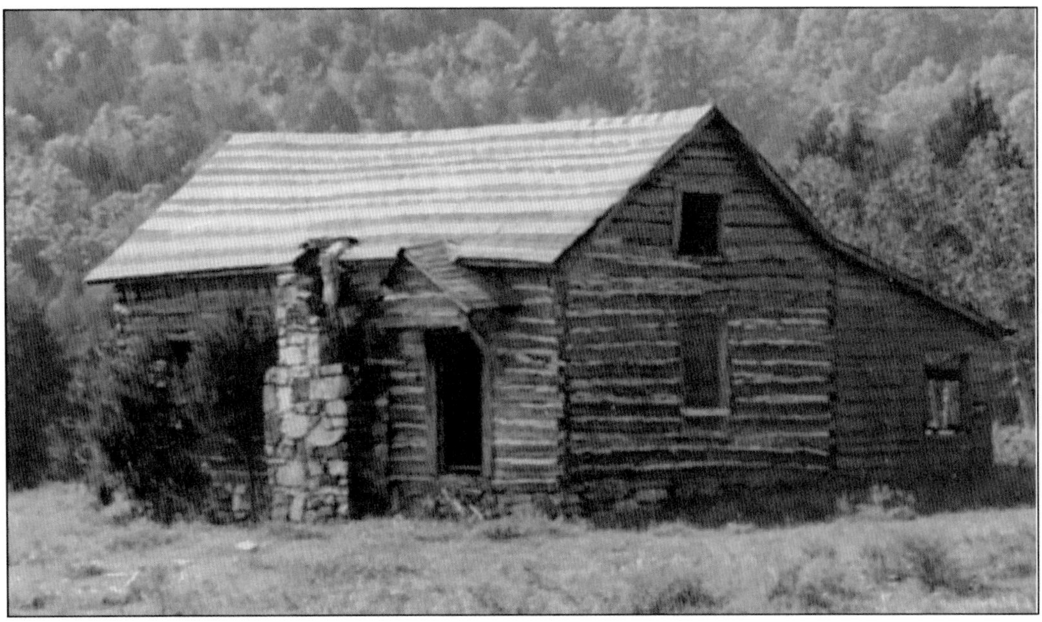

Log cabin similar to the one Peter Smith built. This one is located between Taneyville and Bradleyville on Highway 76.

and slivers in the hand. Every spring the youngsters were given molasses and sulfur to clear the blood. To avoid getting lockjaw after getting scratched or stepping on barbed wire, they would soak the wound for hours in coal oil.

Come the end of summer Mary would gather the grainy seed of the Jerusalem Oak which she boiled with sorghum to make a brittle candy patty. To worm the children she would feed these candy patties to them for three days, and the children thought the candy was a special treat.

Mary Smith was a hard working pioneer woman who faced tough times head-on, meeting every challenge life brought her way. Her faith was strong in God, trusting him always. She raised a family of six children during a time in history when there were no modern conveniences.

She used an old fashioned ash hopper to make homemade soap. She milked cows, and made sweet cream butter in a hand powered churn. She washed the family's clothing at the creek on a large slab rock. Her hands were rough and calloused from hard work. She cooked on a wood cookstove in all four seasons of the year. She carded wool, then wove the threads on her spinning wheel and made their clothing. Her children were taught early to help their parents and were given various chores to do each day.

Life was hard for the early pioneers, but it was also good and simple. They didn't live in such a hurry as people do today. People had time to work and enjoy Mother Earth who supplied all their needs. They visited their neighbors, often staying overnight and sleeping on pallets on the floor. Perhaps even sleeping on a bed tick made of corn shucks.

Mary Smith lived in Kirbyville all her life. She was well known and respected throughout the community by all who knew her. She was a close neighbor and friend to Mary Elizabeth Mahnkey of Mincy. Their children grew up together. Mrs. Mahnkey had the following to say about Mary Smith when she passed away October 17, 1929, after a long and agonizing battle with cancer:

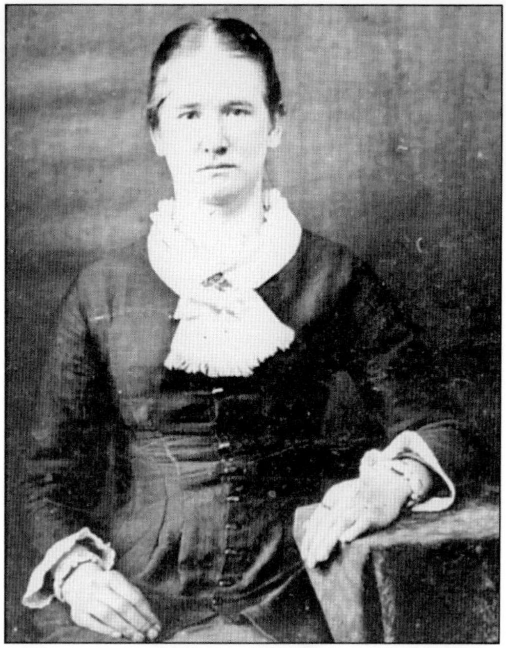

Mary Elizabeth Coggburn Smith, age 18. She lived from June 29, 1861-October 17, 1929.

"My simple words cannot portray the beauty and fullness of this life just closed; the ever ready help and comfort she gave freely in times of sickness and trouble; the fine courage and sweet wholesome wisdom. As I gazed through tears at her folded arms, I thought of the flowers they had planted, the babies they had dressed, the wonderful gardens they had made, the sick beds they had tended, and I grieved that this beautiful service was ended and that we later ones are so illy prepared to carry on.

The house was filled with her many friends and neighbors and the floral offering was magnificent. I thought the sweetest tribute a son could ever pay a mother was when Truman said, "She deserves these flowers."

Aunt Caroline's Encounter With A Panther

Caroline Smith was one of the younger daughters of Peter and Nancy Smith.

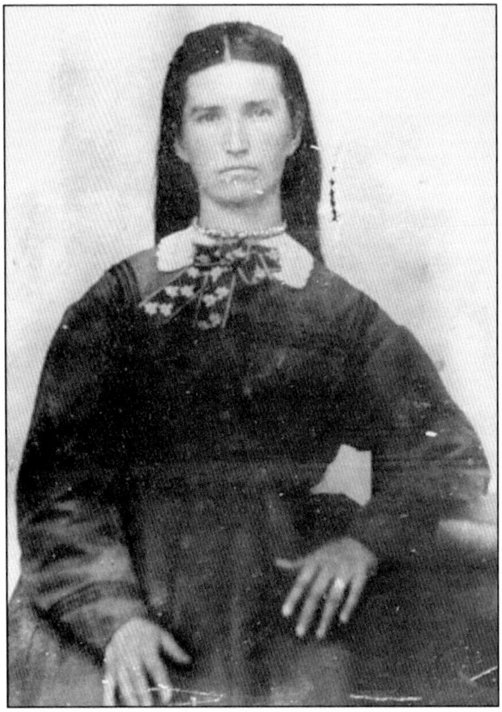

Jane Coggburn Cramer.

When she and her husband first married, they moved to Cedar Creek, Missouri. She was born in June, 1861, and died in February, 1914.

In the early days of what is now Taney County, people often moved to homestead various tracts of land. The place Caroline and her husband moved to needed to be cleared of the brush and timber to make a field. Shortly after their first child was born, the man left his wife and baby at the cabin to return to work in the field.

Caroline sat near the fireplace cradling the baby in her arms. When the baby fell asleep, she would lay him on a pallet near the fire while she worked preparing a meal.

At noon her husband came to the cabin to eat. When finished he returned to the field. While she finished washing the few dishes, she glanced at the baby. She could see the paw of an animal as it reached through a crack in the wall near the child. She ran to the child and swooped it up in her arms. She ran out the door for her husband. She was so hysterical that he had to slap her to bring her back to her senses.

After she told him what had happened, he laid down his axe and picked up the rifle leaned against a nearby stump. As he headed toward the cabin, he circled around it until he found the panther's footprints which were now headed toward the barn. The man could hear the nervous snorts of the mare and foal inside. As he cautiously peeked around the back corner of the barn, he could see the big cat. He pulled the hammer back on his rifle as the panther realized the man was there. The cat turned around and let out it's terrifying scream. The cat made a lunge at the man who quickly took aim and pulled the trigger which struck the cat in the breast killing it instantly.

He then turned, and put his arms around Caroline and the baby as they walked into the cabin. He sat down on the porch and dropped his head in silence for a few moments. He spent the rest of the day patching the cracks in the cabin walls so that such an event could not happen again.

AUNT JANE COGGBURN CRAMER

Jane Coggburn Cramer was one of John and Elizabeth Coggburn's daughters. Shortly after she was married, she and her husband left the community of Kirbyville to start a new life in the north western state of Idaho. The overland move would take a bit of preparation for the long journey. They loaded into their wagon many essential items; a barrel of crackers, a barrel of sorghum, a keg of kraut, a barrel of flour, and some cured meat. They were taking two milk cows, both due to freshen. Her husband had a team of horses and a team of mules.

They also took a tool chest, cooking utensils, and some vegetables. Jane had a new sewing machine she received as a wedding present which they carefully stored in the bottom of the wagon bed. She also had material tucked away to make their clothing once they reached Idaho.

The shelves in the wagon were stacked with boxes of dried fruits, sacks of beans, and cans of honey. They built a bin under the spring seat and filled it with potatoes. A lantern hung on one wagon rod and an iron kettle on another. There was also salt, gunpowder, bed ticking, beeswax, and tobacco.

Important implements packed away in the wagon included: a broad axe, a plow, an iron hoe, an auger, and a saw. After several weeks of preparation the wagon was filled to its capacity. They knew it would take almost a year to reach their destination. Jane realized she would probably never see Missouri again. It was hard for her to leave her family behind, but a lot of young couples were going west to settle in the vast frontier.

Jane had been fortunate enough to marry a man who was, for those times, considered wealthy. He had gone East to purchase a new Conestoga wagon made especially for long journeys. He pulled it back to Missouri with a team of horses and later purchased a large team of mules.

When the last few items were loaded, the two teams hitched into position, the two cows tied behind the wagon, it was now time to leave Kirbyville. Many friends were there with Jane's family as they gathered around her for the last time.

Jane and her husband took their last look at the tiny cabin and the surroundings. Jane hugged and kissed her father, brothers, and sisters. As she hugged her mother, it was sad to tell her "goodbye." Her family wished her well and her husband helped her into the wagon. Tears fell, although they smiled through the sadness. Her husband climbed into the seat next to her. He took the reins in his hands and cracked the whip.

As they traveled away, her family waved until they were out of sight. Soon their thoughts were on what lay ahead of them; the rugged terrain, rivers and streams to cross, unfamiliar territory, the uncertainty of the weather, and the most threatening obstacle of all would be the Indians. But they had several rifles and handguns. They would soon join with a wagon train headed west. They would join the other wagons near the Missouri-Kansas border.

When they reached Idaho, they would homestead 160 acres of land that had never been farmed. They were going to settle about 10 miles from the nearest trading post and settlement. After they would build their cabin, clear some of the land, and plant spring crops, he would become the town blacksmith.

Aunt Jane was a beautiful, young woman when she left her old home place in Kirbyville. She realized when she bid her family farewell they would probably never meet again. The photograph of her was taken shortly before she left Missouri to journey to a land from which she would never return.

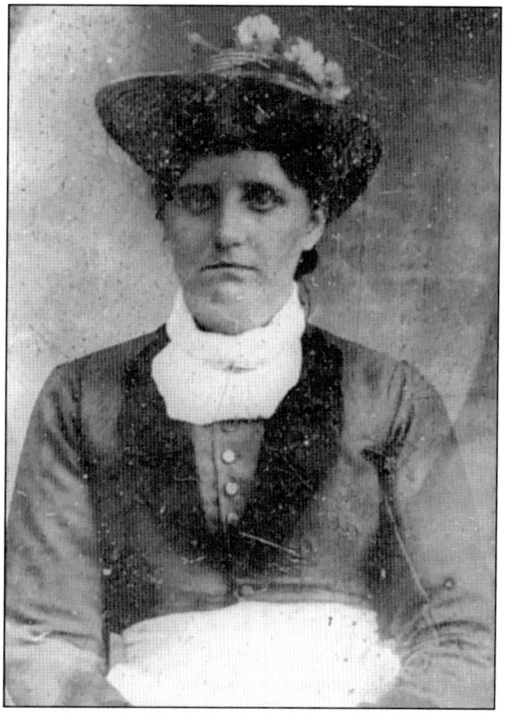

Caroline Smith.

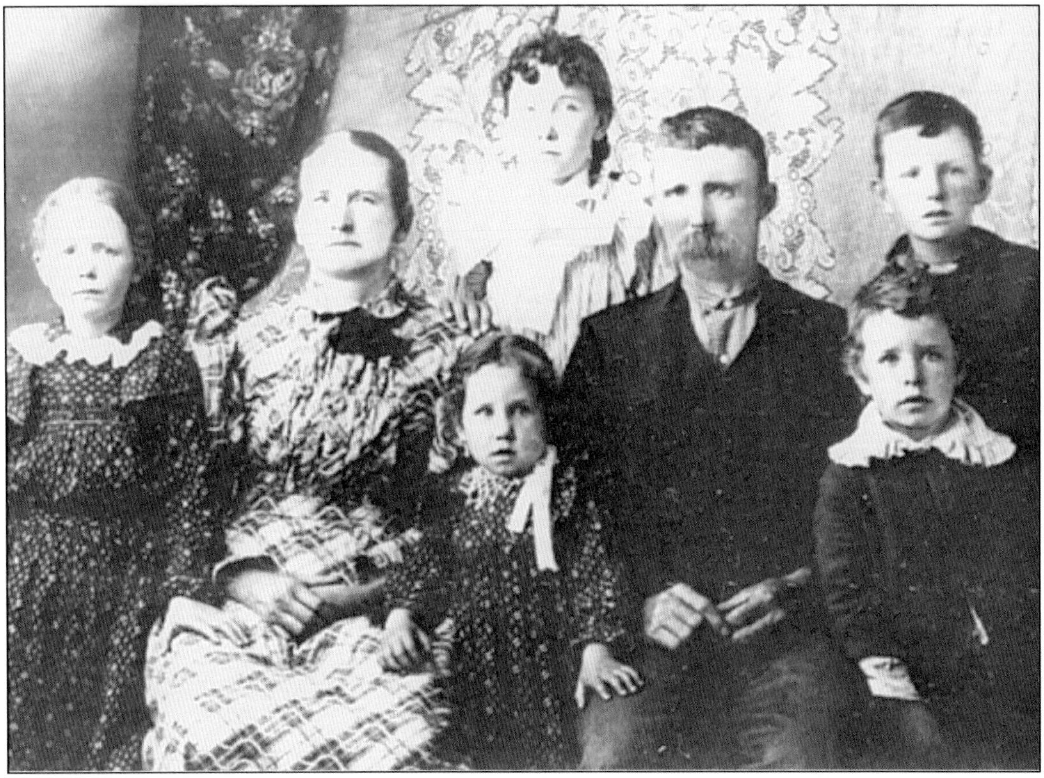

Tom and Mary Smith were their children. From left to right are: Ola, Mary, Ora, June, Tom, Bob, and Truman. Their youngest, Ethel, was not born yet.

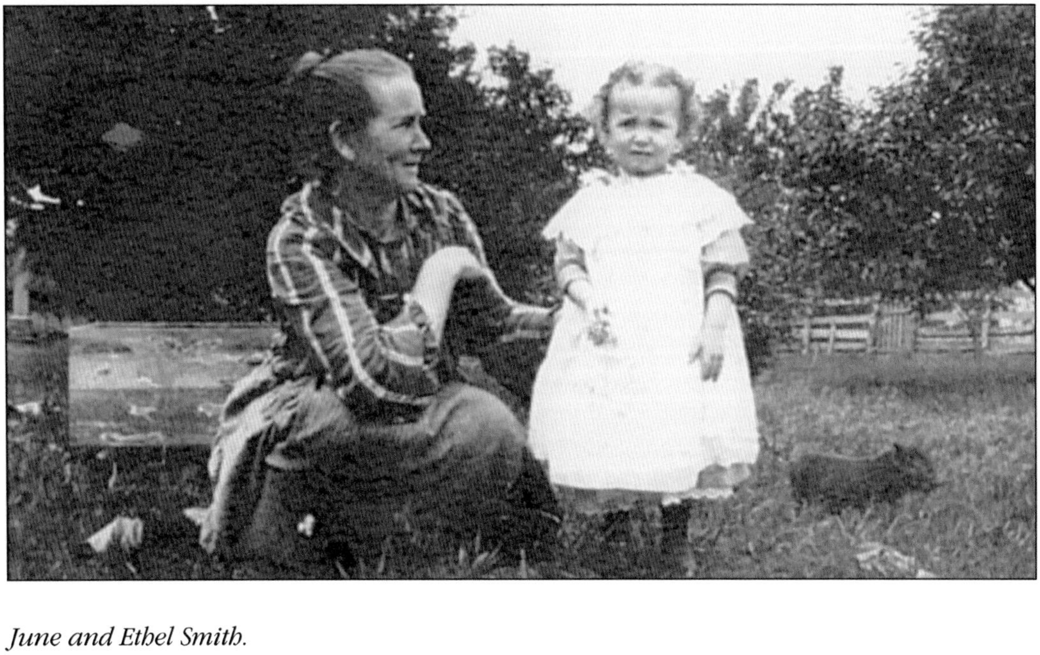

June and Ethel Smith.

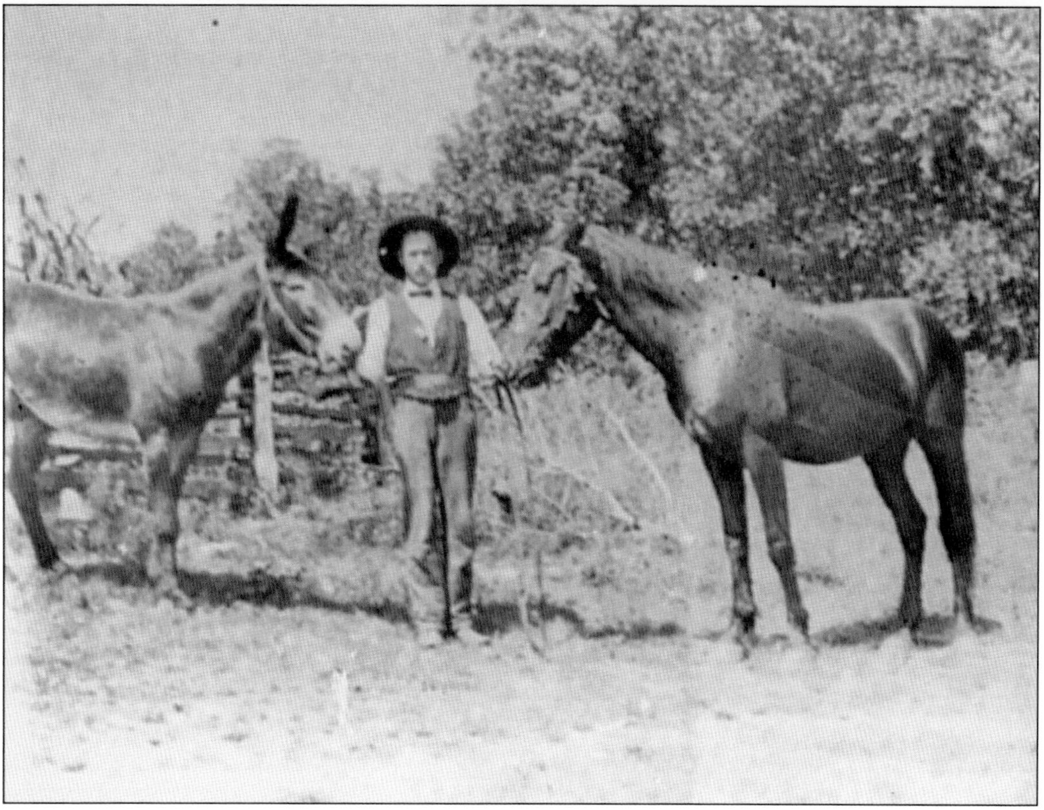

Jepp Whorton with his stallion and one of his mules.

PART THREE

THE WHORTON FAMILY

***Deuteronomy** 11:11-12 But the land, whither ye go to possess it, is a land of hills and valleys, and drinketh water of the rain of heaven. A land which the Lord thy God careth for; the eyes of the Lord thy God are always upon it, from the beginning of the year even unto the end of the year.*

***Psalms** 37:3 Trust in the Lord, and do good; so shalt thou dwell in the land, and verily thou shalt be fed.*

Jepthah and Dollie Whorton

Jepthah and Dollie Whorton lived in Madison County, Arkansas in the early part of the 1840s. They originally came from Georgia. Several of their children were born on the Whorton homestead, and grew up near the creek that flowed through the land and was known as "Whorton Creek."

In the latter part of the summer during the first year of the Civil War, several members of the Whorton family enlisted. They were on the front line of the fighting that took place near the Whorton homestead.

Aunt "Lizzie" Elizabeth Bollinger Whorton (Billy Whorton's wife and Sarah Bollinger Whorton's sister), dreamed three nights that three men rode up on horseback and took her father-in-law Jepthah Whorton and killed him. She went to Jepthah and pleaded with him to go to the Army Post where her husband Billy was with his brothers Randa and John Whorton.

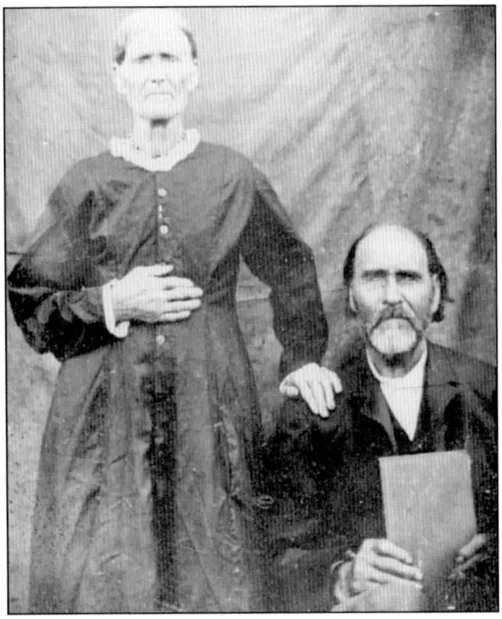

The author's maternal great-great-great-grandparents: Jepthah and Dollie Whorton.

Jepthah listened attentively to Aunt Lizzie as she told him she believed God was fore-warning her of a tragic event yet to happen. He shook his head in amazement as he paced back and forth across the dirt floor of their cabin. He tried to convince her it was just a dream and that he would be all right, then went back out to the wheat field where they were harvesting.

The next day Jepthah got an early start in the field. Then just as Aunt Lizzie had dreamed, three men came riding up the road and ordered Jepthah to get his horse bridled and saddled and ride ahead of them. The women's hearts grew faint at the sight as they tried to keep up with them. Dollie did faint and Sarah, Randa's wife, stayed behind at the cabin to take care of great-grandma Betheny Whorton (Jepthah's mother), who was quite frail. Aunt Lizzie and Gemes Whorton's wife did their best not to let the horses out of their sight.

The three bushwhackers ordered Jepthah to ride into the timber. Jepthah told them he and his family would kill as many of them as they did of the Whorton's if there was any blood shed. The bushwhackers had already taken his gun from him and they now tied his hands behind his back. Then one of them shot him off his horse.

The women screamed in terror! Aunt Lizzie was the first to reach his side as the bushwhackers rode out of sight laughing. She knelt down beside him putting his head in her lap. He managed to whisper a few words to her saying, "Tell the boys to kill 'em." His head slumped into her arms as she closed his eyes with her fingers. Aunt Lizzie sat there cradling him in her arms as her tears overwhelmed her.

Dollie was sick over the brutal death of her husband. The family took his body to the small family cemetery near Whorton Creek and laid him to rest beneath the sod in the hills he loved. He was not the first to die needlessly at the hands of the bushwhackers who stole anything they could get their hands on and killed old men and boys. They even stole some quilts the Whorton women

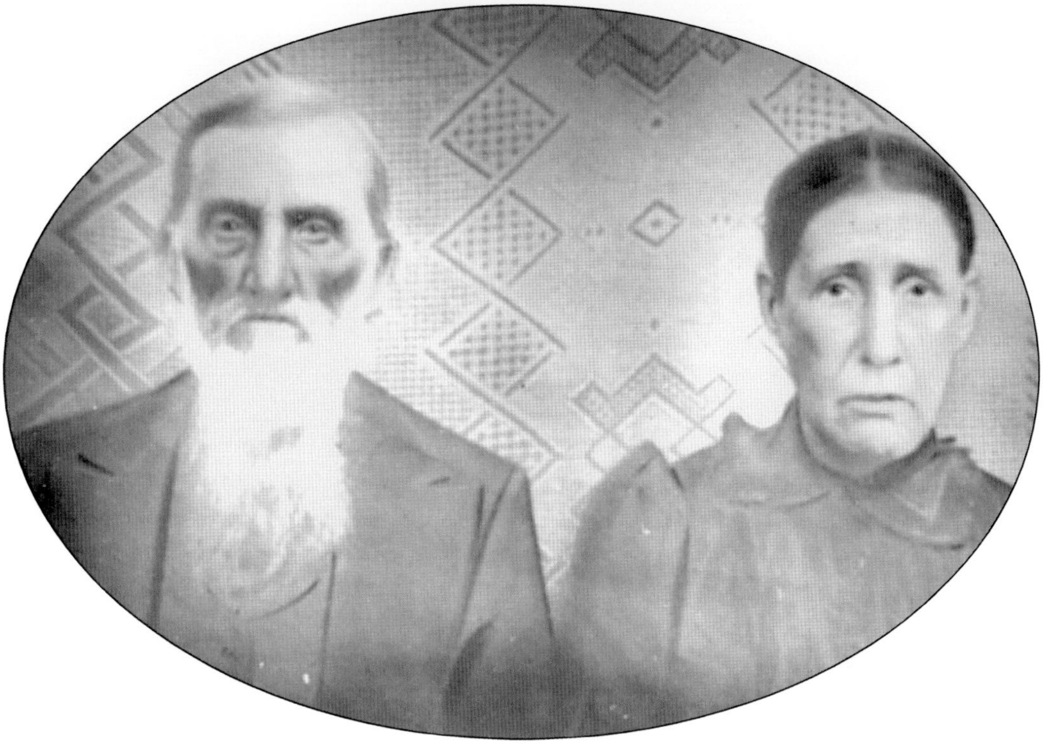

The author's maternal great-great-grandparents: Randa Clinton and Sarah Bollinger Whorton.

had made for their family.

Dollie and the other Whorton women endured the hardships of the Civil War era. She lived to her mid-80s. She was a midwife. She rode her own pony across swollen streams to care for the sick and deliver babies. She managed her own farm, livestock, cattle, and hogs. She pieced a quilt after she was 80 years old. Dollie kept her faith in God. God was with her and gave her a long and useful life. She, too, lies sleeping along side her husband in the Whorton Cemetery of Madison County, Arkansas.

RANDA CLINTON AND SARAH C. BOLLINGER WHORTON

Randa Clinton Whorton was born in Georgia. His family moved to Madison County, Arkansas, when he was ten years old. He had three brothers and five sisters. His parents were Jepthah and Dollie Whorton.

When Randa grew up he met and married a woman by the name of Dotson. They had one daughter, Martha. Sometime during the first several years of their marriage, his wife died.

Later Randa married Sarah Catherine Bollinger. During the first years of their marriage he was engaged in the Civil War as a soldier. In 1881, Randa and Sarah, with four of their sons and eight of their daughters, left the Whorton homestead on Whorton Creek and moved to what is now known as Taney County, Missouri.

When the Whorton's first came to this area they settled at the head of Turkey Creek and bought a farm a mile from what is now Hollister near where Turkey Creek emptied into the White River.

Sometime later Branson had a store and

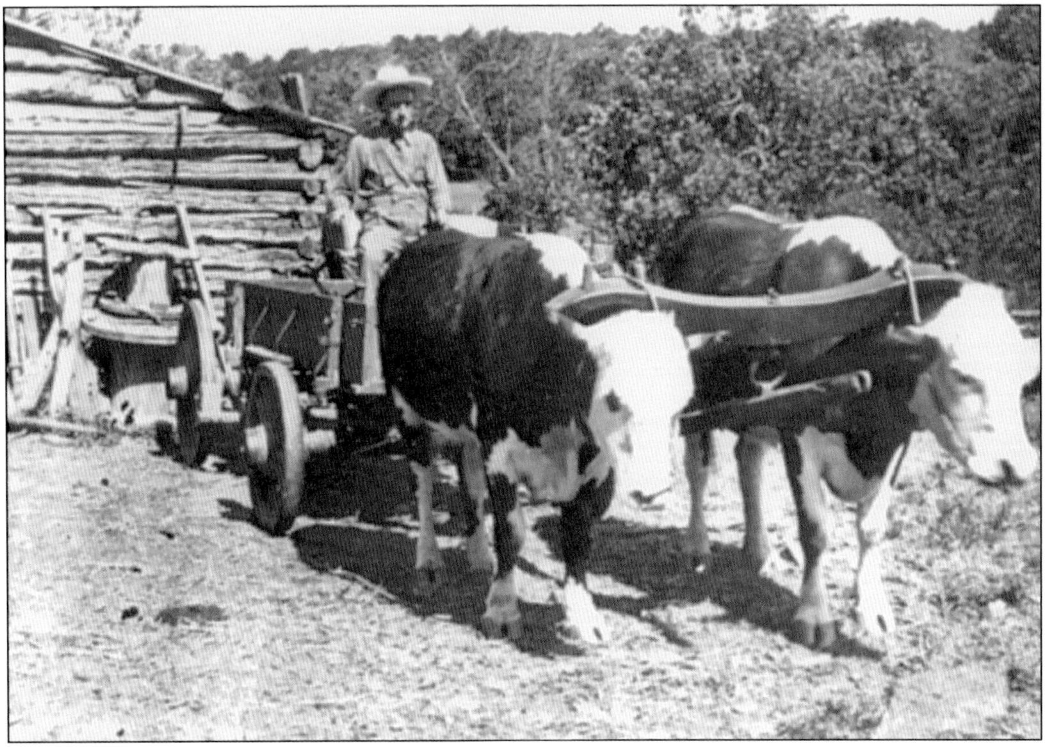

Uncle Jim (Gemes) Whorton with his team of oxen and his wagon. His parents are Randa and Sarah Whorton. This picture was taken about 1936 or 1937.

a Post Office. The Springfield-Harrison Road ran through Kirbyville. That was the main route for travel in the early days of Taney County. It was a common sight to see wagon after wagon rolling along this route. Freighters hauled eggs, bacon, ham, wool, and apples, along with many other items to Springfield, and would transport back needed items for merchants and settlers.

The deer and wild turkey were plentiful which helped lure people to the area. The blue stem grass grew to the horses' shoulders, which was one aspect of the land which fascinated Randa. The Whorton's cleared the creek bottoms and grew corn and wheat which was later taken to the mill to be ground into flour and meal. Sarah had a nice maple orchard and made maple syrup. "It was delicious," Ollie Layton described as she talked about it. Sarah made little cakes that could be dropped into the rich maple syrup, and how the children did enjoy it.

In the fall the Whorton's harvested their sugar cane crop and made it into molasses. If you grew the cane on light soil, the cane would make light colored molasses. If it was grown on dark soil, the molasses would be dark. They cut the cane, pulled the blades from the stalks, then the juice was put in the cane-mill pan and boiled for several hours. The molasses had to be skimmed to remove the green foam from the top. Then the molasses was strained into vessels, usually barrels. Uncle John Hodge and Edd Michel made molasses.

There were several cane mills in the area. Molasses was good during winter months. It was used to make cookies, gingerbread, pumpkin butter, and pumpkin pies. Molasses has iron in it and is a healthy food. If you put two tablespoons in a glass of water and drink it, it will stop leg cramps.

Sarah Bollinger Whorton knew herbs and how to doctor with them. She doctored children with all kinds of ailments. Many home remedies were handed down through the generations of a family, and those who lived in frontier times learned of these life-saving remedies from the Indians.

Lady slipper was a woman's tonic and was very good for a nervous condition. Gusleysmoke was boiled into a strong tea and put into molasses candy and given to the children for a worm medicine. Sarah made cough syrup from wild cherry bark that was boiled in water with a small onion, vinegar, and alum, and finally some honey was added. Mud dobbins from an old log house was used to put on a young baby's navel for powder; they also used parched flour. Pawpaw leaves were bruised to make a poultice to treat bee stings and snake bites. Doctors were scarce in the early days so the early settlers had only Mother Earth and prayer to turn to when there was sickness in the family.

Sarah and her fourteen-year-old daughter, Safronea, would card wool from the sheep in the evenings. They would do the wool from one sheep per day along with the other chores they did. They knitted socks for the family. They had a large loom and wove the material for their clothing, sheets, pillow cases, table cloths, and other items. With the scrap material they tacked together strings and made "hit or miss" carpets for the floor.

They worked hard. They carded their cotton in balls for the quilts, then layered them, overlapping for good warm quilts. Before Fronea married, she had a hope chest full of quilts.

Randa Whorton and his boys butchered the hogs on a flat rock by Turkey Creek. They scalded them, scraped the bristles off, and washed them clean, then cut hams, shoulders, and heads from them.

The flat rock made a good place to butcher. Randa would butcher several hogs at a time. The meat, backbone meat and trimmings from the hams and shoulders were made into sausage.

Those were days of hard work. Lard had to be rendered; sausage, head cheese, and mince meat had to be made. The head was cleaned, cooked, and ground; then the meat put in dish pans. Dried peaches, raisins, gooseberries, and fresh apples were ground and put in the meat. Vinegar, brown sugar, ginger, and cinnamon were added.

Randa would dry some of the meat and pickle some. He would put salt and an egg into a large dishpan. The salt bore the egg up until it showed a place the size of a silver quarter. Then the meat was put in the brine and heated. The meat was placed in a large stone crock and weights were put on it to keep it under the brine. Randa would take a cloth, wet it in the salt water and tie over the crock. It was better to use more than one cloth. This made the best flavored meat. Usually the old-timers would pickle their meat in late spring.

Sarah made cabbage into kraut, and put it into barrels. She also made cucumber pickles, and salt pickles. They grew beans and usually had a mill sack of dried beans. They grew Whipporwill peas and Lady peas to eat, which was a small pea like rice. Farmers grew wheat and a threshing machine would go from one farm to another and thresh the wheat for their flour. The wheat was hauled to the Ozark Mill or Moberly Mill. Mills were scattered here and there. White corn was grown for corn meal.

All farmers put out an orchard. There were no insects like we have today. Peaches, apples, and pumpkins were dried. Apples were buried in the ground as were Irish potatoes, turnips, and cabbage. Large families such as the Whorton's lived well in those days. They worked hard and managed well. In burying apples, Randa would lay the apples on top of straw, cover them with a layer of straw, then dig a trench around them and heap dirt on top so they wouldn't freeze. And a stove pipe was put down in a hole to the straw so the apples could get air. The pipes could be covered with boards to keep rain out. Randa buried their Irish potatoes and turnips the same way. Cabbage was laid out in a trench on straw. The heads were turned down, straw was put over them and dirt over the straw; this was covered with boards to keep them dry. Usually families like the Whorton's did not break into these hills until they had used the food they kept out to use first.

Sarah made turnip kraut, too. She also gathered wild grapes and made them into jelly. They made elderberry jelly—they had to put some wild grape juice in with the elderberry juice. Wild blackberries were plentiful to be picked, canned and made into jelly.

They planted mustard seed and it grew early. Then wild, green narrow dock, hog tongue, lamb's quarter, and other kinds of greens were mixed. Young, tender poke, picked when it first came up, was also used with the wild greens. A doctor once told Sarah a person could live on wild greens and milk if they had to. They are full of vitamins and minerals. Tender polk stalks can be peeled, sliced, rolled in flour and meal, then fried. Poke is rheumatism medicine. Folks gathered the poke berries, washed them, put them in a quart jar, and filled it with Heinz vinegar. You have to use a good grade of vinegar. They let this set a few weeks, then put some water in a glass with two tablespoons of poke liquid and drank it for rheumatism.

The Whorton family and many of the other early settlers in Taney County knew how to use the land, live in harmony with nature, and survive the elements of the wilderness. The account given in these stories show a brief insight into the history of their lives.

Tale of Little Bear

The morning sun was on the eastern horizon as Grandpa Whorton steadied the plow behind his bay mare while her steps worked to keep the rows straight in the corn patch. It was his habit to start the day before the sun had risen. His wife, Sarah, followed behind him. Some of the children helped drop kernels of corn into the fresh plowed

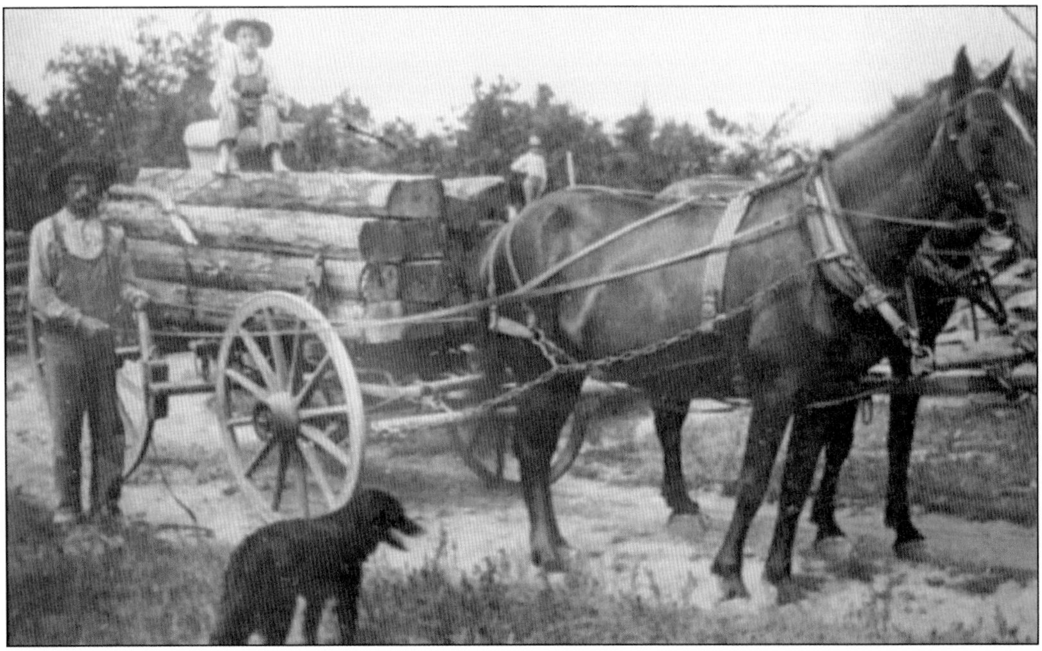

Uncle Jim with his work horse and wagon load of logs. His son Albert is sitting atop the logs. Ben Layton is in the background.

soil. One of the older boys would pull the dirt back over the corn with a hoe Randa had made from a stick of hickory.

Everything had gone smoothly until they heard a wild commotion in a brush thicket nearby. As they watched, a little black bear ran out of the brush with Randa's hounds hot on his trail. As the bear bawled and the hounds howled, the mare spooked and ran away, plow and all. Grandpa carefully climbed the tree and kicked the hounds back as they went.

By the time he caught up with Grandma, he had made a loop in the end of a harness rein. The hounds had run the cub up a tree at the north end of the field. Grandpa carefully climbed the tree and kicked the hounds back as he went.

Grandma watched as she stood below and tried to keep the hounds quiet. Grandpa soon worked his way close enough to the cub where he could slip the loop over his head. He pulled it snug and tried to lower the cub to the ground. As the cub neared Grandma, Grandpa began to climb down. Before he reached the ground, the hounds jumped on the cub and scared it back up the tree, climbing over Grandpa as it went.

Grandpa got his hat on straight and started his second go-round with the cub. This time was successful. With the bear safely on ground, he took Grandma's apron and tied it around the cub's mouth for a muzzle.

They dragged the cub to the house and took him into the barn where they made a place in one of the back stalls for it. Then after seeing that the cub had fresh water and a little something to eat, Grandpa sat down in the hay next to him. He decided to call it "Little Bear."

In the days that followed, Grandpa spent what free time he had trying to get Little Bear to gentle down. Slowly, he responded to Grandpa's gentle hands. Within a week they were acquainted enough so that Grandpa let Little Bear out of his stall to see what he would do. As Grandpa walked out of the barn, Little Bear followed him back to the house and inside. Needless to say, however, it didn't take Grandma long to run both of them right back out the door swatting them on the behind with her broom. So it became apparent to Grandpa that his new buddy would have to remain an outside critter. As time went on Little Bear became one of the family and even the hounds grew to like him. They even developed a game. Little Bear would voluntarily run through the woods just so the hounds could chase him. Not long after this, a few of the neighbor men trained their dogs with the help of Little Bear who enjoyed out-smarting the hounds at their own game. His favorite trick was to get back to the cabin before the hounds, hide under the porch where it sloped and sit down. Then he would box the hounds back one by one as they approached.

One Sunday, some of the kinfolk were to have a dinner at the Whorton's cabin after church. The kitchen table was laden with many good dishes the women had prepared. Placed in the middle was a fresh bowl of honey Grandpa had removed from one of his bee hives the day before.

When there was company around Grandpa always kept Little Bear chained out back of the cabin, since his manners weren't quite up to par yet for such occasions. But Little Bear got a whiff of honey and couldn't resist temptation any longer. He tugged on his chain 'til it pulled loose. This left him free to follow his nose.

Within minutes he had managed to get the back door open and walked in like he owned the place. It just happened that the women folk were out in the front yard visiting. So Little Bear looked around until he found the honey bowl. He then hopped onto the table and began to help himself to the sweet delights. About that time Grandma Whorton walked in. She hollered for Grandpa and at Little Bear. Little Bear wasn't sure what the excitement was about. He raised his head, looked at Grandma, and the honey dripped from his furry chin. The look on his face was as if he asked Grandma if there was something wrong that he didn't know about.

Well, Grandpa ran in the house and just the tone of his deep voice let Little Bear know he was in trouble. Grandpa lifted him from the table, carried him out the back door, and tied Little Bear to his chain. Grandpa went and cut a switch from the hickory tree. He gave Little Bear a whipping he would not soon forget. Little Bear hollered so pitifully; it sounded like he was crying, " Oh, lordy, oh, lordy. "

Little Bear remained with the Whorton family for many years. However, Grandma just about disowned them both over that Sunday afternoon.

The folks that lived near the Whorton's when they were in Arkansas, near Huntsville, were accustomed to seeing Grandpa and Little Bear together. Many times they were seen riding side by side in the wagon as they traveled the country roads. Little Bear was especially fond of trips to the mill where the corn was ground. It's not known how many years they did have Little Bear, but he was with Grandpa Randa Whorton for many years.

RANDA C. WHORTON'S CIVIL WAR STORY

"The most virulent brand of partisan warfare raged beyond the Mississippi, in Kansas, Missouri, and Arkansas. With a head start in civil strife dating from the 1850s, this area lived under a rule of terror during most of the Civil War.

When Randa C. Whorton and his family lived in Arkansas on his parent's homestead, he started as a Confederate soldier in the Civil War in 1861 but soon decided he didn't like the way the Confederate Army handled things. While in camp one night he told a couple of his fellow soldiers he was going to desert the Infantry.

He explained to one friend that at night when he saw him march around his tent a couple of times it meant he was getting ready to leave, and if his buddy wanted to go with him, he could. Randa slipped quietly out of camp without anyone seeing. He headed for the mountains nearby taking only his canteen of water, a few sourdough biscuits, and items to maintain him until he could reach a Union camp. He spent the rest of that night hiding in the thick brush.

At daybreak he saw in the distance a small band of Union Soldiers riding in his direction. He went out to meet them with his hands raised in the air. The Union Soldier in charge asked him what he wanted. Randa replied he wanted to go with them. So they let him ride back to their camp with them, and fitted him up with a Union uniform and rifle.

June 1861: in a further effort to promote the Confederacy in his state, Governor Claiborne Jackson of Missouri puts out a call for 50,000 volunteers. He hoped to repel what he perceived as an attempt by the Federals to take over the state.

July 4, 1861: Lincoln reiterates his position concerning the indivisibility of the Federal Union, once again making clear his stance on declaring war against the Confederacy. He makes a request for an additional 400,000 men to aid the Union.

On the fourth of July in 1861, Randa C. Whorton marched into the area of Springfield, Missouri, headed in the direction of Wilson's Creek Battlefield with his overcoat on. After the war, he often told about how he walked through dead men all day and never stepped by the same dead man twice. And that there wasn't a place on a man's body he hadn't seen a bullet hole.

August 10, 1861: General Nathaniel Lyon is killed at Wilson's Creek, Missouri, where he had led 5200 men to meet the Rebel troops under the command of General Benjamin McCulloch. The Confederates are joined in this encounter by pro-southern Missouri militia under the command of Sterling Price. While Union troops were defeated at Wilson's Creek, they put up a valiant fight, pushing back two Rebel charges on Bloody Ridge, the spot where Lyon falls. After this fatality, the Federals pull back, commanded now by Major Samuel Sturgis, and march to Rolla, Missouri, to the southwest of St. Louis. The Confederate force of 15,000 was depleted by 421 deaths and 1300 wounded as compared to the Federal losses of 263 fatalities and 721 wounded. The battle of Wilson's Creek is the second most important clash between the two enemies and gives the South another significant victory following that of Bull Run in Virginia.

In the fall of 1861 Randa and his two brothers Billy and Gemes went home on a furlough. Randa's wife Sarah was living with his mother on the old Whorton homestead. Shortly after the three men arrived home, Sarah saw a group of Confederate Soldiers coming through the woods at one side of their place. There had been a lot of fighting near their home, and there must have been 30 to 35 soldiers on horseback. She dropped what she was doing and ran back to the house to warn the others. Billy and Gemes slipped out the back door of the cabin and hid in the thick brush in hopes the Confederates wouldn't see them. The Soldiers suspected where they were but held their fire.

Gemes got scared and in his panic started running. The Confederate Captain, whose name was Dawsey, ran his horse along side of Gemes, grabbed him by the hair of his head and jerked him off his feet. Randa, who had moved to the barn, saw this and grabbed his rifle. He shot the Captain off his horse killing him instantly. This started a cross fire between the Whorton's and the Confederates. Randa's mother Dollie kept the children safe in the cabin, and Sarah grabbed a rifle from behind the wash stand and commenced shooting from the cabin door.

When it was finally over and the Confederates signaled to halt all gunfire, four of their soldiers lay dead. Some of the other soldier boys took an old blanket and wrapped the bodies of their dead comrades in it. Sarah said she wanted to see them. The soldiers assured her they were none of her family, but she insisted on seeing them anyway.

Captain Dawsey's head was so shot up that Sarah took the apron she had tied around her waist and wrapped it around the Captain's head. The soldiers took his clothes, boots, and all that he had in his possession. Sarah went inside the cabin for another piece of material and wrapped the dead Captain's body with it.

The Soldiers then secured the bodies of their dead comrades on the back of their horses and rode away leaving behind a bloody trail on the Whorton homestead. For some unknown reason they did not take the Captain's body with them.

After Randa had gotten a grip on himself, surveying the scene of the conflict and the blood stained soil, he sat his gun down by the woodpile. He walked off a short distance and fell to his knees and said, "It is neither the strongest nor the swiftest who gains the victory, it's who God gives it to."

Randa and his brothers later went to the Fyller's homestead to see about getting a casket made. It took old man Fyller several hours to make the homemade casket out of pine. Then the Whortons buried the Captain near the graves of two other Confederate Soldiers in a secluded area near the Whorton place. It was always told to family members following this incident of getting the casket made, that Randa dreamed he saw old man Fyller go to heaven in a basket.

Within a few days Randa, Billy and Gemes left the homestead to return to their outfit. It was hard for Sarah and Dollie to say goodbye not knowing whether they would ever see them again. But the life these early pioneer women were accustomed to made them strong in their faith with God.

As fall moved into winter the fighting raged on. Dollie and Sarah managed to survive the harsh winter months and heard from their men from time to time. Many nights found the Whorton women seated at the small kitchen table near the fireplace with the light of the kerosene lantern glowing in the dark. It could be seen from miles away. Sometimes in the distance they could hear the sounds of cannons being fired.

To pass their time they carded and spun wool. They made clothing and knitted socks for the family. With scrap material they would piece together quilts. They kept the farm going and tended to the livestock. At night when it snowed they would peer out the tiny window of their cabin as the smoke from the chimney rose and disappeared into the cold night air.

March 8, 1862: the Battle at Pea Ridge, Arkansas, the most significant of Civil War battles in the trans-Mississippi west, sees the deaths of both Generals McCulloch and McIntosh, depriving the Confederacy of two able commanders. Federals under General Curtis continue to hold out for a second day of fighting, which ends as Van Dorn and his men retreat to the Arkansas River with orders to leave the state and move to the Mississippi River to aid in defense of Confederate positions there. The tally of casualties for Southerners shows that the Confederacy has lost around 800 men, while the North suffers 1384 dead and wounded.

November 28, 1862: General James Blunt and his Federals stage an attack on Confederate positions at Cane Hill, Arkansas. The 8000 Southern Troops there are under the command of General John Marmaduke. Blunt's 5000 men pursue Marmaduke into the Boston Mountains after beating them back, but this chase is called off due to strategic danger it creates for the Union forces. At this encounter, Federals tally losses at 40 men, while the Southerner's total is considerably higher at 435.

Sometime later in the war, Randa was transferred to a unit of the Union Army which took him further south into the swamp lands near Waldon, Arkansas. Sarah left Madison County at this time and went to stay in Waldon in hopes of being close to where her husband was.

The soldiers had a terrible time in the thick mud of the swamp lands. Randa marched several days continuously in the mud and lost both of his shoes. The weather was still cold and he suffered with aching feet. He got word to Sarah about this and she knitted him a thick, heavy pair of wool socks to wear until Mr. Ball could make him a new pair of leather shoes and get them to him.

Sarah had stored wheat in the tiny outbuilding near the cabin she was staying in. One night in the early hours of morning a band of Confederate Soldiers came by and stole all of it. Any food she had on hand had to be hidden carefully so she could feed herself and her small son, Jeppie. One time she even had some hidden beneath the wooden planks of the floor. Some soldiers took their bayonets and poked around the floor until they found a soft spot, tore back the planks and took all she had.

Sarah also had her spinning wheel, a bunch of yarn, some handmade handkerchiefs, and a jacket she had made for Randa out of a fawn's hide. The Soldiers took her yarn and handkerchiefs, then tried to take the jacket. But she fought them off, kicking and screaming at them until they finally let go of her and the jacket. Randa told her later it was a miracle they hadn't knocked her down or even killed her.

The day following the robbery of her food and other items, Sarah decided to take herself and her young son Jeppie to the Army refugee camp which was close to where Randa was. So she started on the long journey walking and carrying Jeppie on her hip. Somewhere on the road a man came by on horseback. He offered to give her a ride to the camp; she gladly accepted.

They had to cross several creeks and it was so cold that Sarah's shoe froze to the stirrups. Before she could dismount the man had to take a rock and knock the ice loose from her shoes. Her feet were almost frost bitten. When she finally got to the camp, the doctor there had to take care of her feet for several days before she could walk.

During the time Sarah and Jeppie remained at the Refugee camp, peace was declared and the war came to an end. The South had been devastated and it would take a long time for the deep scars to heal for both the North and the South. The scars inflicted upon the Whorton family would never heal. Randa's father had been killed by the bushwhackers. His brother, Gemes, was killed while fighting, and this left his wife, Bethany, and their little girl alone. Randa and Sarah lost three children, John, William, and Nancy.

When Randa was discharged from the Union Army, Sarah hadn't seen him in almost two months and barely recognized him as he marched into the refugee camp with his comrades. He had lost weight and the war had aged him several years. She stood quietly and watched the weary soldiers come into camp for the last time. Some were bandaged and bleeding. Some were helping those who couldn't walk on their own. Some were carried in on cots. Although it was a sad time, there was a peaceful atmosphere about the soldiers as they joined their voices together in a song:

After the toil and the turmoil, after the strife is past, Cometh the peace God giveth, cometh rest at last.
Rest, sweet rest for the weary, after the toil and the pain. Rest for the well beloved, crowns shall the victors gain.
They who have fought and conquered, waging a war with sin, Into the heavenly city, gladly will enter in.
Rest for the worn and weary, shelter for all the lost, And in the blessed Haven, anchor the tempest toss'd.
Rest, sweet rest for the weary, after the toil and the pain. Rest for the well beloved, crowns shall the victors gain.

Randa looked around and caught sight of Sarah as she stood near the command post. He dropped his rifle and ran to meet her as she, too, ran to meet him. As they fell into each other's arms they wept bitterly as loss of loved ones flooded their minds as well as the ordeal of the war itself.

After their joyful yet sad reunion, they made arrangements to leave as soon as possible to return to the old Whorton homestead in Madison County. Randa had managed to save quite a bit of his Soldier pay. He gave it to Sarah and told her to go to the supply tent and purchase whatever she thought they would need for the journey home.

She bought some loaves of bread and cured meat. She also got ten yards of material at 10¢ a yard to make some clothes once they got home. Randa had a horse, so they had a way to travel. They would take turns riding the horse with Jeppie. Sarah gave Randa the jacket she made for him out of the fawn's

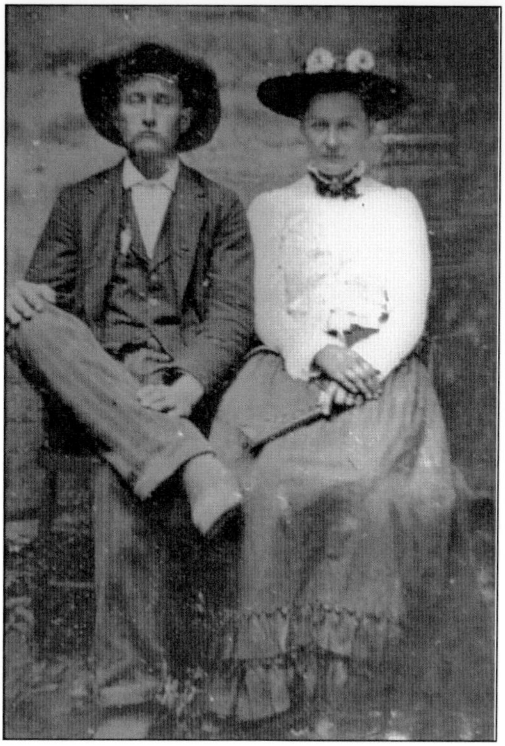

Jim and Almeda when first married.

hide that the soldiers tried to steal. He was so proud of it and the way she stood up to those Confederates.

After a day or so of resting and clearing up Army business, the Whortons left the refugee camp bidding farewell to the other Soldiers and their family members. Randa led the horse slowly through the gate while Sarah held Jeppie in front of her on the horse's bare back. After getting a little way along the road Randa stopped long enough to turn around and look one more time in the direction of the camp. Perhaps in the back of his mind he was thinking, "Could this all have been a nightmare?" Or was the reality of it so overwhelming that he needed that last look to reassure himself of what God had brought him safely through.

With the passing of time the Whorton's arrived safely back at the homestead and rejoined the rest of the family. Sarah went to work making new clothes for Jeppie and Randa out of the new material she brought home with her. There was even enough to make herself a new dress and apron. It was like starting all over again for them as they tried to pick up the pieces and go on.

The war had made the hair on Randa's head turn gray. Lines from worry had left their mark on Sarah's face. Dollie had grown weak and spent much of her time sitting in her rocking chair near the fireplace as she held Jeppie and read the Bible. Sometimes she would just close her eyes and hum peacefully.

The war changed everyone's disposition as well as their outlook on life in general. Randa became more quiet. The war and the loss of loved ones made him realize more the uncertainty of one's life here on earth.

In time, life once again came to the Whorton homestead as they slowly put the war years behind them. Soon the flowers were blooming again in the south and the birds began to fill the air with their music. The deer and the wild turkey once again fed from the land that had been bathed with blood. The fields began to grow again with corn and wheat where there had been the foot of many a soldier as he marched off to battle. And life once again for Randa and Sarah would become peaceful.

The men who were unfortunate enough to have to serve in the Civil War fought during a time when medical treatment was very remote. The soldiers on both sides saw a rough time, and it was hard as they struggled to survive just the daily elements not associated with the actual fighting; like the need for shelter, clothing, and food, as well as medical care when they were injured during the fighting, or when they got sick from the unsanitary conditions of the camps.

The Armies needed all manner of goods; uniforms, underwear, boots, shoes, hats, blankets, tents, muskets, swords, revolvers, cannons; a bewildering variety of ammunitions, wagons, canned foods, dressed lumber, shovels, steamboats, surgical instruments, and so on.

During the first year, industry was not geared up to turn out all these things in quantities required, and heavy purchases were made abroad while new factories were built, old factories remodeled, and machinery acquired and installed. By 1862, the government practically stopped buying ammunition abroad because its own manufacturers could give it everything it needed or wanted.

For the unfortunate Civil War soldiers, whether he came from the North or from the South, not only got into the Army just when the killing power of weapons was being brought to a brand-new peak of efficiency; he enlisted in the closing years of an era when the science of medicine was woefully, incredibly imperfect, so that he got the worst of it in two ways. When he fought, he was likely to be hurt pretty badly; when he stayed in camp, he lived under conditions that were likely to make him sick; and in either case he had almost no chance to get the kind of medical treatment which a generation or so after would be routine.

Both the Federal and Confederate governments did their best to provide proper medical care for their soldiers, but even the best was not very good. This was nobody's fault. There was simply no such thing as good medical care in that age—not as the modern era understands the expression.

Randa C. Whorton and the Bushwackers

When the Whorton's were still in Arkansas, they lived near Kingston. Randa and two of his brothers had made a trip to another town 20 miles away. On the journey home, one of Randa's brothers was shot in the stomach by Bushwhackers who had hid in the brush by the roadside.

After an exchange of gunfire, they decided they would continue toward home. They tried to stop the bleeding enough to where he could ride his horse. It didn't take long for him to realize he would never make it, so he told his brothers to go on and that he was dying.

They discussed it and finally did. They

went 100 or 200 yards on up the hill and hid behind a log. From there they could keep an eye on the brother left to die. A short time passed and the Bushwhacker found him. Within minutes they killed him. Then they stripped his clothes from him, even his boots. One of them turned a boot upside down and poured blood from it onto the ground. To witness that nearly broke Randa's heart. The Bushwhackers mounted their horses and rode away.

The Civil War had ended years before but there were Bushwhackers still terrorizing many people along the state lines between Arkansas and Missouri.

The brother with Randa said he knew one of the men was from a neighboring community. Randa was broken-hearted at the way his brother had to die, then the humiliation of being left naked. But what hurt Randa the most was to see the blood poured from his boot.

The other brother said since the war was over they'd have to take his body home for burial and forget about it. They wrapped a blanket around him and tied him to the saddle on his horse and took him home.

When they arrived home, the family was grieved over the tragedy. They buried him in the family cemetery near Whorton Creek. In the nights that followed, Randa lay awake, his memory haunted by the death of his brother.

Randa told the rest of the family he would seek revenge. But the other brother said he did not want to be a part of it—that they would have to go on with life. Determination led Randa to pack his saddle bags with some food, take his bedroll and rifle. He left the cabin, though his mother pleaded him to stay. He went to the crossroad and hid in the brush for three or four days waiting for the Bushwhackers to ride by.

When several days passed one of them finally did ride to the crossroad. Randa shot him with his 32.20 where his overall galluses crossed his back. The man slumped over the saddle and soon fell to the ground dead.

Several days after this the other Bushwhacker heard of it. He and his family got together, loaded their wagon with their belongings and left the country fearful for the man's life.

Then the Whorton's got together and had a meeting. They decided the same thing might happen to Randa; some friends of the man he shot might lay in wait somewhere to shoot him. So the Whorton's loaded their wagon with their belongings and herded their livestock behind as they left Madison County en route to what today is known as Taney County, Missouri.

They traveled from 40 to 50 miles. One wouldn't think much about that distance today in a car. But, then, traveling by wagon it would take two or three days or more to make a journey of that distance. They moved far enough from Kingston, Arkansas, that they did not encounter any problems over the shooting. And that is how the Whorton's came to Taney County.

Randa C. Whorton and the Survey Crew

After the Randa Whorton family settled near Hollister in 1881, they had to clear the land. The family worked together clearing the timber, brush and sprouts off an acre or two of ground to create a field. They used an axe and rubbed it down with a rubbin' hoe. The combined efforts of all soon produced a fertile plot of ground near the creek.

Around the turn of the century the railroad survey crew came to survey the right-of-way for the railroad that was to be built. According to their calculations it would go through the Whorton's field they had worked so hard to clear. It is where Ira Rittenhouse's place is today.

This angered Randa and he told them they could not go through his field. They, in turn, told him they had gone through every other place they wanted to for miles and miles, and had never changed the right-of-way for anyone.

Randa told them they could have their

right-of-way, but they could not destroy the field. They didn't need as much as they claimed. If he let them go though, they would have to narrow the right-of-way.

Randa sat down on a stump and clutched his single-shot 32.20 tightly in his hands. He told the survey crew they would have to shoot him off the stump, and he would kill the first man who set foot in his field with a survey instrument. He admitted he knew there was enough of them to kill him but he intended to fight to protect his land.

The survey crew backed down and discussed the situation with their boss. Later, when they returned to the field, Randa was still sitting on the stump holding his rifle. His long white beard blew in the wind as he shaded his eyes with his Union soldier cap. His determination and grit paid off. The railroad agreed to by-pass the field and narrow the right-of-way.

According to family history, Randa's wife Sarah also encountered conflict with the survey crew. She refused to cooperate with them because they wanted to run the railroad through her beautiful maple orchard that was near their house. The crew spent an entire day trying to convince her to sign the deed.

After they negotiated with her all day they reached a mutual agreement. They would run the track along the rear side of the orchard, so she could still walk from the house to the orchard and not have to cross the railroad track. She settled for a sum of money and signed the contract.

Randa C. Whorton and Sarah Bollinger Whorton's Children

The following is information on the children and grandchildren of Randa and Sarah Whorton.

1. John Henry Whorton died during the Civil War.

2. William Whorton Whorton died during the Civil War.

3. Nancy Whorton died during the Civil War.

4. Jepp Whorton was born in 1861. He married Martha Cuthirth. Their children: Charlie, Rosa, Mollie, Nora, and Andy.

Jepp Whorton's second marriage was to Kezia McGown. Their children: Alvin, Les, Miranda, Sarah (died young), Mallie, little Johnny (died young), Elmer, Wilbur, Mildred, and Francis.

5. Gemes (Jim) Clinton Whorton, October 13, 1865–October 14, 1937. He married Margaret Cutbirth. Their children: Dollie, May 11, 1885. Walter, November 30, 1887. Gemes' second marriage was to Almeda H. Thorpe, September 1874. Their children: Albert Ray, July 23, 1895–November 13, 1977; little Randa, died when young; Elbert Clinton, January 18, 1905–October 10, 1955; Delbert, November 11, 1912; and Margie Whorton, December 28, 1898–June 9, 1901, Gemes'(Uncle Jim) and Almeda's daughter.

6. Safronea C. Whorton Layton, January 25, 1867–June 2, 1958. Married William (Dank) Layton February 1892. Their children: Ben, Randa, Sarah, Lonnie, and Ollie.

7. Millie Whorton married Jim Burks. Their children: Maudie, Mattie, Tilda, and Becky.

8. Mary Whorton married Bill Breshears. Their children: Martha, George, and Lester.

9. Eva Whorton, died at the age of 14 years and was the first to be buried at the Whorton Cemetery.

10. Newton Whorton married Lydia Rittenhouse. Their children: Clem, Clyde, Esby, Lige, Augusta, Goldie, Jepp, and Herbert.

11. Amanda Whorton married Dave Rittenhouse. Their children: Emma, Annie, Alford, Ray, Elzea, and two died in infancy.

12. Maude Whorton married John Rittenhouse. They had one child: Ira.

13. Sinea Whorton married Isaac Strahan. They had one child: John Henry.

14. Wilbur (Dick) Whorton married Millie Breshears. Their children: Oscar, Austin, Alford,

Sylvester, Orville (deceased when young), Clifford, Della, Lula, twins—Faye and Jaye, Beulah, and Ruby.

15. Ollie May Whorton married Jason Burks. Their children: Jesse and Lena.

Maude, Sinea, and Ollie Whorton

Maude, Sinea, and Ollie were Randa and Sarah Whorton's last three daughters. They were born on the Turkey Creek homestead near Hollister. Maude married John Rittenhouse and they lived on a farm near Turkey Creek. Maude lived her entire life there. She and John were farmers and lived on her parents' farm. They took care of her parents when they were no longer able to care for themselves. Her father passed away in her home.

John and Maude had one son, Ira. The three of them enjoyed raising cattle on their farm. Ira taught school for several years at Oak Grove. Ira and his wife Linnie (Savage) raised chickens and sold eggs to the chicken hatcheries around Springfield, Missouri.

Sinea Whorton met and married Isaac Strahan, who was a Baptist minister. They owned a farm on Turkey Creek one mile from Hollister. Sinea enjoyed churning cream in an old time butter churn. She made good country butter and sold it to the merchants in Hollister.

They had one son, John Henry. In later years they sold the Turkey Creek farm and bought one close to Mincy near the store, Post Office, and school. The family members are buried in the Mincy Cemetery. The grandchildren still live on the farm there and at Kirbyville. A grandson and a great grandson own the Strahan Feed Mill in Hollister, Missouri.

Ollie May Whorton was the last daughter to be born on the Turkey Creek farm and attend school at Cedar Springs. Ollie would make trips with her mother, Sarah, back to the Whorton homestead in Madison County, Arkansas near Kingston and Huntsville. Many relatives, Whorton's and Bollinger's, lived there and many friends.

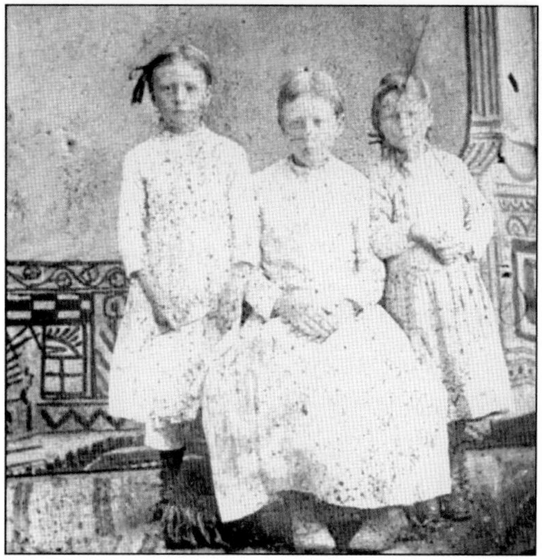

Maude, Sinea, and Ollie Whorton.

On one trip Ollie met Jason Burks, a local neighbor and friend of the Bollinger family. Shortly after the two got acquainted they were married and made their home in Madison County. They had two children, Jesse and Lena. Jason and Ollie were farmers. They raised cattle, sheep, hogs, and horses. They grew crops of corn and wheat which furnished them with plenty to eat and to sell. They lived out the remainder of their lives on that one farm. After their deaths, they were each buried on the Burks homestead in the family cemetery.

The Johnson's

Randa C. Whorton had a younger sister named Lavica. She married John Ralston. They had a daughter named Mollie. John and Lavica lived on a farm by Turkey Creek in Hollister, Missouri, near her brother Randa's farm. Mollie grew up by the creek. Her parents farmed, raised cattle, chickens, and hogs. They traveled in a horse-drawn wagon.

John became seriously ill and passed away on the farm where his wife and daughter cared for him in his last hours. After his

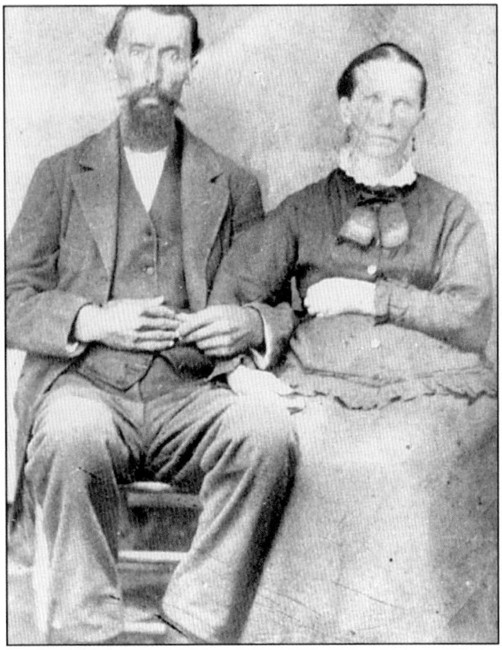

Mollie and Jehew Johnson.

death Lavica remained on the farm and raised their daughter. They managed the farm well as they continued raising cattle and chickens.

When Mollie grew up she married Jehew Johnson. She left the Turkey Creek farm and went to live in Rogersville with her new husband. They had one son, Tom. Tom grew up and married. His first child was Opal. Later his second marriage bore him a son, Henry.

After Jehew died, Mollie lived to be in her mid-80s. From time to time she would travel back to Taney County to visit her Whorton relatives. Mollie and Jehew are both buried in Rogersville.

Jepp Whorton

Jepp Whorton was Randa and Sarah Whorton's fourth child. He was a baby during the Civil War. When Jepp became a young man he married Martha Cutbirth. Their children were: Charley, Rosa, Mollie, Nora, and Andy. Jepp and his family were farmers and raised cattle, hogs, horses, turkeys and chickens. Jepp was especially fond of the work mules he raised. He plowed in the spring with a pair named Mack and Daisy.

Often during hard times he would have to pull the fodder from the corn and cut the tops to feed roughage to his mules with what grain he could raise. Every day Jepp would curry his mules, then use a soft-bristled brush.

If anyone in the country needed good advice when it came to the subject of mules, Jepp Whorton was the man they asked. Jepp used mules instead of horses to operate the sorghum mill. He broke many to work and to ride. He sold them throughout the country.

Jepp grew corn, wheat, hay and sorghum each year. When he made sorghum, he made a barrel or two. In those days sorghum was a sugar substitute like honey. Real sugar was expensive and cash money was a commodity the pioneers lacked.

Jepp hunted and trapped like Daniel Boone. He traded in furs throughout the country. When he had acquired a wagon load of furs he would go to Springfield, Missouri to sell the hides. He brought back many needed items for his family and neighbors.

When his first wife died, she left him with five small children to raise. His sisters helped, and his mother took care of Andy who was the baby. Andy and his grandmother had a great love for each other. She was like a mother to him.

Not long after Martha died, Jepp met and married Kezia McGown. They had ten children: Alvin, Leslie, Mallie, Miranda, little Sarah (died young), Mildred, Francis, little Johnny (died young), Elmer, and Wilbur. All 15 of Jepp's children grew up on the same farm and attended the same school. Jepp also had bee hives on his farm. Many times when the family would sit down for a meal, there wouldn't be enough honey in the bowl for that meal. Jepp would take a long butcher knife and a bucket and go out to the hives with his protective clothing on. He would cut off a slab of honey into the bucket and take it back to the kitchen.

Jepp lived to be an old man who looked

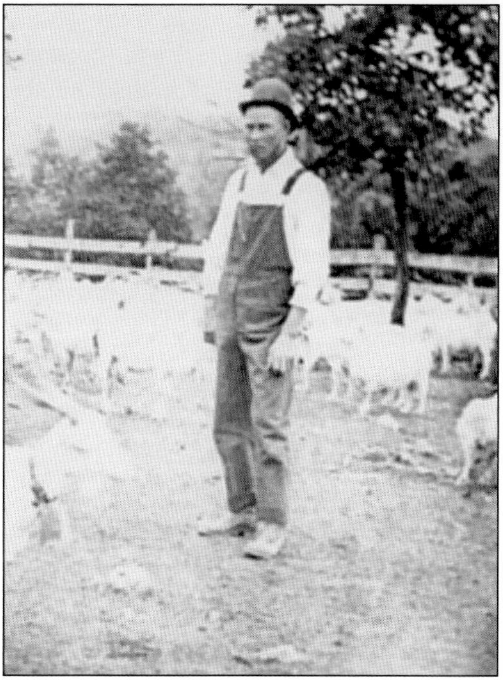

Jepp's son Andy with his herd of goats.

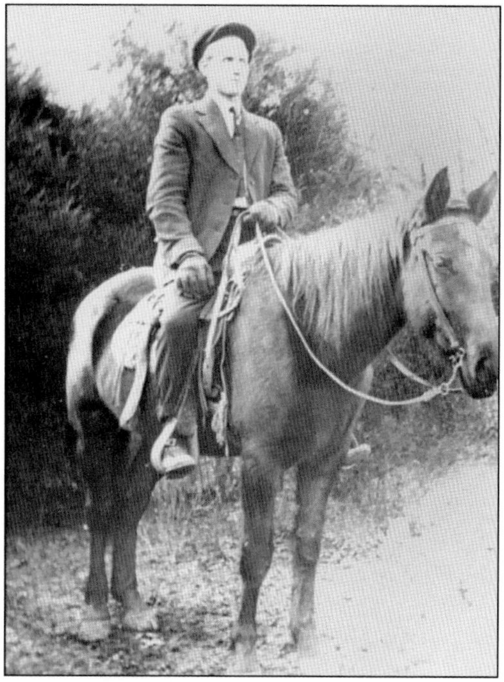

Jep's son Alvin with one of his horses.

back over his life and was well pleased. He lived to see many grandchildren come into his home. He was well known and respected in the land of Taney County, Missouri.

ANDY WHORTON

Andy Whorton was Jepp and Martha Whorton's youngest son. Martha died while he was a baby. Jepp's mother cared for him. When Andy was in the first World War, Sarah prayed faithfully for him. In time he came home after he had been gassed on the battlefield. He had to crawl to safety while his best friend was killed by his side.

After he came home he married Blanche Brittain. They became farmers and went to Mena, Arkansas, to live. They had four sons. Andy enjoyed the goats they raised and let them roam freely over the farm. They would kill one for their meat supply and sell some at the market in Fort Smith. They would sell the hides which were tanned and used for all kinds of leather items from shoe laces to bull whips.

Andy and his wife are both buried at Mena.

ALVIN WHORTON

Alvin Whorton was Jepp Whorton's son by his second marriage to Kiza McGown. Alvin took after his father in many ways, especially in his great love for horses and mules.

Alvin married Dice Lynch, a Taney County native. They had four daughters and lived in Kansas. Dice worked in a nursing home for many years. Alvin worked in the wheat harvest every year as well as other farm related jobs. They lived on a small farm and raised chickens, cattle, horses, and a few hogs. They attended church and were well respected citizens of the community.

Remembering Uncle Jim (Gemes) Whorton

Gemes Whorton was named after one of his uncles who was killed during the Civil War. But he was well known by the name of Uncle Jim. He was born October 13, 1865, and died October 14, 1937, at his home near Branson, Missouri. He was one of 15 children of Randa and Sarah Whorton.

Uncle Jim and his first wife had two children: Walter and Dollie. When Jim and his first wife separated, Uncle Jim was suppose to get Dollie since she was a baby at the time. But his first wife decided she wanted Dollie after all. This change of mind led to some trouble for the Whorton family with the Bald Knobbers.

One day Jim's sister, Fronea Whorton Layton, sat on the back porch of her log house with Dollie on her lap and saw old Sam King come through the lot headed toward the front of her cabin. Sam was one of the Bald Knobbers.

Fronea knew Jim's wife had sent Sam to get Dollie back for her. Fronea slipped quietly away from the house and went into the cornfield. From there she watched Sam King for a while and then decided to take Dollie into Arkansas to stay with some of the folks there where she would be hidden safely. Fronea walked to her parents' farm on Turkey Creek and her dad took her and Dollie down into Arkansas.

While Fronea was gone the Bald Knobbers took Uncle Jim. When her father returned to his farm, the Bald Knobbers got him, and took him to the place where they held Uncle Jim. On the same day Uncle Jepp saw Jerry Youngblood who was also a Bald Knobber. Uncle Jepp was carrying his rifle when Jerry stopped him on the side of the road and asked him what he thought he was doing with that gun. Uncle Jepp, not the least intimidated by Youngblood replied, "I'm carrying this gun, that's what I'm doing with it!"

After that the Whorton's and some friends united and wrote the Bald Knobbers a letter which said, "there wouldn't be any of them left in the country if any harm came to Uncle Jim or Grandpa Whorton." They all signed their names to it and sent it to Capt. Kinney.

The Bald Knobbers took the warning seriously and let Uncle Jim and Grandpa Whorton go home. After that incident the Whorton family didn't have any more trouble from the Bald Knobbers. Grandpa Whorton had a reputation for the way he avenged his brother's death at the hand of a Bushwhacker. The Bald Knobbers left the situation alone not wanting to stir up trouble further than it already had gone.

Uncle Jim got to keep Dollie and his first wife went on back to Arkansas to her folks. Later on Uncle Jim met and married Almeda Thorpe. They had four children; Albert, Elbert Clinton, Margie, and Delbert.

One of the most fascinating aspects about Uncle Jim was the oxen team he drove hitched to his wagon. He and Aunt Almeda went to church in it. They would go to the grocery store with eggs and maybe a can of cream to sell for a little income. To sell a few eggs meant a few dollars. And to get a new dress from print feed sack material was pure luxury.

The Whorton children and other children would ride in the back of the wagon seated upon a pretty quilt made by either Aunt Almeda or Grandma Whorton.

Aunt Almeda was a wonderful cook. She and Uncle Jim loved children and were very kind people. He was a Baptist preacher. Aunt Almeda was devoted to the Lord and often shouted in church. Those were the days when all the kinfolk went to church at Oak Grove. Of course, today all the old congregation is gone. Those who were children then are now the senior citizens.

The little building at Oak Grove still stands today, weather-beaten and lonely, with only cobwebs and silence within. The flowers still bloom in the church yard. There's a well in the yard where they all used to get a good, cold drink of water. They used to have old-fashioned pie suppers there on Saturday nights. Christmas was celebrated there, and the new year was greeted, too. Christmas was a special time for the children.

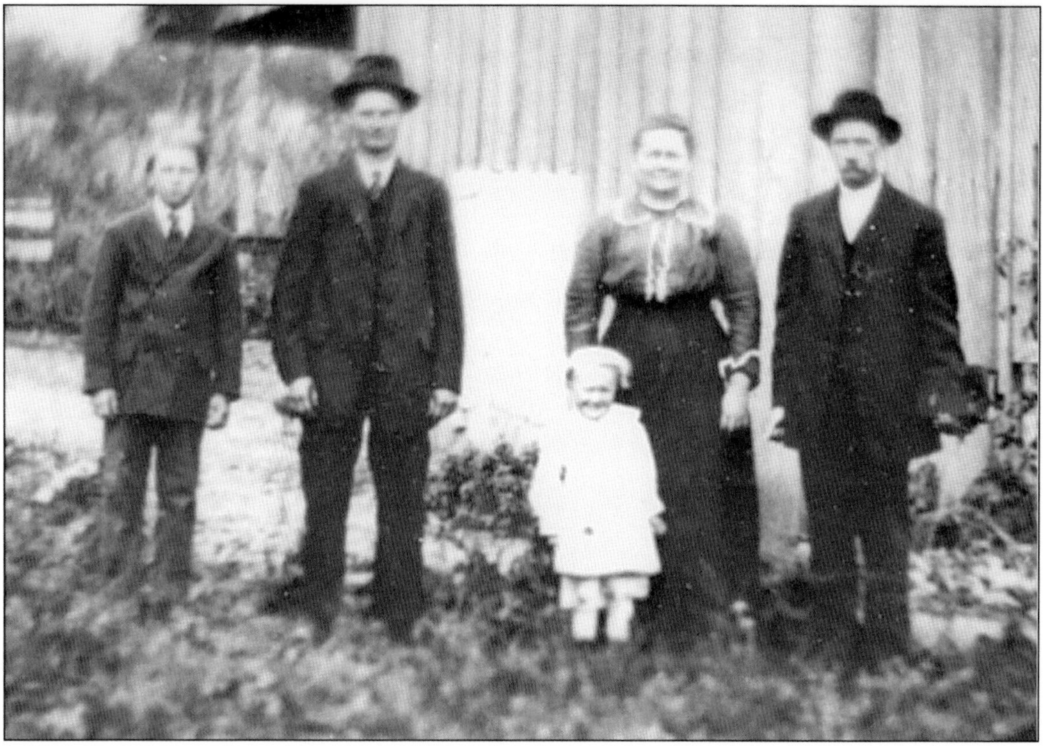

Uncle Jim, Almeda, Albert, and Clinton. Clinton (January 18, 1905-October 10, 1955) married Anna Bull on July 4, 1927. He became a water well driller at the age of 18 and worked in partnership with Albert.

They would all get a present from under the beautiful tree that was decorated with homemade ornaments.

Uncle Jim died October 14, 1937, near Branson and was laid to rest in the Whorton Cemetery near many other family relatives. Each year on Memorial Day the family members walk and lay flowers on each grave in loving memory of those who are at rest.

The author's mother, Hazel Layton Cobb, told a funny story about Uncle Jim. When Hazel was about the age of three or four years, her dad, Randa, and Uncle Jim were dehorning some cattle. As she came upon the sight she said, "Please, Uncle Jim, don't cut my ears off!" as she put her hands over her ears. Later she was teased by her brother Bill, who was older than she.

G.C. Whorton, Old Time Resident in County, Passes to his Reward

Neighboring communities were saddened last Friday to learn of the death of "Uncle Jim" G.C. Whorton. Mr. Whorton had not been ill for a long time and hoped that he would recover and be active again.

Funeral services were held Saturday at the Mt. Branson Baptist Church at 2:00 p.m. with Rev. Bob Grady in charge of the service. His burial was in the Whorton Cemetery south of Hollister and Rev. Troy Compton conducted the burial service.

Mr. Whorton was a very well known citizen of Taney County, having come here from Arkansas in 1881. He had lived on the present place near Kirbyville since 1900.

Mr. Whorton often created a bit of

excitement on the streets of surrounding towns with his team of oxen. He often drove them into Branson and the Leader ran a feature story about it at that time. A few paragraphs follow:

"A yoke of oxen! And on the streets of Branson. Bransonians were treated to this rare spectacle Monday morning. Mr. and Mrs. G.C. Whorton of Kirbyville, pioneer residents of Taney County, drove their ox team to town.

So rare was the sight that a slight traffic jam resulted when Mr. Whorton pulled up to a stop across the street from the Leader office. Business on the south side of Commercial Street came to a virtual stand still as shop keepers, shoppers, motorists, and tourists stopped to see the oxen. Several picture seekers produced cameras and took pictures.

The ox trip to Branson was not meant for publicity said Mr. Whorton, but was made because other equipment at the farm became unavailable at the time. In fact it could be said the trip was quite a utilitarian one, for on the wagon with them the Whorton's brought 97 dozen eggs and a can of cream to market here, and returned with feed and supplies.

Besides his widow, Mr. Whorton leaves to mourn his passing three sons, Albert and Clinton, who live in Taney County, and Delbert, who is a resident at Altamont, Kansas.

Mr. Whorton was the son of Randa and Sarah Bollinger Whorton. He was born October 13, 1865, in Madison County, Arkansas. He died October 8, 1937.

He gave his life to Christ at the Oak Grove church in the year of 1901 and was united in the Baptist church. He was ordained as a minister of the gospel on April 5, 1914, and lived a faithful servant up to the time of his death."

(Author's note: This article was published in the Taney County paper years ago.)

She Didn't Go Home

One time a piano and organ instructor named Ragsdale came to Oak Grove from his home in Arkansas, to teach those interested in learning to play the piano or organ. While he was in the community, Aunt Almeda Whorton wanted to learn the organ so she could play at church on Sundays. Ragsdale began to teach her with her favorite song, "The Great Physician."

Uncle Jim and their daughter Margie, who was three years old, came with Almeda one day during practice. Several hours later it was time for all to go home. As they left the church Almeda got on her horse and Jim attempted to put Margie in the saddle in front of her mother.

Margie fought getting in the saddle and repeatedly cried out, "I'm not going home, I'm not going home!" After some persuasion, Jim finally got her to get in the saddle. But she kept repeating those same words, "I'm not going home, I'm not going home!"

Jim mounted his horse and the three started home with Almeda and Margie's horse in the lead. Suddenly, and without warning, a wild hog ran from the brush across the road directly in front of Almeda's horse. The horse reared and threw Almeda to one side knocking her unconscious. Then the horse fell backwards on top of Margie pushing the saddle horn through her chest and killing her instantly.

This happened so close to the church that when Jim screamed, Ragsdale, who was preparing to leave, heard the commotion. Jim leaped from his horse and ran back to get Ragsdale to come help. In an intense state of shock, Jim laid down in the middle of the road and cried out, "Why did she have to say she wasn't going home! " Could it have been possible that Margie's spirit had been forewarned from her guardian angel of the danger which awaited her?

Ragsdale hurried to the tragedy, but Margie lay dead. Almeda had a terrible gash on her head and he wrapped his handkerchief around it to control the bleeding. Some of the other relatives drove up in their wagon and tried to help. Jim came to his senses and cradled Margie in his arms as he wept.

Almeda was laid in the back of the wagon

as Jim sat near her with the child still in his arms. They were taken to their home a short distance away and the neighboring relatives were notified. Soon their home was filled with concerned relatives and Almeda was taken care of by someone. She was still unconscious. Someone took Margie from Jim and laid her lifeless body on a pallet in the corner where she would be prepared for burial the next day in the Whorton cemetery.

Randa Layton, a nephew of Jim and Almeda was there when this happened. He was four years old and was playing with his cousin Albert who was about the same size as he was. They were on the bald near the church when this happened. Afterwards someone told Randa to carry Albert home. As they started down the road Randa dropped Albert. Someone spanked him for it, so he left and walked on home.

Whorton Cemetery

The following is a list of names and dates of those buried in the old Whorton Cemetery near Turkey Creek in Hollister, Missouri:

1. Chauncey and Emily Adams, in an unmarked grave.

2. David L. Rittenhouse: born March 21, 1874; died November 9, 1934.

3. Sara A. Rittenhouse: born January 26, 1876; died May 12, 1914.

4. Maggie Rittenhouse: born December 7, 1903; died February 10, 1904. (David and Sara were husband and wife, Maggie was their child.)

5. Infant of Dave and Sara Rittenhouse: born and died March 16, 1902.

6. Margie Whorton, daughter of G.C. and A.H. Whorton: born December 28, 1898; died June 9,1901.

7. Martha A., wife of J. H. Whorton: born April 22, 1864; died in 1884 or '94.

8. Nora, wife of S. J. Spruce: born February 20, 1889; died March 5, 1916.

9. RCW and OW (2 babies).

10. Eva Whorton: born June 18, 1873; died September 17, 1886. The first one to be buried in the Whorton Cemetery.

11. Mary E., wife of W.R. Breshears: born June 3, 1868; died May 6, 1894.

12. Randa Clinton Whorton: born December 30, 1836; died December 19, 1907. CO. B 1st Arkansas Infantry.

13. Sarah C. Bollinger Whorton, wife of R.C. Whorton: born March 27, 1841; died January 3, 1916.

14. Orsvil Whorton (Mallie's daughter): born August 16, 1903; died December 16, 1905.

15. Josephine E. Layton: born November 3, 1897; died March 22, 1938.

16. Lee Layton: born May 17, 1928; died August 24, 1964.

17. Fronea Catherine Whorton Layton, wife of W.D.: born January 25, 1867; died June 2, 1959.

18. Wilma Lucille Layton, Ben and Rosa's daughter: born March 11, 1921; died December 5, 1929.

19. Rosa Victoria Layton: born April 12, 1894; died October 19, 1962.

20.Ben Layton: born November 12, 1892; died March 19, 1978.

21. Harold Layton's infant: born and died October 29, 1964.

22. William D. Layton: born March 14, 1857; died January 1, 1903.

23. Virginia June Layton, daughter of R.D. and Ethel: born October 5, 1925; died October 8, 1925.

24. Sarah, daughter of J.H. and K. Whorton: born February 23, 1908; died January 28, 1909.

25. Johnny, son of J.H. and K. Whorton: born December 23, 1903; died June 9, 1904.

26. G.C. Whorton: born October 13, 1865; died October 8, 1937.

27. An unmarked grave near to Margie Whorton.

NEWTON AND LYDIA RITTENHOUSE WHORTON

Newt's parents were Randa and Sarah Whorton. Lydia Florance was the daughter of Eli and Elizabeth Rittenhouse. Newt and Lydia married on December 24, 1893. Their children were: Clem, Clyde, Esby, Lige, Jeppie, Augusta (Johnson), and Golda (Wade). Newt died in 1944. When Lydia died she left two sisters, Susie Kelly and Cora Gloyd.

Newt and Lydia's home place is on Highway 76 East between Kirbyville and Forsyth. The log house once sat on the north side of the road but was recently torn down. But their old barn is across the road and still stands today.

Lydia was a housewife. She was a wonderful cook and sewed by hand. They raised many fine gardens and canned all they were able to for the long winter months. Newt raised cattle and crops on his farm, with hogs, chickens, and horses.

Randa Layton has spoken many times that he and cousin Albert Whorton would spend the night in Newt's old barn. They were young men and would be out on a night's hunt of opossum, coon, fox, even panthers. They both lived at Oak Grove and would get caught out in a rain storm and seek shelter in the barn.

Sometimes way in the night—past midnight—they would slip into the barn and bed down in the hayloft. They would tell stories of their huntin' trips and varmint tales. Sometimes they would lie there listening to the music of the hounds runnin' their prey while the night creatures filled the air with the sound of their music.

If that barn's hay loft could talk it could tell many a good huntin' story of days gone by when the young men of Taney County roamed the beautiful hills and valleys.

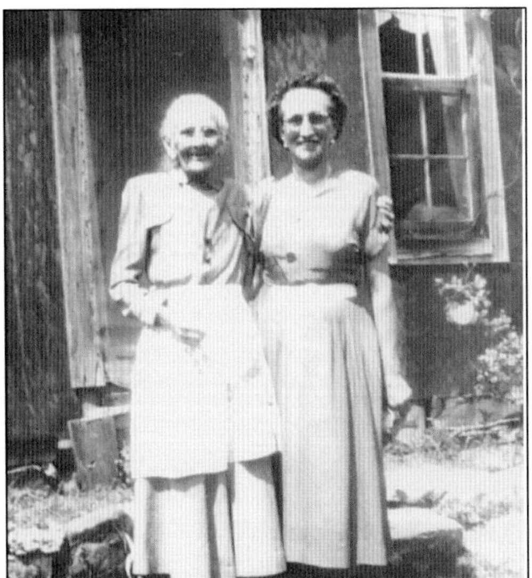

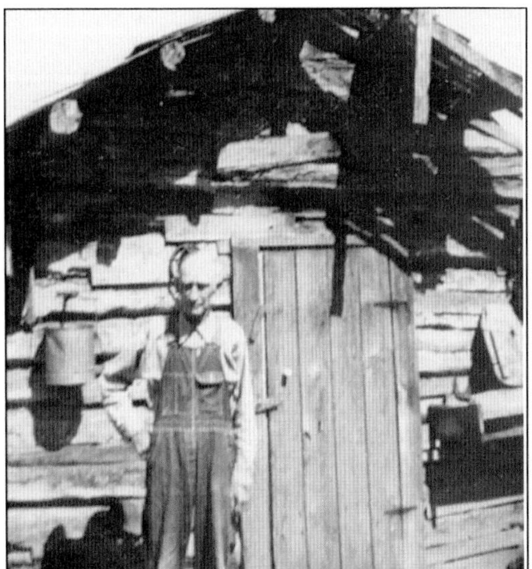

Newt (right) and Lydia Whorton (left) at their old homeplace. The other woman's identity is unknown.

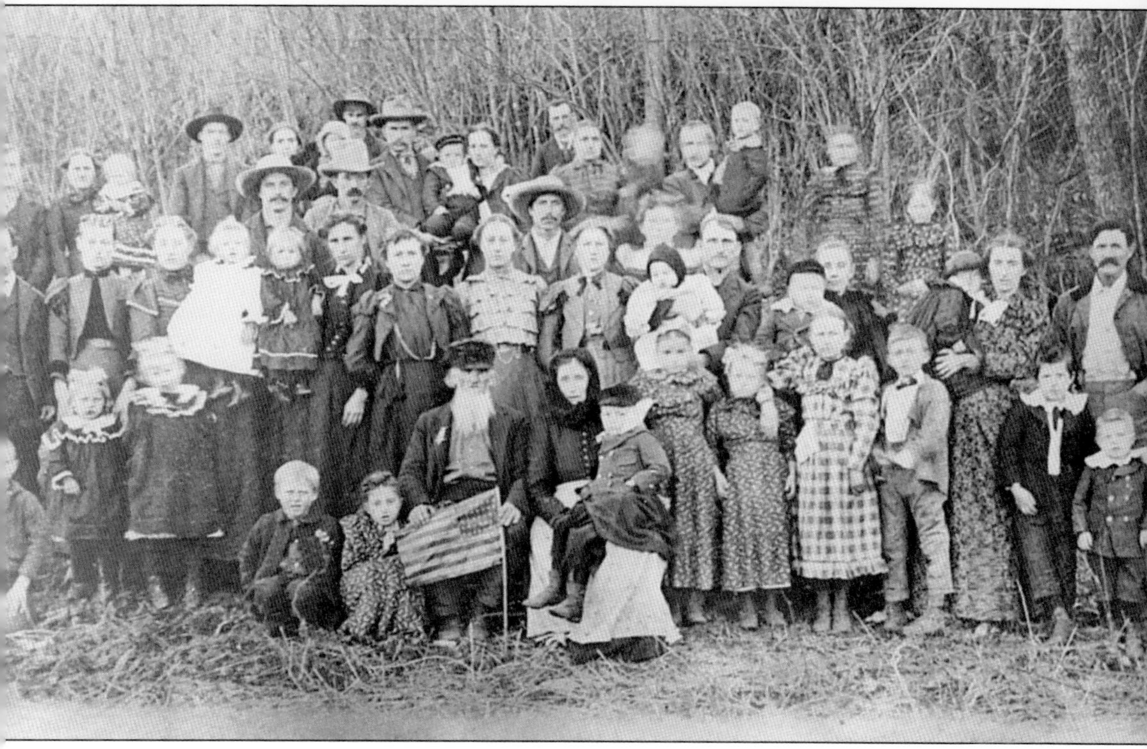

THE WHORTON REUNION: The "Whorton Reunion" photograph was taken in 1900 when many family members and friends gathered at the home of Randa and Sarah Whorton on their homestead near Turkey Creek in Hollister, Missouri.

Front row, left to right: boy kneeling is Tommy Strahan, two girls are Annie and Emy Rittenhouse, boy and girl kneeling are Andy Whorton and Mattie Burks, Randa C. Whorton is holding the flag, his wife Sarah is holding Clem Whorton, three young girls are Maudie Burks, Tilda Burks, and Mollie Whorton, Lester Breshears, Ben Layton, Randa Layton, and Walter Whorton.

Second row: Isaac Strahan, Sinea Whorton Strahan, Mandy Whorton Rittenhouse, two babies are Alford Rittenhouse and Becky Burks, Mallie Whorton Burks, Martha Breshears, Ollie Whorton, Dollie Whorton, baby is Esby Whorton being held by Newt Whorton, small boy is Clyde Whorton held by Lydia Rittenhouse Whorton, Edna Layton Brittain held by Safronea "Whorton Layton, and William David Layton.

Third row: boy is Albert Whorton held by Gemes Whorton, Almeda Whorton holding Margie Whorton, two men with hats and mustaches are Dave Rittenhouse and Jim Burks, next man with hat and mustache is John Rittenhouse, Maude Whorton Rittenhouse.

Back row: Man with hat is Dick Whorton, Millie Whorton is holding Oscar Whorton, two men with hats and mustaches are George Breshears and Johnny Whorton, child is Paul Whorton held by Mrs. Johnny Whorton, Green Brantly, Kezia McGown Whorton, Les Whorton, Jepp Whorton holding Alvin Whorton, Rosa Swartz and Nora Spruce.

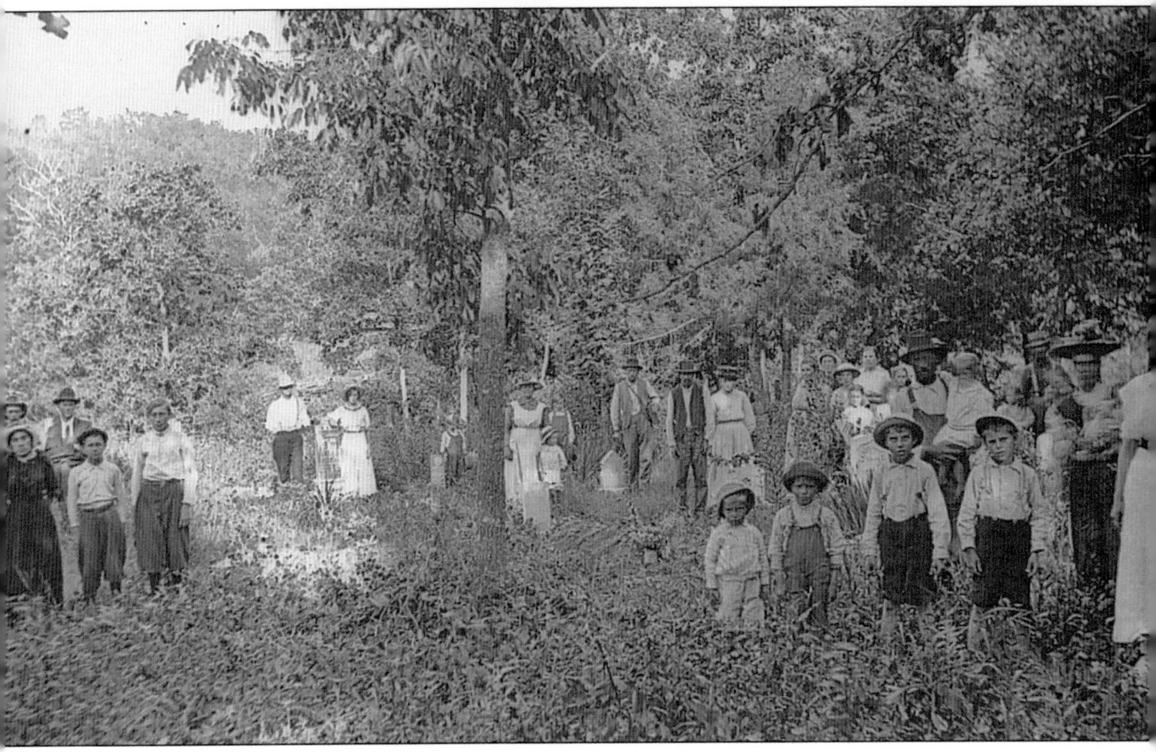

The Whorton Cemetery Gathering: The "Whorton Cemetery Gathering" photograph was taken in the early 1900s at the Whorton family cemetery by Turkey Creek in Hollister, Missouri. Family members gathered that day as one was laid to rest. This lovely little cemetery is almost forgotten but is a part of Taney County's past. It is visited each Memorial Day by today's family members who still remember and cherish the memory of loved ones at rest.

Pictured left to right: Edna Layton Brittain, Rosa Kaneaster Layton, Clinton Whorton, Ira Rittenhouse, Randa Layton, Austin Whorton, Oscar Whorton, Dave Rittenhouse, Anne Rittenhouse, Elsie Rittenhouse, Almeda Whorton, Delbert Whorton, Gemes G. Whorton, John Rittenhouse, Mrs. Stewart, Annie Gibson, Millie Whorton, Alford Whorton, John Whorton, Clifford Whorton, Richard Whorton, Uncle Dick Whorton holding a child, Aunt Maude Rittenhouse, and Emy Rittenhouse.

Gemes (Uncle Jim) Whorton took stones from cedar glades near this area, then chiseled the names and dates on all the older graves.

Author's note:
Randa Clinton Whorton's brothers and sisters:
Gemes Whorton (killed in Civil War)
William Billy Whorton
John Whorton
Polly Ann Whorton Johnson
Tilda Whorton Reves (Morgan Reves)
Lavica Whorton Ralston (John Ralston)
Heatha Whorton Clark

PUBLIC SALE

I WILL SELL AT PUBLIC AUCTION AT MY PLACE KNOWN AS THE G. C. WHORTON PLACE ABOUT 3 1-2 MILES NORTHEAST BRANSON, 3-4 MILE OFF HIGHWAY 80 ON LONG BEACH ROAD

FRIDAY, NOV. 16

BEGINNING AT 10:00 A. M.

—LIVESTOCK—

1 Jersey Cow, 4 yrs. old, will be fresh
1 Jersey Cow, 7 yrs. old, dry
1 Black Mare, 8 yrs. old, broke to work
Some Chickens

—MACHINERY AND TOOLS—

1 Hay Rake 1 A-Harrow
1 Section Springtooth Harrow
1 Peg Tooth Harrow
1 Double Shovel Plow
1 Single Stock Plow; 2 Turning plows
1 Two Wheel Cart
2 Sets of Harness; 1 Leather halter
1 Rope Halter; 2 Pitch Forks
1 Potato Fork; 1 Pair sheep shears
1 Spade; 2 Long Handle Shovels
2 Other Large Shovels One a scoop Shovel; 1 Large Anvil
1 Large Shop Blower
1 Large Vise and lots of shop tools
2 Mattocks; 1 Hoe and Rake
1 Almost new Garden Plow
1 Buck Saw; 1 Cedar Buck Saw
Crowbars; 1 Maul Ax
2 Other Axes and Wedges
1 Wagon Jack; 1 Hay Knife
1 Broad Ax; 1 Foot Adz
1 Good Foot Tread Grind Stone
Horse Shoeing Tools; Cow Bells
Hand Saws and Other Carpenter tools
Log Chains and Other Chains
1 All Metal Wheel Barrow
1 Royal Blue Separator; Lariat rope
Several Metal Feed Barrels
2 Twelve-Dozen Egg Cases
2 Wooden Barrels; Counter Scales
Hand Sickles, Stone Jugs, 1 gal. red Paint; Metal top for brooder heater

—HOUSEHOLD GOODS—

3 Bedsteads & springs; 1 Dresser
3 Cotton mattresses; 1 pr. coil springs
1 Metal couch can be made full size bed
1 Chicken feather bed; Bed clothes
1 Sewing machine, World's Rotary, in Good Condition; Quilting Frames;
Lard Stands; 1 ice box; 1, 4-Gal. stone Churn;1 3-Gal. stone churn; 1Camera to made post card size & larger pictures; 1 Coffee mill; 1 10-gal.
Stone Jar; 1 5-gal. cream can; 1 2-gal
Cream can; dishes, cooking utensils
Some buckets; Hand washing machine, all metal with wringer; 22 Rifle
1 4-Tube R.C.A. Battery Victor radio
2 Commodes; 1 stand table; wash stand
1 Dining Table; Kitchen Table; 2-door Safe; 1 Cast Iron cook stove; Chairs
1 New Iron Wood Heater; 1 Pressure Cooker, 22 qt. Improved Kook Kwick
Small Cabinet; Telephone, Western Electric; 1, 15 gal. iron wash kettle & iron stand; Canned fruits & vegetables
Empty fruit jars; 3-gal. Stone Jar; several 1-gal. milk jars; 1, 20-gal iron Wash Kettle; 1, iron kettle to cook in
Good ironing board; library table
Divan, 2 matching rockers; oak rocker
Cane Rocker; Three quarter Bed;
2 Beds, springs & mattresses; 3 good as new mattresses; Iron bedstead;
Stand Table; Dining table, 3 extra Leaves; 6 Dining chairs, Large safe;
2 500-Chick size electric brooders
Other things too numerous to mention

TERMS—CASH

LUNCH ON THE GROUND

ALMEDA H. WHORTON, Owner

HILLHAN & HILLMAN, Phone 70M
Auctioneers

MRS. CLINTON WHORTON
Clerk

49

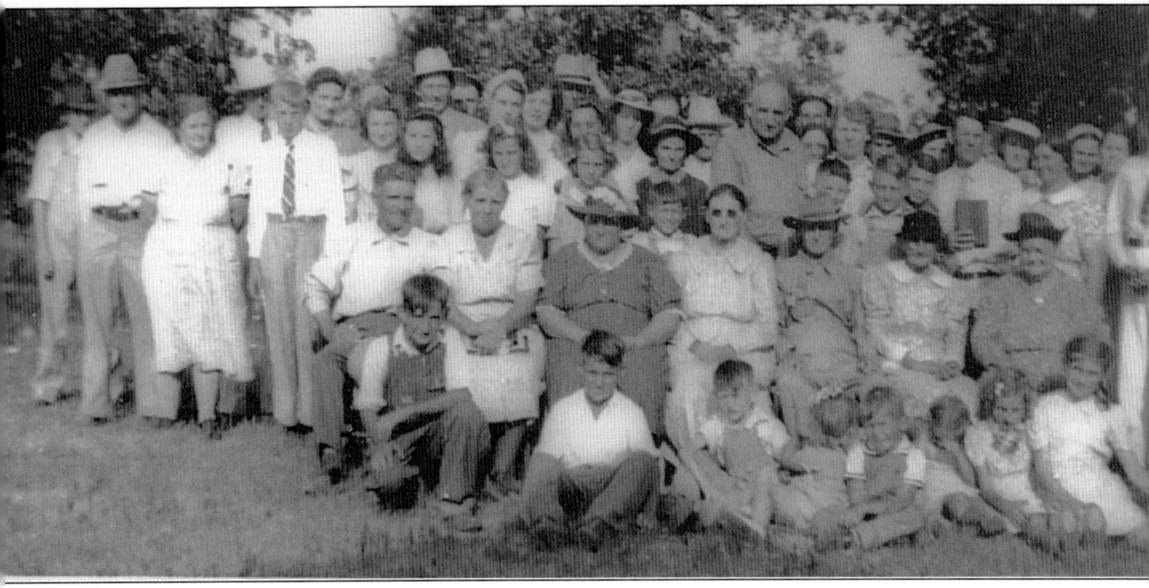

The 1942 Gathering at Clyde Whorton's: Many of the relatives got together at Clyde "Whorton's in the summer of 1942 for this gathering of the Whorton family. It was a hot day as many of the kinfolks and friends enjoyed the day visiting and fellow shipping with God, as well as the dinner on the grounds.

Their identities in this photo are as follows: (front row, let to right) Francis Thurman Rittenhouse and her sister, Charles Whorton, a couple of the Dickey girls, and the other identities are unknown; (second row) Almeda Whorton, Lydia Whorton, Newt Whorton, Fronea Whorton Layton, Edna Layton Brittain, Mamie Littig, and Art Littig; (third row) Esby Whorton, Beatrice Sims, Luther Sims, three of Lee Collier's boys, Don Whorton, Junior Yarnell, Elly Whorton, Clyde Whorton, Ollie Lord, Pheobe Sims Snapp, Bonnie Christian, Maxine Yarnell, Geneva Collier, Kenneth Whorton, Ethel Smith Layton, and Randa and William (Bill) Layton; (fourth row) Vinita Dickey, Eva Whorton, Salley Pickett, Winnie Collier, next two are unknown, Esther Whorton, unknown, Goldie Thurman, Stella Hunt, Lois Whorton, Claude Hunt, Frieda Hunt, and Clarence Collier; (fifth row) Austin Brittain, Douglas Hines, Jaunita Collier, Albert Whorton, Ollie Layton, Emil Fletcher, and Bobby Layton.

Some others are: Bill Hensley, Frank Davis, Francis Davis, Price Brittain, Charlene Layton Rowland, Hazel Layton Cobb, Frank Pickett, Augusta Whorton Johnson, Ernie Johnson, and Lonnie Layton. The two oldest ones there were Fronea Layton and her brother Newt Whorton.

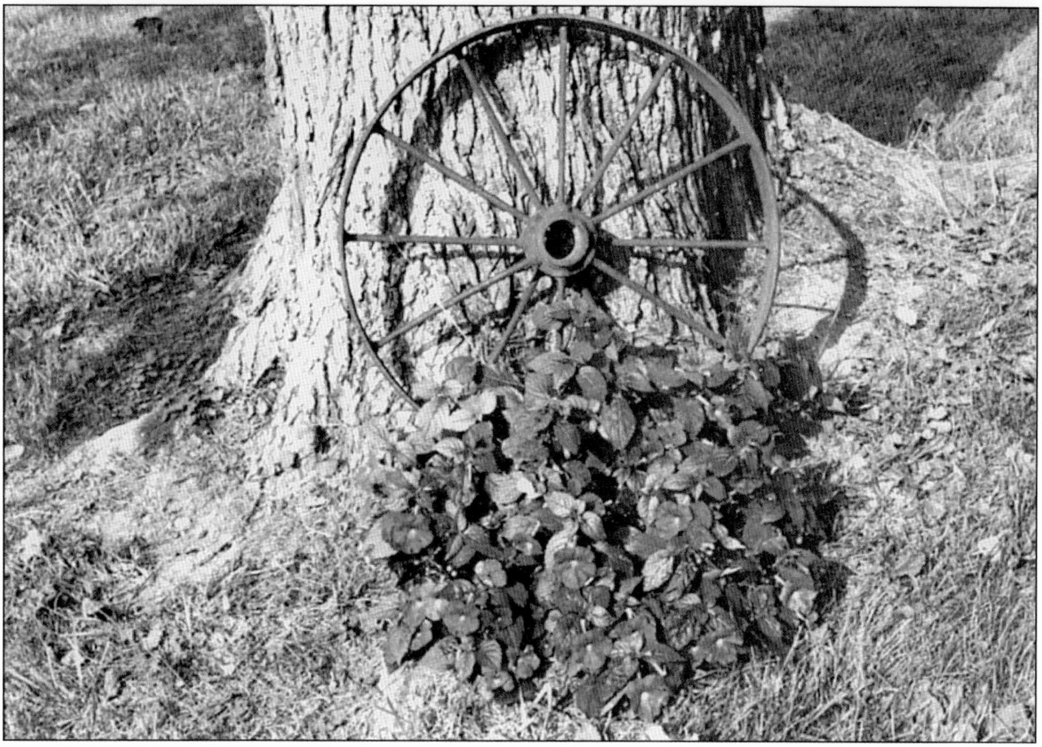

A wagon wheel from yesteryear now still and silent with a bouquet of flowers as if a grave marker to yesterday's forever gone.

PART FOUR

THE BOLLINGER FAMILY

Psalms 89:15 *Blessed is the people that know the joyful sound: they shall walk, O Lord, in the light of thy countenance.*

Psalms 100:3 *Know ye that the Lord he is God: it is he that hath made us, and not we ourselves; we are his people, and the sheep of his pasture.*

Sarah C. Bollinger Whorton spent many evenings not knowing where her husband Randa was fighting during the days of the Civil War. She had two sons of her own involved and two brothers-in-law. There isn't much recorded in the family history about the Bollinger family involvement in the War. But it is evident that the war touched the lives of every family in one way or another during this era.

According to family history, Sarah's grandpa, Dave Bollinger, rode his horse into the town of Huntsville, Arkansas, when he was 107 years old.

The following are two songs Sarah found herself quite familiar with as she sang the ballads of the Civil War era.

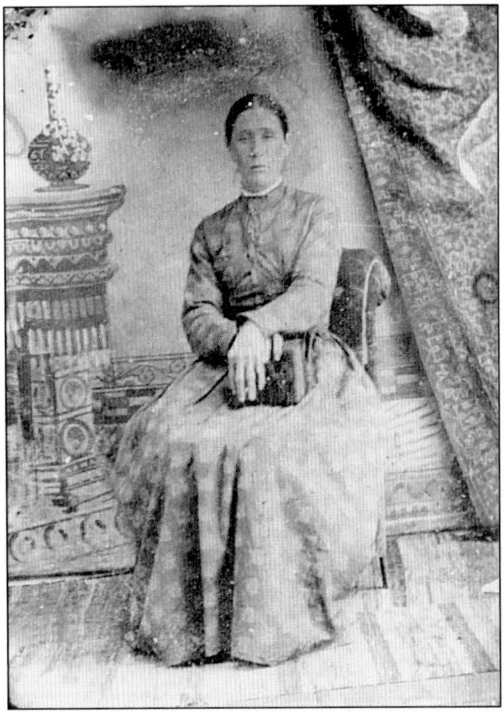

Sarah Catherine Bollinger Whorton. This was taken some time the Civil War.

<u>*Lay flowers Lovingly*</u>

Lay flowers lovingly over the dead
Leave not a loved one to grieve by the bed.
Of a darling forgotten, for God bore away.
Some shrouded in Blue and some shrouded in Gray.

Over them all, Angels are watching,
Over them all, over them all.
Let the bright flowers, Lovingly lay
Over them all, over them all.

Lay flowers lovingly over the dead
Garland its portals and hide all its gloom
For the heroes are resting from honors today
Some shrouded in Blue and some shrouded in Gray.

Lay flowers lovingly over the dead
Weave a bright chaplet to cover the head
And while thou art weeping for the loved born away
Lay Garlands of peace o'er the Blue and the Gray. 10

Welcome, Brave Soldiers, Welcome

Who risked your lives to save
The country from its ruin
And also free the slave
You left your home and dear ones,
The Civil War to fight.
And amid the roar of cannon,
You the wrong did right.
So this is why we welcome you,
Who did the country save
You left your home and dear ones
And who did free the slaves.
What mean these flags and decorations
That we see all through the land?
'Tis to celebrate the memory
Of that brave and fearless band
Who sailed forth to battle
Left their homes, kith, and kin.
They sought to stamp out slavery
And the Civil War to end.
This they did and now we gladly
Honor them who bravely gave
All they had, to bring together
North and South, and free and slave."

Jap Bollinger's Brutal Discovery

One time there was a young woman with a small child who lived in Yellville, Arkansas, at the time of the Civil War. After she had received word her husband had been killed in the fighting, she decided to travel to Huntsville to stay with some relatives. The only means of transportation she had was to travel by foot and maybe along the way she could hitch a ride with someone in a wagon.

She gathered up a few belongings, put the child on her hip and began her journey. At the end of the first day in the evening, the woman stopped at a lone cabin near the edge of some timber. She asked the elderly man who lived there alone if she could spend the night and resume her journey about daylight. The old man wasn't in his right mind and denied the hospitality of his home and requested that she move along.

Discouraged and frightened the woman said if he wouldn't let her stay would he just let her have a chunk of fire from the fireplace. Then when he obliged her this request, she left and went to the edge of the timber and built a fire for the night. As she found a suitable spot for the baby to lay down and sleep she began the task of preparing for the night. As the fire blazed successfully, she sat down and sang a lullaby to the child. Already frightened to be alone in the woods, she heard the scream of a panther coming from the dark shadows of the night. With no means of protection, the woman was totally helpless. As the scream drew nearer she picked up a chunk of fire and threw it in the direction of the scream. This angered the cat, and as it let out another terrible scream it made a lunge for the woman and child. Within a matter of seconds they were both killed.

The next morning Jap Bollinger along with two neighbors were running their line of traps in that area. As Jap checked a trap near a spring he glanced in front of him about one hundred yards and could see a panther drag something on the ground. Jap's first thought was the cat had robbed his trap and he would check to see what it had. He tied his horse and yelled for the other two to come quickly. Jap took his rifle and walked through the brush quietly.

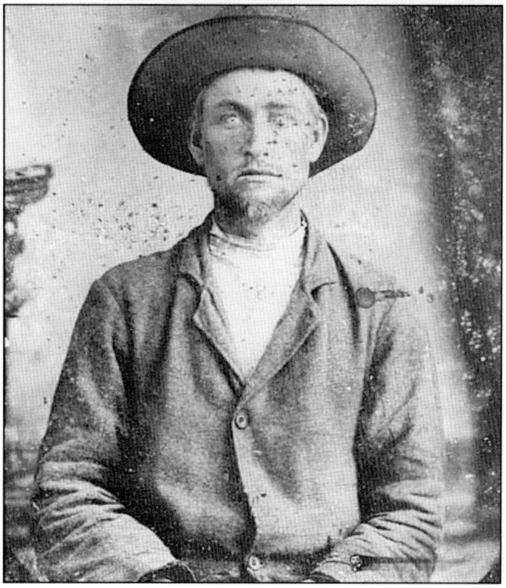

Jap Bollinger.

Less than 40 feet from the cat he could make out what the grisly sight was. The panther was dragging the partial remains of the young woman. With careful aim he sighted in on the cat, pulled the trigger. The cat jumped into the air, screamed, and turned to face its foe. As a second shot came from the right of Jap, one of his neighbors fired and killed the panther.

Close to the mother by a log they found the remains of the child. They dug a grave and buried them together. Jap and his friends were not far from the old man's cabin so they rode there to tell him what happened. They asked him if he had heard the cat scream out in the night or if he had seen the woman.

The old man was stunned by the news. He confessed he denied her the comfort of his home for the night and made her go on. He was so upset that he sat down on his front porch and cried.

Fredrick Bollinger's Panther Tale

One time there was a man with a small son about six years old. They left their cabin early one morning to go out in the woods and chop down a bee tree to rob the hive of honey. All the man took with him was his double-bit axe and a hunting knife that he carried in a sheath on his belt.

While the man was busy chopping at the base of the tree he heard the scream of a panther come from the timber in front of them. He motioned for his son to get behind him as the panther ran straight at him. As the big cat made a lunge at the man, he threw his chopping axe at it. The axe only stunned he cat.

The cat landed on the man, dug it's claws deep into his shoulders and neck and tore at his sides. He man knew he wouldn't be able to stand much longer as he fought the cat. The little boy screamed out, "Daddy, oh Daddy, don't you want your knife?" He pulled the knife from its sheath and handed it to him. The man was able to grab the cat's tail and position it where he could kick it. Holding one side with one hand, with the other he managed to stab the panther to death. When the cat finally stopped kicking, the man fell along side of it. His left side was so gashed open that some of his entrails were hanging out. The little boy took his shirt and tried to tie it around his dad's waist.

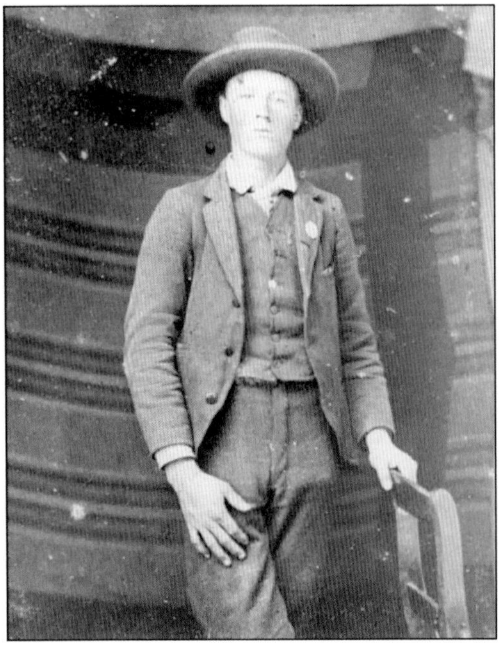

Frederick Bollinger.

After helping the man to his feet, the two of them started walking back to the cabin. The boy hollered for his mother when they got in sight. She opened the door, saw them walk up the path and ran to meet them. As she reached her husband, he collapsed helplessly to the ground. The woman told her son to get the horse bridled and ride over to the Whorton place for help.

The woman was able to get her husband inside the cabin and onto the bed near the fireplace. She began to cleanse his wounds and tried to stop the bleeding. He was in an awful shape and she feared he would die.

Soon the cabin door swung open as Randa Whorton and his brother-in-law, Frederick Bollinger, walked in. They rushed to the young man's side as Randa began to help the woman cleanse the man's wounds with some home remedies he brought from his home one tablespoon of a mixture consisting of the root, leaves, and berries added to a pint of boiling water. The proper dosage of this was to drink one teaspoon. Wild clover blossom was made into tea and the dosage was one half cup. Catnip tea required a teaspoon of the herb to one cup of boiling water. Besides giving these dosages to the man internally, the solutions were also used to cleanse the external wounds.

His wounds were so massive, it would be a matter of time. By now he was unconscious from loss of blood. Randa went on home after doing what he could. Frederick remained behind. He sat up with the man for several nights. On the third night in the early hours of morning, the man died.

At daylight Frederick dug a grave in the cemetery near the cabin. He made a pine box casket from boards he found in the barn. Noon came and the man was laid to rest. The woman and child asked Frederick to stay with them until they could make it on their own. He agreed but made a trip home to get a few belongings.

In the days that followed they began to harvest the corn crop, and took a wagon load to the mill to be ground and sold some to the merchant of the general store. What corn was left in the field would be harvested to feed the cattle and hogs.

Frederick chopped several cords of wood for the woman to cook and heat with. He returned several times throughout the winter to replenish her wood supply. After he moved back home he made frequent trips to visit and to do work the boy wasn't old enough to do. The three of them remained friends. Frederick taught the boy how to plow the fields and to fill the shoes his father left vacant.

In the years that followed the woman and boy managed their farm and crops as they continued to live in the Arkansas wilderness.

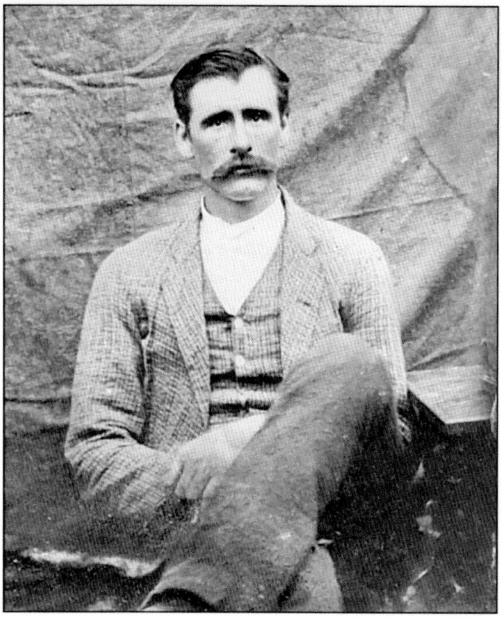

Newt Bollinger.

The Night Newt Bollinger Was Attacked

In the 1800s and early 1900s in the hill country a vast number of panthers roamed the wilderness. The panther was one of the most feared and dangerous wild animals in the woods for the early pioneers. Panthers followed people as they traveled by foot, horseback, or by wagon.

One time a relative of the Whortons' and Bollingers' named Gep Bowman had a daughter who lay sick at home in bed in need of a doctor. Gep asked Newt Bollinger to ride to the neighboring community 12 miles away and bring back the doctor.

Newt rode on a well-traveled road for those times. When he got halfway there, his horse began to spook and balk. It was still daylight but it was evening, and the dense timber made it difficult for Newt to see clearly. The horse reared several times as it tried to turn itself around toward home. It almost fell over backwards with Newt. The horse became uncontrollable and Newt realized he was in trouble.

The scream from a panther nearby made cold chills come over Newt as he tried to urge the horse onward. As they came to a short bend in the road with an overhanging ledge on one side, the horse reared up again. Within seconds a panther peered over the ledge. Then came another spine-chilling scream and the cat jumped onto the back of the horse.

Unable to reach his rifle now, Newt reached for his hunting knife he carried on his belt. As he felt the panther's teeth sink into his shoulders he began to stab it repeatedly. The pain Newt felt was excruciating, but he continued to try to stay in the saddle. The horse reeled around out of control as it tried to rid itself of the cat. Newt was about to give up when the blade of his knife broke off in the cat's chest. All he could do now was fight it with his fists. As an urgent prayer passed from his lips he was finally able to kill it with his fists.

The cat slid from the horse's back as Newt fell out of the saddle. Holding his side he tried to tear his shirt and wrap it around his waist to stop some of the bleeding. The horse's hips were badly gashed, and it was so frightened that it shook and trembled. With one hand clinging to the saddle horn Newt huddled close to the horse.

They began to walk down the road again. A short time passed until a man in a wagon came by and offered Newt a ride. Newt accepted and the man tied his horse behind the wagon. They arrived at the doctor's and Newt was taken in for treatment. Luckily, his wounds were not massive. After the doctor patched him up, he persuaded Newt to sleep awhile. He gave him some medication to help ease his pain and help him rest. The doctor also patched up the horse's hips and it was bedded down in a stall at the livery stable.

Newt had managed to give the doctor directions to Gep's house as he explained the girl's situation. The man who brought Newt in agreed to stay with him the next day as soon as the doctor left at daylight to go to Gep's. It was late now and the doctor did not want to leave Newt.

The next morning the doctor left in his buggy en route to Huntsville. Newt was doing well but needed further bed rest before the journey back home. When the doctor arrived at Gep's he took the girl's vital signs and gave her medicine. He stayed the day and night there sitting up with the girl who showed some improvement by morning. He decided she would be well in a few days so he left some medicine instructions with the girl's parents.

The doctor had explained Newt's condition when he arrived at Gep's and word was sent to the Whortons and Bollingers. When the doctor left Gep's home to return to Newt, one of the Bollinger boys and Randa Whorton were in a wagon to follow the doctor to pick up Newt.

The buggy and wagon left the Bowman home and arrived at the doctor's home where his office was located. They were surprised to see Newt up and walking around. He seemed quite anxious to return home and see the little girl.

The doctor explained to Newt he needed plenty of rest and told him how to take care of his wounds. Bowman and Whorton helped Newt into the back of the wagon where he was laid down on some soft quilts. They tied his horse to the back of the wagon and left. The doctor said he would be around to check on Newt in a few days.

On the journey home they had to travel slow. The horse walked slowly with a limp and Newt could not stand to be bounced around. When they came to the place where the panther attacked them the horse became frightened and they had to blindfold him and lead him through.

When they arrived home Newt rested for several weeks and the doctor visited him several times. His wounds soon healed and he became active again. The horse's wounds healed but it was permanently damaged in its hind quarters and could no longer be ridden by anyone but Newt. The horse spooked badly at night and was just used in light work.

Dave Bollinger's Journey West

In the 1870s and through the years after, wagon trains headed West toward the open country in the Pacific Northwest. There was plenty of unoccupied land offered to those who wished to settle in the West.

One of Sarah Bollinger's brothers, Dave, joined a band of wagons heading from Missouri to the West. Dave didn't have a wagon but had his belongings tied onto a pack horse which he led.

There was one man among the travelers who bragged that he would kill the first Indian he saw. Very few of the travelers associated with this man who traveled by himself. One day, after they were past Dodge City, Kansas, about two days journey, the wagons passed a beautiful Indian girl as she sat on a log. Soon, there was a gunshot heard, and the young girl fell backwards, dead.

The wagon master was the first to reach her. He checked her pulse and found none; the young girl was dead. Others ran from their wagons to where she lay on the blood-stained ground. The women hung their heads and cried. Then the sound of laughter and a shout of victory was heard as the man who bragged of killing an Indian walked up to view his victim. He commented on how good she looked dead and how he longed to see the next Indian. The wagon master warned him the Indian tribe would not let this go unanswered. The man laughed and walked back to his wagon.

That evening the wagon train made camp by a creek that flowed near the trail. The talk that evening consisted of the day's journey and the death of the Indian girl. Many of the travelers feared retaliation from the Indians.

The next morning the wagon train was surrounded by warriors and the Indian Chief wanted to speak to the wagon master. The Chief questioned him about the girl's death and demanded her killer be handed over or all of their lives would be in danger. Without hesitation, several of the men grabbed the man and escorted him to the Chief saying, "This is the man you want."

The man began to sense he was in grave danger and demanded the wagon master plead to the others to protect him. The wagon master sadly reminded him that he had been warned and now the time had come. The Chief ordered all those on the wagon train to line up in front of the camp and watch.

The warriors hung the man upside down from a tree as if he were a wild animal. They stripped his clothing from his body as he kicked and screamed in fear. The warriors took their hunting knives and began to skin the man's hide from his body starting with his feet and worked their way down. The man kicked and screamed for mercy, but none was shown. Many of the women fainted at the gruesome sight while the children became hysterical. Some of the men could not bear to witness such an ordeal.

When the warriors finished skinning him, they cut the ropes and let him fall. As he screamed and moaned in agony the man crawled along the ground to the creek where he got a drink and hung his head into the waters. No one would go near him as he begged for someone to shoot him. They just stood back and watched as the Indians ordered. After an hour, the man died.

The Chief warned the rest not to let anything like the girl's death happen again or they would return. As the Indians rode out of camp, some of the travelers loaded their wagons after making the decision to return to their old homes they had left behind.

Dave Bollinger helped dig a grave for the dead man. He also changed his mind about continuing West to the Oregon frontier. About four or five wagons headed back to Missouri and Arkansas. Dave became the guide back East.

When the wagons passed by the place where the girl had been killed, they could see the monument the Indians left to remind

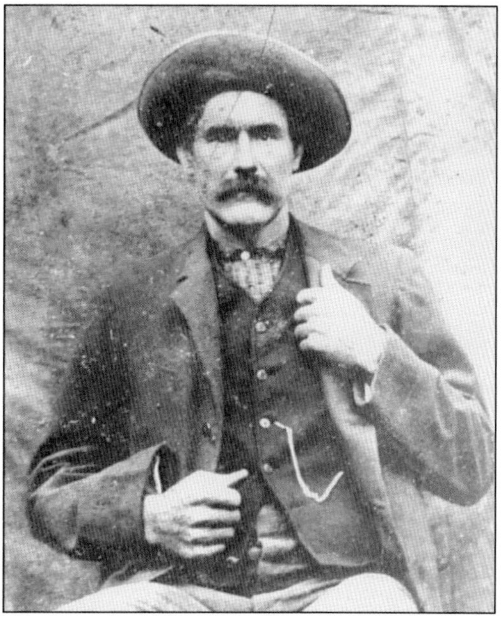

Dave Bollinger.

those passing by of what happened. Hanging from the limb of an oak tree was the dead man's hide. The women tried to shield the children's faces from the gruesome sight. It had been a terrifying experience, one they would never forget.

After a long journey the wagons reached Missouri safely and Dave journeyed on to Arkansas. Many of these travelers never ventured from their homes again. Dave finally returned to Huntsville, Arkansas, where he lived out the remainder of his days. Dave never married. His sweetheart died when she was young and he never went with another woman after her death.

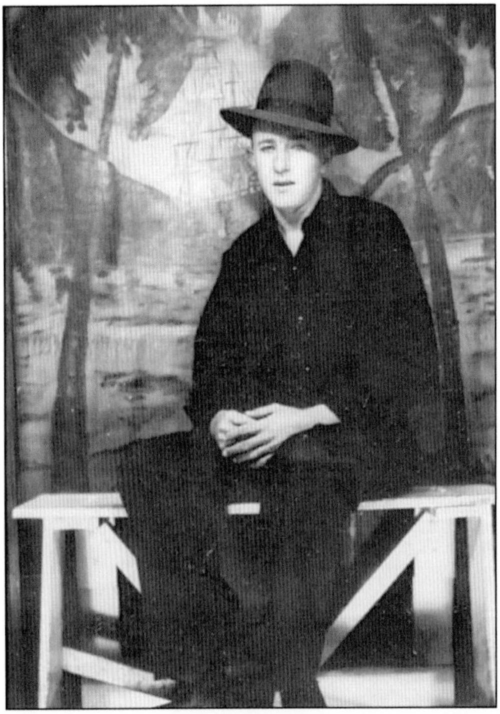

This young man is William (Bill) Thomas Layton, a great-grandson of Randa and Sarah Bollinger Whorton and a grandson of William David and Safronea Whorton Layton. The picture was taken in 1945.

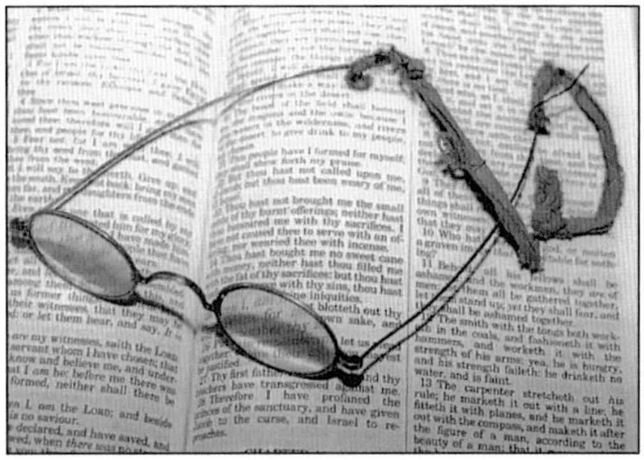

These wire rimmed glasses were worn by Sarah.

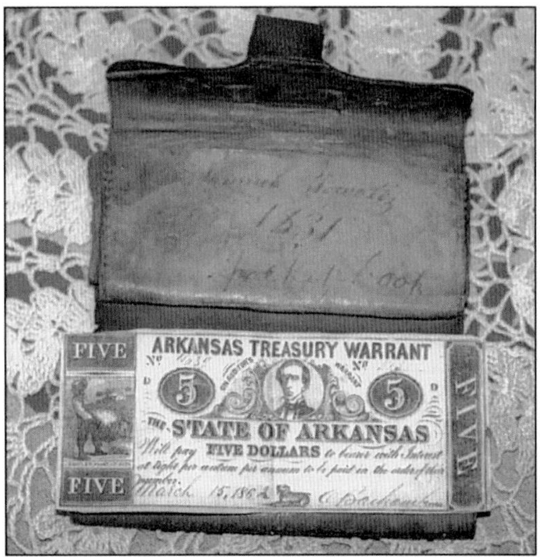

This billfold belonged to Sarah's grandfather, Dave Bollinger. He rode his horse through the town of Huntsville, Arkansas when he was 107 years old.

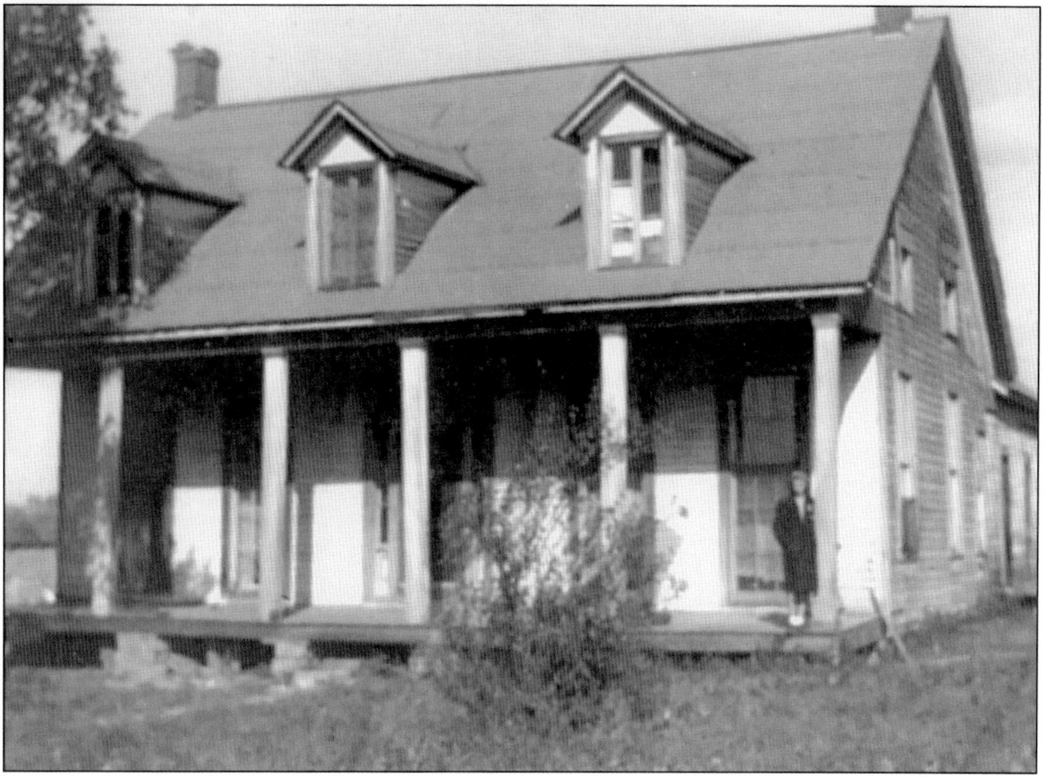

Original home built by Thomas Layton and Julia in the 1850s. Charlene Layton Rowland is standing on the porch.

PART FIVE

THE LAYTON FAMILY

***Isaiah* 65:22** *They shall not build, and another inhabit; they shall not plant and another eat: for as the days of a tree are the days of my people, and mine elect shall long enjoy the work of their hands.*

***Ruth* 1:16-17** *And Ruth said, "Entreat me not to leave thee, or to return from following after thee: for whither thou goest, I will go and where thou lodgest, I will lodge, thy people shall be my people, and thy God, my God. Where thou diest, will I die, and there will I be buried, the Lord do so to me, and more also, if ought but death part thee and me.*

Layton-Foster

(Article: Your Family Tree: Ozark Genealogy.)

Mrs. C.F. Ammerman, 2331 South Virginia, Springfield, Missouri 65804, would like to contact all branches of this family, some in Springfield as early as 1843, later moving to Taney County, Missouri. Charles Layton (1791 Va., d. after 1860), m. 1813, Sarah Foster, Spotsylvania Co. Va. Children: Ann (m. Edward Almond); Susan (m. Robert Lowry); Thomas Foster (b. 1820, d. 1899 Taney Co., Mo.—m. Julia Ann Foster); Sarah (m. Thomas Jefferies); William; Archibald; John F.; Marana (m. John Bedford); Virginia (m. James Forrester); Charles R. Layton; and Robert Dudley Foster (b. 1795 Va., d. 1868 Va.—m. Elizabeth Mitchell, 1802 Va., 1900 Springfield, Mo.). Children coming to Missouri were: John A. (killed at Wilson's Creek); Julia (m. Tom Layton); Robert; Amanda (m. William Peacher); Joseph Moody; Mary Ann (m. Dr. William Hughes II); — Fullen (first name not known); James; and Ellen (m. Dick Stone); and Thomas.

This letter was written by Thomas F. Layton to his father and mother, Charles and Sarah Layton, living in Springfield, 1849. The original is in the possession of Mrs. Wesley Hawkins, Shreveport, La. Permission to print this in "Ozark Genealogy" was given by Mrs. Betty Ammerman, Springfield. The spelling is as it was written.

California Gold Diggings
November 13, 1849

My Dear Parents: It is with much pleasure that I accept this opportunity to address you, though I have but so short a notice that I cannot give you much information and will defer giving in detail my trip account until I find a more convenient season. We arrived here about the 13th of October, after a long and tiresome trip. One that I would not attempt to perform again for no small consideration. We had a hard trip of it at best, but thanks to kind Heaven we have gotten through and find prospects quite flattering. James Myers died on the 20th of October after a long illness of typhoid fever. The Doctor, Dutchman, and myself have had our health and are very well at present for which I feel thankful. We have been mining for some 20 days and have made an ounce per day to each with the most temporary machine. We have not made our Backwasher yet as we have not procured quicksilver. But the Doctor is going down to the city of Sacramento in a few days to lay in our winter stock of provisions and will get some quicksilver. Then we intend to make our machine. They sell for from $500 to $1000 and are being used by many. The miners find that the small cradling loose a great deal of the gold and a great many are using the backwasher. I intend to make one on a small scale and make it quite light in order that we may pack it up the mountains. Where it is very difficult to get along. Early in the spring we plan going up the Yuba River where it is very rich, but it is so cold now that miners have to leave. We are on the Yuba River at present where we expect to winter. It is quite pleasant.

The rainy season has set in and it is raining more than one half the time, which prevents us from working but it is not cold by any means. I think it is a healthy and pleasant climate. We passed through the finest yellow pine, fur and cedar in crossing the California Mountains that I have ever seen. I saw a number of trees that were 10 feet in diameter and 100 yards high.

Lumber is worth from 75¢ to $1 per foot and everything else high that requires laborers. Flour is worth 60¢ per pound, pork 75¢, beef 50¢, Bacon $1, dried apples or peaches $1.25 to $1.50, Irish potatoes $1, Onions $1.25, and everything else in proportion except clothing. That is cheap. I expect you can learn a great deal more about the country through the papers than I can tell you. I don't think that the gold *accounts have been exaggerated at all as some lucky fellows find large quantities while others are not doing so well. One ounce is about average. We can make one and a half ounces and ???? when we can work and should be so fortunate as to strike one of those rich places we may make quite ... [unable to read]...I promised to write to Messrs Lain and Kimbrough but I am so far from where the post office is that I don't know when I shall get the chance, but say to them that they are doing good business but still if they had 12 or 15 hands out here they would be certain of a fortune and I wish they had and I was partner with them.*

I advise all who wish to come to this country to come by the Isthmus of Panama as the time they would save, would more than pay the difference in the fare or pack mules. To start early in the spring with 100 days provisions, but I don't recommend the route across the plains at all.

I also promised to write to Capt. Bedford and Mr. Farmer (His sister Marana Layton married John B. Bedford) and will do so if I meet with a chance. Nothing would give me more pleasure than to write to my friends but I assure you that it is very difficult to get letters off and more so to receive them as I have not had a line nor heard one word from any of you in the states since I left and am now the most anxious to hear from my family, friends, and relations than I ever was. But I hope the Doctor will bring me some letters when he returns.

I find the Doctor to be everything that I could wish and am agreeably disappointed in him. I have taken John Kimbrough's advice. Tell Capt. Bedford that I don't know where Thomas Bedford (Capt. Bedford's son) is but if he has him a claim near Sacramento City he is sure of a fortune. I know he may do well. Archibald (Thomas Layton's brother) is in California but I have not seen him nor do I know where he is. I did not know that he was coming out here nor would not have known had Dr. Perham not seen him. He was then going up the Yuba

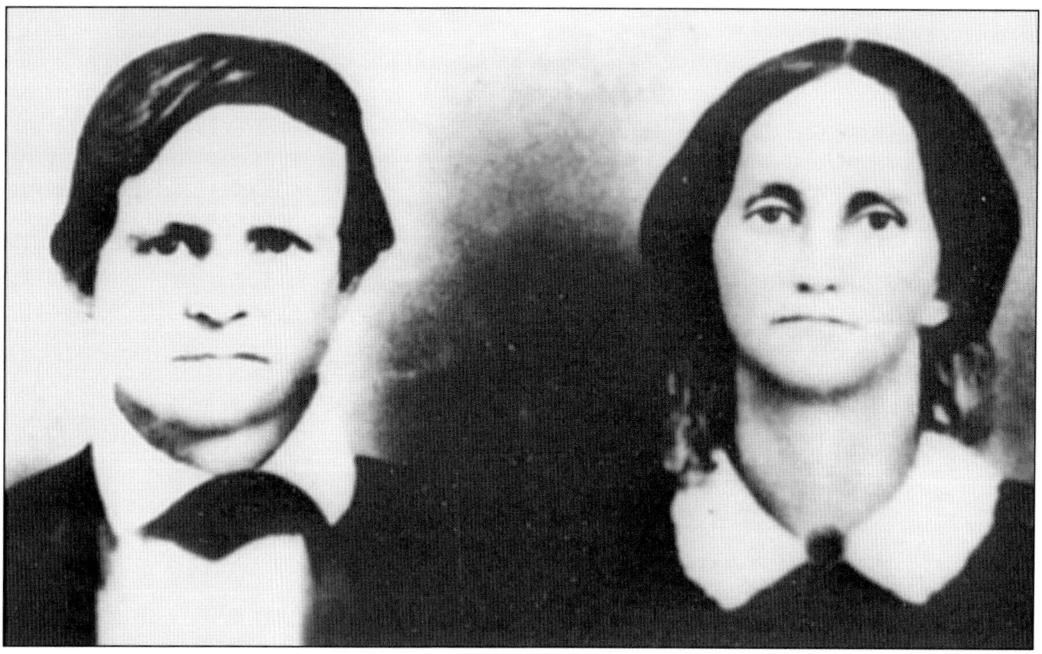

Thomas Foster and Julia Ann Layton.

River to work. That was before I got in as the doctor went ahead of the wagon before we crossed the Calif. Mountains. I have not seen John Foster (Brother of Thomas F. Layton's wife. Prosecuting Att. Greene Co. Mo. 1860, Confederate Colonel, died from wounds received at Battle of Wilson Creek, buried at National Cemetery, Springfield.) either nor do I know where he is. I have addressed him at Sacramento City but don't know when I shall see or hear from him. I wish I could see him and Archibald and wish that William [another brother] and Lowry and yourselves were out here and John also. I know you could make considerable in the course of one season and I would be most willing—if I had it—sent you the money to come. I have enclosed an order from Dr. Perham on Thomas Tiller for one hundred dollars which I wish you to get and send to Julia Ann (his wife who had gone with their children to Virginia to be with her folks) as soon as possible as perhaps she may need some for I wish her to send the children to school or teach them herself. You may take $25 for yourself and apply it to any purchase you please but if you need the necessaries of life apply it to that, all but $6 I wish Sarah (his sister, Mrs. Thomas Jeffries) to pay to Mr. Farmer and take in the letter due bill I gave him which she was to pay. I will send some more when Dr. Perham hears from Philadelphia, where he has deposited money. You must enclose this letter to Julia Ann as it may be some time before I can get a chance to write again. Direct your letters to Sacramento City. Give my love to all my relations and friends for I feel a warm regard for them and except for yourselves a full share.

From your affectionate son
Thomas F. Layton.

The view from Layton hill is a magnificent sweep across several thousand acres in the southwest corner of Taney County. It overlooks new Highway 65, the School of the Ozarks, and the ancient trail downward along Turkey Creek toward Hollister.

It includes the new home of Wanda and Vernon Layton who were among the seven Taney Countians to receive an award from the American Revolution Bicentennial Missouri Committee of Agriculture. The plaque stated:

"In observance of the American Revolution Bicentennial the Centennial Farm award is presented to Thomas Foster Layton, homesteader; Vernon Layton, owner. This award is in recognition of those farm families who have maintained an active interest in agriculture by owning and operating a Missouri farm for one hundred years or more. May this recognition also be a symbol of priority that a productive agriculture is vital to the health of this nation and to the world. Signed this Bicentennial year of 1976, James B. Boillot and Elmer R. Kiehl."

Vernon Layton is understandably proud of this honor but, of course, it doesn't tell the full story. Even Vernon isn't sure he knows it all. He is certain that the family is one of the oldest in this area and that his home rests on the original foundation of the old mansion built by Thomas Foster Layton over a century ago and became, in this county, a symbol of the Layton family's perpetuity.

The first of the Layton family to migrate to this part of the country was one of the seven children born to Charles and Sarah Foster Layton of Spotsylvania County, Virginia. In 1843 he followed the acceptable and prudent custom at the time by marrying his cousin, Julia Ann Foster. Both the Layton and Foster families originally came from England. Their lineage is buried in antiquity but is known to have been from Scotch nobility. They were people of substantial holdings and community standing when this country was just getting established. In Virginia, the Fosters owned not only vast lands but fleets of sailing ships and the Laytons were equally prominent. It was traditional that each individual member forge his own link in the family chain and there were no spoiled scions or favored sons.

Shortly after their marriage, Thomas and

Julia Ann put their personal possessions in a wagon, hitched to a yoke of oxen, and headed for Greene County, Missouri. Springfield, the Ozarks' Queen City, was a mere mud-streaked urchin but Thomas Foster saw its future promise. His faith in it and himself was such that he opened a mercantile store, the first in the town, and supplemented his income as a cabinet maker. Julia Ann contributed by sewing for the wealthy men of the area and in the rosy glow of ambitious youth, it looked as if they would make it on their own.

When news of the great gold discovery burst on Springfield, groups of men banded together for the trek westward. Under the banner of the Greene County Argonauts, many headed toward California to make their fortune. How many died of disease, accident, or foul play may never be known but the hazards soon became apparent to all.

Thomas Foster was among a group of 100 men, most of whom made it through safely. There is no doubt he hoped to find gold for he staked a claim in the hills above San Francisco. He was also a practical man and as agent for the firm of Kimble, Shepard and Kimble, he drove a herd of 1,500 cattle across the mountains to furnish meat for the 49ers. Since he anticipated being gone at least two years, Julia Ann went home to Virginia to stay with her family while he was away. His letters to her carried instructions as to the education of the children during his absence and included drafts to cover expenses and pay off debts. They were filled with details of what he found and did in that far-off land. He wrote of opening a store there and making investments, most of which were successes.

Although he abhorred it, personally, the trip West had been generally uneventful but the return was another matter. His father, who had gone with him, refused to recross the mountains and plains so they booked passage on a ship to sail around by way of South America. The voyage was a near disaster. The sailing ship was becalmed for six weeks and the food ran out. The men became so desperate with hunger they decided one of their number must be killed in order that the others might live. They drew lots for the sacrifice. However, before this cannibalistic act could be completed, a wind came up and, realizing there was a good chance another ship would come by and rescue them from starvation, they discarded the ballot. This decision proved correct and the remainder of the trip was without further incident.

In 1854, Thomas returned to Poker Flats, California, to check on his claim and the business he had established there. As before, he headed another cattle drive to pay his way. The claim had not produced anything of value and he felt himself fortunate to find a buyer—only to see the man strike gold the following day. This stay in the Golden State was an unhappy period. Thomas Foster was a man reared in the Southern tradition of decency and honor. A man's word was all that was necessary in a business transaction and a gentleman consorted with others of his kind. There he found himself in the midst of thieves, gamblers, and murderers. A man of strict moral convictions and church affiliations, he found the absence of any religious life nearly intolerable. His letters to his parents and to his wife were full of despair at what he saw and he noted with extreme clarity the conditions of the era and the absolute baseness of human nature. When vigilante groups took charge and hanged murderers in ever increasing numbers, he began to dispose of his holdings and wrote that he could not willingly be part of such an existence.

Probably his most pleasant memory was of a boat he had seen there. At least it made enough impression on him to give his next child its name, Sacramento Belle, and to her eventually went his only known memento of his trips, a ring made from a gold nugget.

Julia Ann's brother was also in the gold fields at this time and he wrote to his parents of his impression of the immorality there, stating there wasn't a Virginian in the area. They must inform Julia Ann—"I am far from ridiculing the people with whom she has been living for so long a time but must say that Missourians are among *the* greenest set of people in general that I ever saw and if the people here are a fair example of the Western people, I say, Lord, deliver me from a life's residence among them!"

How she received this message is unrecorded but her unselfish endeavors throughout her lifetime to comfort and assist her neighbors establish her concern for all humanity. In the best Southern tradition, no one was ever refused lodging or went hungry from the Layton home. She was waiting when her husband arrived back in Greene County, having spent this last vigil in her adopted land.

Thomas Foster's homecoming was too an equally unpleasant situation shaping up. He had little time to adjust his affairs before the outbreak of the Civil War. He joined the army of Sterling Price and fought valiantly for what he believe to be right, the Confederate cause. At the Battle of Elkhorn Tavern (Battle of Pea Ridge), he was wounded in the leg, captured and sent to Rolla, Missouri, for the duration of the war. For the rest of his life he walked with a limp.

There was relief if not gladness at the war's end. The feeling among many Springfieldians at the assassination of Lincoln was mixed. The city was under martial law. Quintus Richards reported that the citizens there were informed of the president's death and ordered to put out flags of mourning. One southern sympathizer hung out a blood red tablecloth and when a Yankee Captain rode up with his squadron and demanded the meaning of such an outrage, the lady replied she was doing as ordered. "Red is not mourning," he said. "Red is mourning for the devil and the devil is dead!" she snapped.

How strongly Thomas Foster's personal feelings were he never said, (at least for posterity). He took advantage of Mr. Lincoln's Homestead Act, homesteading 160 acres in Taney County. The property bordered one of the main north and south travel arteries used by the stage and freight lines between Springfield and Harrison, Arkansas. His neighbors were to be families who created Taney County history: the Ellisons, Olivers, Keiths, Whortons, Jacksons, Holidays, Coggburns, and a couple of Yankees he admired and respected, Dr. A.J. Storms and Hardin Warren.

He established a saw mill known as the Pinery, and it became a successful business. It was important enough to expand to a store with a Post Office, which made the area come to be known as the town of Layton. Andrew Brown, father of Lee Brown and Winnie Stottle, courted Susie Bryan with letters mailed from this place and to this area came his cousin, the great statesman, William Jennings Bryan, to visit during his campaigning. It became a favorite picnic spot in the 90s and "many a name is carved on the wall of the huge cave nearby."

Elizabeth Mahnkey describes the original power used at the Mill as "tread power" and writes of "an immense wheel placed in an incline, driven by 24 head of cattle, each tied to a place behind another. As they walked they turned the great wheel that made the power. Later, machinery was bought and installed and the mill became famous throughout the country."

It was the Layton mill that furnished the lumber to build the old mansion, "cut from Ozark oak and pine, so immense that the two 52 inch saws, one above the other, were required to make the cuts and only the heart of the logs were used," wrote Mrs. Mahnkey.

The house was styled in the old Colonial fashion of the Virginia plantations with stately white pillars on the veranda. They supported the high roof and dormer windows and cast oblique shadows onto the grounds below. There were beautifully carved woodwork, false fireplaces and a magnificent stairwell. Quoting a Layton, Mrs. Mahnkey wrote of the family ghost: "not a creepy, spooky ghost, but one who makes its presence known in the dark hours of the night with a pleasant tinkle of glass and silver in the grand old dining room."

It was a lofty, alien neighbor to the hand-hewn log cabins and salt box clapboards scattered through the county but to its owner the house was a monument to remind his sons and daughters of their prestigious heritage. It took seven years to build and so remarkable was the workmanship that it withstood the ravages of the elements and the onslaught of numerous descendants over a hundred years.

Originally there were two enormous trees flanking the entrance (one is dead), twin barns in the rear (one remains), and a handsome cellar built of square rock quarried on the place which is still in use. The customary burial ground is behind the house where Thomas and Julia Ann rest among their kin. Close by, the slaves who chose to ignore emancipation are buried.

Thomas also brought to his homestead the first and finest dairy cattle of the Ozarks to pasture on the luscious and plentiful native bluestem grass. He raised jet black saddle horses, prized as the ultimate in luxury by breeders and riders, alike, and easily identified by the tiny white forehead star that was their trademark. But his greatest feat was bringing in the Morgan quarter horse from New Hampshire. Those he bred and trained and they introduced into the West the fabulous cutting horse of the great cattle roundups.

He was a man of good judgment with a reputation for fair dealing and was often asked to settle disputes or act as administrator. (He was one of the three men appointed by the court to appraise the value of Malinda Fortner's property following her death—the land that became the center of Hollister.)

He was foremost in many fields and endeavors, setting the social trends and customs, and helping establish better educational standards. He employed teachers, paid their salaries and boarded them free of charge, allowing anyone who desired to attend classes. His own family received the best education available and they were taught to understand its values. All made good use of this. One son became a lawyer and a daughter married an educator who established Clarke Academy at Berryville, Arkansas.

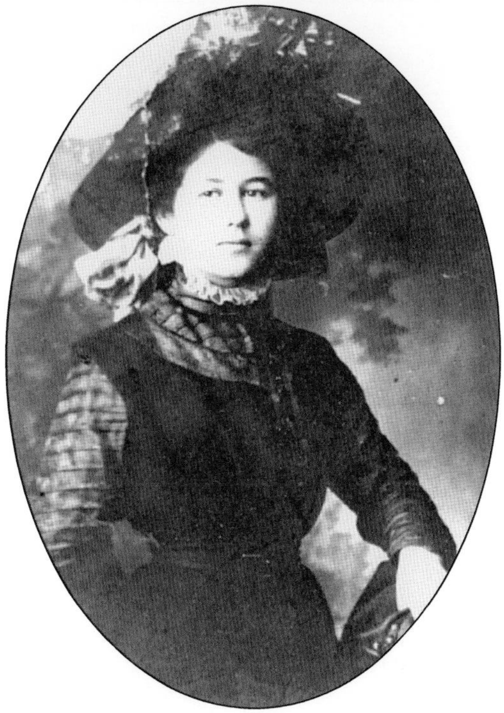

Louisianna Layton, daughter of Thomas and Julia, born June 24, 1861, died December 16, 1903. In the 1880's she was listed as an epileptic.

Obviously he had help in these matters and his strength and moral support no doubt came from his constant companion and equally strong wife. The couple seemed invincible. They had conquered near insurmountable obstacles, recreating a genteel southern way of life in a raucous new environment. Their dreams were unfolding and they saw the future a serene and happy fulfillment.

When their 12th child was 2 years old, Julia Ann developed "congestive fever" and died. While the world did not end, for Thomas Foster it changed and was never again the same. (He did remarry—a widow with a small child, 26 years his junior.) Years later, he had a magnificent portrait of Julia Ann done by a Chicago firm, an expensive and lengthy process. The day the portrait arrived he wrote his daughter of his satisfaction with the result and said he had taken it to show Uncle Hardin Warren.

Thomas Foster Layton died July 20, 1899, at the age of 67, but his mansion continued to house his children, grandchildren, and great-grandchildren. It was they who added to the original homestead until now the aggregate acres number nearly a thousand.

THE LAYTONS (PART II)

The Foster/Layton story began in Spotsylvania County, Virginia. Thomas Foster had belonged to the nobility of Scotland and England and was a direct descendent of the English Dudleys who owned large estates and ship lines that ran to several countries. He was a neighbor of George Washington and served in the fourth Virginia Regiment of Foot Soldiers during the Revolutionary War. His wife was Susannah Mitchell from Aberdeen, Scotland, and their families were of equal prominence. Susannah's sister, who had gone to live with an Aunt in Scotland, told her folks there was enough wealth in the family here to buy the entire state of Virginia. Certainly it was apparent in the Mitchells' lifestyle for John Mitchell's home was built of old stock wear, bricks, nails, and glass imported from Scotland and graced with cut glass and sterling. He was a proud and haughty Tory aristocrat down to his solid silver knee buckles.

The Horace Layton family was also from England and, like the Fosters and Mitchells, were descendent of the Cavaliers, members of the court of Charles I of England. They had developed a profitable freight business in the same Virginia county. Part of the route passed through the Manassa area, scene of two Confederate victories, the battles of Bull Run and also where the Civil War Battle of the Wilderness was later fought. At that time it passed the home of John and Susannah Foster and their seven children. Thus it was that Horace's son, John, met and on December 27, 1810, married Susannah (Sukey) Foster; his brother, Charles, married her sister, Sarah, on August 4, 1813.

After Horace died in 1841, the two couples and several of the Layton brothers and sisters immigrated to Greene County, Missouri. Among them were Thomas and Julia Ann and their little daughter Sarah Elizabeth, who was to grow up to marry first her cousin, Leonidus Layton, and then Walter Hopper. They brought with them a touch of southern elegance and a way of life quite the opposite of the northern pioneers for the Laytons as well as the Fosters brought along their slaves. They were in Greene County through most of the Civil War, fighting gallantly for the Confederate cause while Sterling Price occupied the city of Springfield. It was Col. John A. Foster, brother of Julia Ann who raised the first Confederate flag there. He died of gangrene, the result of a minnie ball wound in the leg received at the Battle of Wilson's Creek.

The elder Foster, Robert Dudley, remained loyal to Virginia. He had fought in the War of 1812 with the Virginia Militia at the age of 19. His six sons, five sons-in-law and four grandsons were all on the side of the South. Quintis Richards reported that his mother, Cordelia Foster Richards, told him of the Missouri branch inviting Grandfather Foster to visit with the idea of moving here. He came in 1868 and stayed but briefly. The trip had been hard and he was ill as a result. After returning home, he told his wife, "Betsy, I would not live there if they gave me the entire state." He died in Virginia on August 6, 1868. His widow did move to Missouri to live with her children and enjoy the pension she received through the latter part of her 98 years.

Some of the family came to Taney County during the war years, including Thomas Foster Layton and Julia Ann Cordelia and her husband, Rufus Richards, lived on the Layton property (the men being in the service). She and Julia Ann ran the Union blockade at Forsyth on several occasions, bringing badly needed supplies from Springfield for the Confederate Army to the south. She stuffed

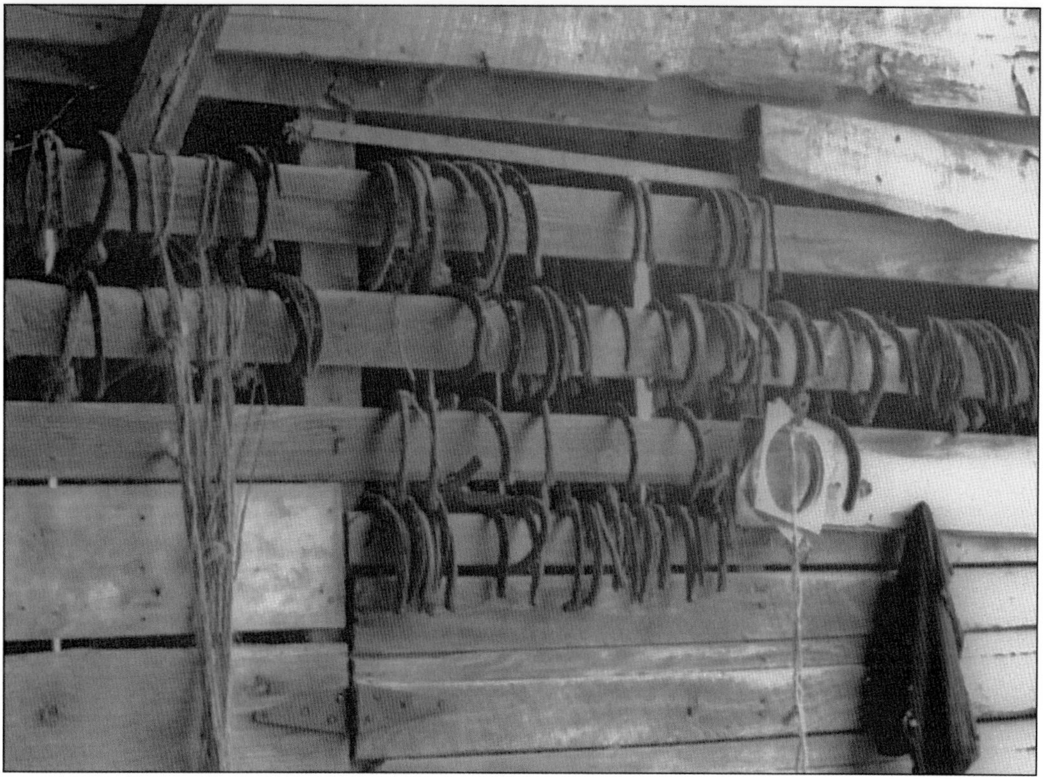

Inside view of the barn built by the Layton's in the 1850s.

dolls with quinine for the "gallant Missouri Soldiers of the Malaria Brigade," and brought salt and soda also. She had horse shoe iron cut in shoe lengths and tied the strips in bundles of straw and hid them under more layers in the wagon. Both nearly fell into the hands of the German mercenaries who fought with the Union Army. Halted at Forsyth by the Captain in charge, they were advised of the imminent arrival of the foreign soldiers. "I have a wife, mother, sister, and daughter," the Captain told them, "and I would not allow them to proceed tonight for I'm expecting a large number to start coming in and I cannot say what might happen to you."

He went on to tell them he would have a tent put up near his quarters for them and two guards to protect them and insisted they have supper with him. The meal, they said, was a good one but they could not sleep for worrying about what might happen should the soldiers examine their wagon. They left camp as early as possible the next day and met many of the foreign troops between the encampment and home, reporting their contacts were "simply awful" but they were not molested. It might have been different, they conceded, if they hadn't been befriended by and indebted to the enemy they were in the act of betraying.

The Richard's home was often visited by the Alf Bolen gang and sometimes by Bolen alone. The huge cave on the land is alleged to have been their hideout. The story of the outlaw's death has been written by many historians and the details vary little. However, most do not mention that the killing of this infamous monster took place in Cordelia's home and that she was the lady involved.

The family version is that government officials were trying to capture Bolen to end the continuous cycle of robbery and murder by his gang along the heavily traveled road between south Missouri and Arkansas, a Union supply route. Whether they believe there was sympathy for the outlaws, or realized there was little that could be done but tolerated the visits if they hoped to live, remains unclear.

But in any event, the officers arrested Rufus and to insure Cordelia's cooperation, told her that when they had Bolen in custody, they would release her husband. They then sent a soldier, disguised as a Southerner trying to make his way back home and pretending to be too ill to travel. When Bolen next came to her home, Cordelia told this story to him and after satisfying himself that the man was what he
seemed, Bolen accepted it. Mealtime came and she served the food, following which Bolen filled his pipe and turned to the fireplace for a light. The rest is history. The soldier struck him with a poker, knocking him unconscious. He started to hitch up a wagon to take him to Forsyth but Bolen began to regain consciousness and the soldier shot and killed him. Then he dashed to Forsyth to get a Union Captain and squad. They severed the head and took the body to Forsyth where they buried it in a large cracker box in an unmarked grave. The head went to Ozark where it was impaled on a pole in the square, a message of relief to travelers, and a warning to those who might entertain thoughts of continuing Bolen's practices. Finally, they packed up the Richards' belongings and moved them back to Springfield lest the gang try to seek revenge.

John F. Layton, son of Charles and Sarah, was 14 at the time the family left Virginia. Eleven years later he married Elizabeth Jarrett of Knoxville, Tennessee, who was also of Scotch descent. He, too, homesteaded on land near Cedar Springs close to his brother Thomas F. Layton. The period was tense and the area still primitive but the couple coped with the situation quite as well as Thomas and Julia Ann. Elizabeth refused to be intimidated by the roving bands of bushwhackers and guerrillas or the wildness of the region. The story is told of a stalking panther, squalling threateningly near the cabin where she and her slave woman were alone. Elizabeth's companion was terrified but, with staunch courage, the Rebel lady refused to leave and threw her feather bed into the fireplace to create a diversion, knowing the odor and fierce smoke would drive him away. Then, having proved her point, she sat down and calmly smoked her pipe.

John and Elizabeth raised a family of 10 children, instilling in them the virtues of honesty and thrift, manners and decorum, and never did they lose sight of the fact that they were Laytons, and southern. And while some eventually married to the north of the Mason Dixon Line, it was a situation the family frowned on and one Yankee member relates the story of an incident in which a relative was arrested in Illinois on a charge of horse stealing. His lawyer was a young man named Abe Lincoln who proved the charge to be false and unfounded. When the story was told, cousin Sacramento Belle echoed the family sentiment by saying, "Better to have hung for horse stealing than to have had Abe Lincoln for a lawyer!"

Whatever the viewpoint, the descendent and inter-marriage relationships of the Layton family run into astronomical figures. Their individual stories are vividly interesting, adding considerable material to the volumes of American history. The pride in their heritage is as strong in this year as when they first set foot on American soil.

John F. Layton died in 1880 and was buried on his property, in a field near the road by the School of the Ozarks. Next to him lies his son-in-law, Edward Reese, a German immigrant. About ten years later, his widow sold the place to a Mr. Vinton of Kirbyville and the family moved to Caddo County, Oklahoma. Elizabeth kept a restaurant in Union City for many years and died September 1, 1917 at the age of 79. She is buried at Pocassett in Grandy County, Oklahoma.

The couple's second son, William David (Dank) Layton was born in 1857 at Springfield and grew up in the Cedar Springs community of Taney County.

By now, conditions had improved to the extent that bears and panthers were not as prevalent, although wolves roamed freely and destructively through the countryside. However, the economic situation had worsened and law enforcement was a complete farce. Taney County was noted for its lawlessness and was the favored rendezvous of bushwhackers and guerrillas who followed in the wake of the Civil War. Murder went unchallenged and a life could be snuffed out easily and with little or no justification. There was no protection from and no punishment for crime. In rebellion, the Bald Knobbers organization was formed and members took matters into their own hands. Right or wrong, it was the beginning of a new way of life. No doubt each side had its stand and its story and, as historian Elmo Ingenthorn stated, "The truth lay somewhere in between." This was the framework in which William David Layton began his career.

He became a farmer/stockman, raising mostly sheep and, as did most local residents of that time, worked at whatever odd jobs were available to supplement his income. Although hard times had developed, he held to the family tradition of honor and always gave a good day's work to his employer. One of these was his uncle, Thomas Foster Layton, who now owned considerable property. For him, William hauled corn from the land that was later to become the YMCA Camp in Hollister and also worked at the Pinery. He is known to have split 100 rails a day during the period he worked for Dr. Storms with whom the family attended church at Gobbler's Knob and prayer meetings in the homes of neighbors. It is noted that he "loved little children, people, and had faith in God." Interestingly, and perhaps prophetically, he met Fronea Kathryn Whorton at the Layton mansion and the fine old Foster/Layton and Bollinger/Whorton lines were merged when they married.

Meanwhile, life continued its ever-changing pattern at the mansion. Most of the children had gone. Cornelius had been wounded in the Battle of Hartville in January of 1863 and died the following day. Julia Ellen had married John J. Jeffries and moved to Carrolton, Arkansas. Thomas Allen became involved in politics and was in the County Courthouse at Forsyth for many years. Laura Marshall had married Jasper Newton Stephens, a Christian minister of the Kirbyville area and Alice Monroe, after having taught school in old Warnersville (Kirbyville) married Andrew Jackson Stephens.

Louisiana remained a spinster and Ona Mae married Conred Kiesiech. Sacramento Belle, always unpredictable, married attorney Henry Glitsch of Hesse Dornstabt, Germany, in a Civil service, the bride and groom both on horseback. Claude Wesley had married in October of 1890 and he and his wife were there taking care of the place when Thomas Layton died of a heart attack in the portico of the mansion.

She was also from an old pioneer family, the daughter of Paralee Hopper and Washington McCormick. Wash's sister, Prudie, married the distinguished Gillum Hopper; thus the children of these couples were double cousins. Lula McCormick and Annie Belle Hopper were prominent in early Hollister history—Nannie Belle as the wife of Professor J.W. Blankinship and Lula as the mistress of the Layton mansion.

The Laytons (Part III)

The prominence of the Layton family at the turn of the century was unquestionable. On Layton hill, the mansion with its high ceilings and carved fireplaces was the setting for fancy parties and social affairs of western Taney County. The great parlor, filled with elegant furniture that had come all the way from St. Louis, was still the most impressive in the area. Its surrounding grounds held the interest of the younger set and to small visitors the twin haylofts were irresistible. From the open mows they jumped to the piled hay below and cared not at all for the history that had been created by the land's owners.

However, the family knew, and the sons and daughters, nieces, and nephews wore the name with pride. By now the custom of wedding their own cousins had died out and they married into the intrepid pioneer stock of the hills. Their partners brought to the family the fresh and stimulating character facets that kept the Layton line powerful and strong. They were active and interesting, their vibrant personalities a driving force that lifted them above the humdrum of ordinary existence and made them leaders—outstanding and unforgettable.

When Randa and Sarah Whorton left Madison County, Arkansas, and took up residence in the Turkey Creek area not far from Layton hill, their daughter, Fronea, was fourteen. In 1891, at the age of 25, she became Mrs. William David Layton. She was tall and slender with brown hair and eyes—quiet, gentle and deeply religious. With the solidarity of their combined ancestral background, this couple had every right to expect that their future would bring happy fulfillment to their dreams. For a short while they lived in the Oak Grove community, a few miles to the north along the White River.

As soon as they could afford it, they bought an 80 acre farm near her parents and settled down to raise a family. In those first days, they got milk from their neighbors, Hardin and Lou Warren (Aunt Lou claimed it was sweeter because she fed her cows sweet bran), and a good portion of their meat from Dr. A.J. Storms who raised hogs in great numbers. This was the usual barter system with neighbors helping at "killing time" and being paid off in meat. Still it was a happy period as compared with the life of a decade or so earlier. The county, now with some 6,000 persons, was more law abiding with a sheriff who meant business. A new courthouse replaced the one that burned December 19, 1885, and functioned according to standard regulations. And some of the Laytons were employed there as public servants.

Then a severe drought struck and the young couple was forced to find more acreage as pasture for their stock and try to raise enough produce to feed themselves. Further up the creek, near what is now S of O, they located a farm belonging to Bob Powers and rented it, leaving their own place idle for more than a year. When the weather finally normalized, things began to improve, and when the crops were laid by and the work caught up they decided to move back to their Turkey Creek home and prepare the ground for the coming spring planting.

While Fronea prepared a farewell dinner for the neighbors she had grown close to, the Jess Oliver and Marion Ellison families, William saddled his horse and rode to Forsyth to pay up the taxes. He had caught cold and on his return trip through Silver Creek, near what is now Powersite, he began to feel feverish. By the time he reached the farm he was too weak to do more than fall into bed. Already weakened by a previous bout with pneumonia, William didn't have the strength to throw off this latest attack and all of Dr. Storms' valiant efforts to pull him through were to no avail. When he realized he had reached this point, William counseled Fronea as to what she must do for she would now be without his help and on her own.

She should dispose of the Springfield wagon (or borrowers could wear it out), sell the stock, (being careful who set the price), be sure each child received a fair share of the property (when it reached maturity) and, above all, keep her faith with God. He died on the day of the new year's arrival, 1903, leaving her with five small children; Ben, Randa, Edna, and ten-week-old twins Lonnie and Ollie.

Sorrowfully, Fronea laid him to rest in the Whorton Cemetery. Mindful of his advice, she did as he had outlined and also sold the farm to the St. Louis Iron Mountain and Southern Railroad for use as a right-of-way, taking her children to her parent's home for a year. Remembering William's warning, she priced her own stock as she sold it—a fact that was to remain a point of pride with her for the remainder of her days. Then with the money she received from the railroad she bought 160 acres of timbered ground back in the Oak Grove area near her brother, Rev. G. C. Whorton and close enough for the children to walk to school.

Still it was an uphill climb all the way. The two older boys helped with the chores, took care of the horses and cut wood for heating and cooking, even did the washing for the younger children. As they cleared the land she planted apple and peach orchards and kept a garden. Then she canned the fruit and produce, raised cotton which she transformed into shirts and dresses and quilts, sheared her sheep, carded the wool, spun it and made the cloth with which she sewed the family's winter clothing. She also knitted socks and filled special orders for Dr. Storms who insisted they be long enough to tuck under his toes to keep them warm. She was a good mother, teaching her children what she knew from her own experiences and reading books to them as they grouped around the fireplace in the evenings. On Sundays she took them to the old church, wanting above all for them to grow up to be as honorable as their father had been. And, as William had desired, she kept her faith and lived to the age of 91 years and 4 months. Today, her daughter, the tiny twin, is still in possession of the home place.

The days of sailing ships, gold mining and enormous private enterprise became largely a thing of the past by the beginning of the 20th century, yet, in many ways the life of Ben Layton paralleled that of Thomas Foster Layton. He was as ruggedly individualistic, self-reliant, and productive, and bridged the eras of his famous ancestors and his own descendants, comfortable with each and as much at home in yesteryear's saddle as today's mechanical conveyances. His life made a great impact on this area and his influence is still an important part of the lives of a number of people. His domain covers 240 acres on the perimeter of Layton Hill. In the modest rock house on what was once the "Jackson Place," built just after the town of Melva was destroyed, he lives alone with his memories and the comforting presence of his eight hounds.

He has much to remember for he has known Taney County from the growing pains of its adolescence to its maturity, from the aftermath of the Bald Knobber era to its present position as the sophisticated center of the nation's tourist playgrounds. And, like a strict and caring parent, he helped to discipline its unruly exuberance through the many phases of its development. He has worn a lawman's badge for most of his 84 years and still carries a deputy sheriff's commission. He views the world with a more tolerant attitude than perhaps he did in his younger days and he seems to have arrived at an understanding truce with life. His humor is delightful and contagious. There's a twinkle in his eye as he recalls the numerous struggles throughout that long period and one can sense the satisfaction he feels at having won the majority of them. He is tall and erect, a bit reserved, but altogether a handsome and impressive man. His recollections and anecdotes flow in a continuous stream of the charming combination of a soft Virginia drawl and an Ozark dialect. In his talk the grace and dignity of another age is apparent. At 84, he still refers to those who were his elders with deference and respect. The courtesy titles of "aunt" and "uncle," with "miss" for maiden ladies, reveal the quality of his rearing. Today he is the oldest member of the Layton family, the patriarch of the clan. He is a remarkable personality whose name is prominent among the elite group of pioneer families of Taney County, the real hill people of the Ozarks.

Ben was ten years old when his father died and much of the family responsibility fell on his shoulders. Although he had to forsake the luxury of a full formal education, he had the inborn benefit of the Layton heritage. From the time he started to walk he had been at his father's side, learning the lore of the hills, the mark of good stock and storing away the knowledge and training that was to help him through the trying periods to come. He inherited a love of fine horses and a natural aptitude and instinct for selecting the best breeds, a fact that was to be one of his great advantages. And, having experienced the thrill at his father's side, he adopted the Ozarkian's urge to follow the hounds in the star-lit pursuit of fox and coon.

"I was something like seven or eight years old when he used to take a horse and we'd do coonin' down in the corn fields on the creek," he said. "That's just before the railroad started building through Hollister. I think that started about 1902 and that's when they went to work cutting the right-of-way. They were two or three years building and at that time there was nothing much there. The Ellison's lived at the top of the hill on the country road (now Bus. 65); Uncle Marion Ellison had a big family—I was raised up with them. We all lived here together and always got along well. They were wonderful people. The Lewallen's lived in a house about where the north end of the viaduct is now, a great big white building. Uncle George Caldwell owned the place up the hill, Pa Whorton and Uncle Tony Keith, the Strahans—all right up the creek. I knew everybody clear to the head of it and after awhile, most everyone in the county.

"The first fella ever put in a store in Hollister was a man named Rube Kirkum. Big fellow, and he had one daughter, Willard. Same name as Bessie Ellison's girl—that's who I named my daughter for. We were all about the same age and all went to school together. The store was a big, long frame building, not much by today's standards but for the time it was good. He sold lots of groceries. There was plenty of teamwork going on up and down the creek and the teamsters and everyone were buying there. Well, things got to building up and then there was some trouble—Rube got into it with a fella—sort of a personal matter, knocked him in the head and hurt him pretty bad. But back in those days folks didn't go to court over such things; they just 'fit' it out."

He paused, obviously enjoying the memory of that action. "Well, not long after, the store burned and the Kirkum's left. Tom Jennings had a new building put up and went on with business. Then they moved over a bunch of buildings from Kirbyville. One big one stood on the northwest corner (Broadway and 4th) and Pete Kite put in a drug store on the bottom floor. I worked for him quite a while, sold candy and tobacco, ran the soda fountain, that sort of thing. The tourists used to come to Hollister on the train then—you'd see them all over the roads, afoot. This was before the arrival of automobiles and people walked. "There wasn't much to do," he said, "except hunt or fish and not everyone cared for those sports. Uncle Dick Whorton put in a little stand down on the creek, sold cold drinks and the like. Soda pop was kind of a treat then and used to be in big, thick bottles with no caps but a sort of push-down stopper." It was the one modern concession to the untouched charm of the hills.

He said as things began to grow, disputes arose. The railroad, viewing the expansion of tourism, wanted an idyllic area with no unsightly or disturbing influences. Merchants whose income depended on those customers also wanted a pleasant, uncluttered village. But the stockmen, long accustomed to free range and all that it implied, wanted to bring their animals to town for shipment without any restrictions. Thus, the stock wandered at will through the town and interfered with any attempt at order, to say nothing of sanitation. The newly written ordinance calling for the penning up of the animals to be shipped was reinforced by the building of stock pens in which to hold them until they were loaded on the railroad cars. The pens were torn down and carted away overnight, presumably by the stockmen, and tempers on all sides flared. The man hired as marshall to enforce the law was a miserable failure and the situation was utter chaos.

It was at this time that the young Ben Layton asked for the job. "I was 17," he said, "but Pete Kite knew me and knew I could handle it. He wasn't much older than I was and he, Bill Johnson, and Bill's brother-in-law, Dick Everette, used to go hunting with me. Anyway," he said succinctly, "I was hired and I got the job done." From then on things were generally peaceful. There were some problems but nothing like there had been in the past.

There was other work going on. The passenger depot was being built and Ben helped on that—hauling rock and sand with John Keith for a man named Shoemaker. "Didn't get too much but, times were poor. We all worked at whatever we could to make a dollar."

To Bill Johnson it seemed the time was at hand to handle those dollars. "He wanted to put it in a bank. He didn't have enough money so he went out to see Dr. Storms and see if he'd back him—put some money in the bank. The doctor was a mighty nice old man and worth a lot of money but he had some funny ideas. He judged a person by the number of bumps on his head. [The doctrine of Phrenology, originated by Franz Joseph Gall, had its heyday in Storms' youth and he adhered to its use.] Bill said the doctor wouldn't do a thing until he'd felt all over his head and guessed that it proved to his satisfaction. Anyway, Storms let Bill have the money and he became president of the bank and had his picture enlarged and it hung on the wall there for many years."

Presbyterian Hill was the setting for the great Chautauquas and church affairs and was one of the main attractions in the area. It was from a Sunday evening service that 21-year-old Ben Layton escorted the daughter of Ida Berry Waugh and Alexander Kaneaster to her home in the vicinity of his mother's Oak Grove farm. It was the beginning of a new life for him for he was suddenly and irrevocably in love. Rosa married Ben and was his "Rosie" from that day on.

Rose Victoria was born when Alexander, the champion of Robert E. Lee, was 60 years of age. He had huge peach orchards and considerable property but she knew little about him for he died shortly after her birth. Her mother then remarried (for the third time) another Missouri pioneer of age, Joe McGill. She had two daughters by Waugh: Mary Florence and Grace; and three by Kaneaster: Betty, Bessie, and Rosa. Theirs was a happy life for there was unity in the large family. They were involved in school functions with old-fashioned spelling bees and the hundreds of wholesome no-cost parties and entertainments to be found in the hills. They read good books and Ida read to them from magazines she subscribed to, keeping up with what was going on in the world outside the Ozark hills. She was an elegant lady, well educated and fond of swishing skirts with fashionable blouses and wore colorful ribbons in her hair. She was stately and tall and devoted to her family. She dressed her girls in lovely feminine styles and they were the envy of the crowd. All the nieces and nephews vied for the affection which she graciously and generously bestowed. She gave

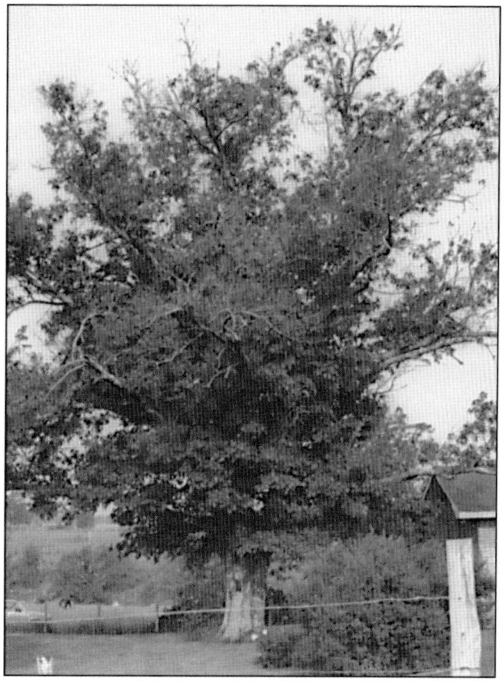

The tree planted by Thomas and Julia Layton in the mid-1850s. The story goes: someone put a tin can in top of it when it was a sapling, then shot it out, that is the reason it is so straggly looking today.

each of her daughters the name of a queen, (Mary, Anne, Victoria, etc.) and said she expected them to act like one.

Whether Rosa came up to Ida's expectations may never be known but certainly to her own children she was a queen—a diminutive, joyous individual with a great zest for living and a fondness for playing pranks. She was petite and pretty with velvet brown eyes, full of music and tinkling laughter and an air of expectancy as though she were always anticipating something better to come along. She turned her misfortunes into jokes and retained the childlike quality of her girlhood throughout her lifetime. Fortune, good or bad, she shared with Ben. On trips that necessarily took him away from home she could not go but was the welcoming beacon to which he returned.

He bought stock all over Arkansas and Oklahoma: cattle, hogs, and horses. "Whatever I thought I could make money on. We used to have rough times in this country," he said. "If folks today were up against them, they'd die."

He recounted his adventures driving a herd of hogs across the Boston Mountains in a blinding snowstorm; numerous cattle drives, many of which were accomplished with just the aid of a good saddle horse and his favorite stock dog, Snide, who "could do everything but talk," and the particularly exasperating chore of driving a pair of mules to the Springfield mule barn. He told the hilarious tale of driving the first *Model T* Ford into the town of Mincy and scaring the school children (about 18 of them) who had never seen one, away from the playground and into the hills. He recalled the bleak winter when he was hauling railroad ties (at 10¢ a tie) and took time off for a chance at hunting wolves. It was one time when he was lucky, for he shot a female with six pups and got paid off by the various stockmen's clubs in the area to the tune of some $350, enough to fence his place, buy seed for planting, and an extra pair of mules.

He was involved in or observed many tragedies: the holocaust when Branson burned; the brutal murder of Sheriff Newt Boles; and probably his most memorable experience, rescuing the bodies of the children who were swept into Turkey Creek when a tornado destroyed the town of Melva. His account of that day, from the appearance of Uncle Marion Oliver running down the railroad tracks, hatless, his face streaming blood and yelling. "The house is blown away and Sarah's a layin' in the yard with her hip broke," through lashing his huge mule into a frenzy of haste through the storm and into a torrential stream, was a spine chilling tale. His locating of a final body and diving for the child whose "stiff fingers seemed to reach up and meet mine," was an act far above and beyond the responsibility of an Officer, a neighbor, or a friend. But those who know Ben agree it was typical of him and add, "he's a Layton."

He was acquainted with the famous and colorful personalities of the area—Rose O'Neill, Jim Holiday, Josie Barnes, Hardin Warren, Dr. McIntyre, Jerry Butterfield, Professor Blankinship, Bethel Eiserman, Charles Moore, the Hoftneisters, the Plymptons, Otto and Mattie Kohler, and Jessalle Blankinship Nash, to name a few.

He is still a man admired and respected, consulted on matters vital to the life of an Ozarkian, whether it be the value of a stallion, a herd of stock, a piece of ground, or more likely, a hound dog. He holds court in his cozy rock home with its ancient fireplace and a few necessities for "batchin'." Old friends drop in to share a few hours and strangers, dog lovers, and stockmen come from as far away as Texas to seek his advice. The list of his friends is endless and they visit frequently. The names of Dawson, Linkous, Yarnell, Snowden, Holiday, Miles, Burnett, Lowry, Simmons, Hillman, Oliver, and Allen Pleake are household words. Often they bring their wives, for the women are an important part of today's fox hunts and they are "into dog stories." One woman who visits is his cousin, Pearl McFarland Hodges, who claims relationship on both sides of the family.

It is his son and daughter-in-law who took

over the mansion in 1939. His grandchildren and great grandchildren have played beneath the huge trees, in the old barns, and on the grounds around the intricate rock-faced cellar. They take the ancient cemetery as a matter of course. Times are better now than they were in Ben's youth. His descendants, like the old Virginia ancestors, are making the most of their opportunities and for them, Layton Hill is the personification of their heritage.

They Passed This Way

The south wall of the barn Thomas and Julia Layton built in the 1850s contains a collection of relics to their past. The eyes of today's modern generation would look upon these old horseshoes as if they were nothing. But these horseshoes came from Thomas and Julia's stock of horses. They hang suspended from a time in which their original value has become obsolete, yet they are a mirror to the past. They represent a time when the ways to travel were either horseback, mule, wagon, or by foot; some even traveled in ox-drawn wagons.

The Laytons brought to Taney County some of the finest horses this area had ever seen: the black-as-jet horse with a tiny star in its forehead, the Morgan horse, the first of its kind in this part of the country.

Gazing at the horseshoes, one might wonder which shoe came from the hoof of the horse Thomas rode while he surveyed the beauty of the hills which surrounded him in the land that was his final home, or which shoe came from the dainty mare Julia rode while using a side-saddle.

They surely enjoyed exciting rides, galloping through the fields of lush, beautiful blue stem grass that grew to the horses' shoulders. They enjoyed the simplicity of the peaceful, flowing country stream, while they rode near Turkey Creek.

One might wonder how many times Julia Ann rode by herself over the hills and valleys as she let her hair blow in the freedom of the wind. She could sense the majestic strength of her horse as it made its way up one hill and down another.

The collection of horseshoes are but souvenirs our Layton ancestors left behind to remind those of us who follow, that at one time, they passed this way.

The Cemetery On The Thomas F. Layton Homestead

When the Laytons homesteaded near Hollister, they set aside a small plot of land to be used as the family cemetery. It is secluded within the original boundary lines today as it was when Thomas and Julia were alive. Some of the stones are difficult to read, but the names and dates as they currently are, follow:

1. Julia Ann, wife of Thomas Foster Layton, born March 2, 1826. Died September 8, 1873. (The inscription of her tribute reads as follows, although some words could not be made out).

I would not live always
nor welcome the tomb.
Since Jesus hath lain them
I dread not its gloom
Till he bid me rise
to hail him in triumph
ascending the skies.

2. Clyde C. son of Thomas Allen and Florence A. Towns Layton. Born, January 24, 1876. Died, September 4, 1884. Age 8 years, 7 months, and 10 days.

3. T.C. Layton (Thomas Clay), son of T.F. and J.A. Layton. Born, August 20, 1891. Died, October 5, 1895. Age four years.

4. Lula, daughter of T.A. and F.A. Layton. Died, May 31, 1891, age 14 months and 8 days.

The lovely bud so young and fair
called home by early dawn just come
to share love in sweeter flower
in paradise would bloom.

5. Virgie McGrath, daughter of T.A. and F.A. Layton. Born, October 3, 1887. Died, January 1, 1888. Age 2 months and 29 days.

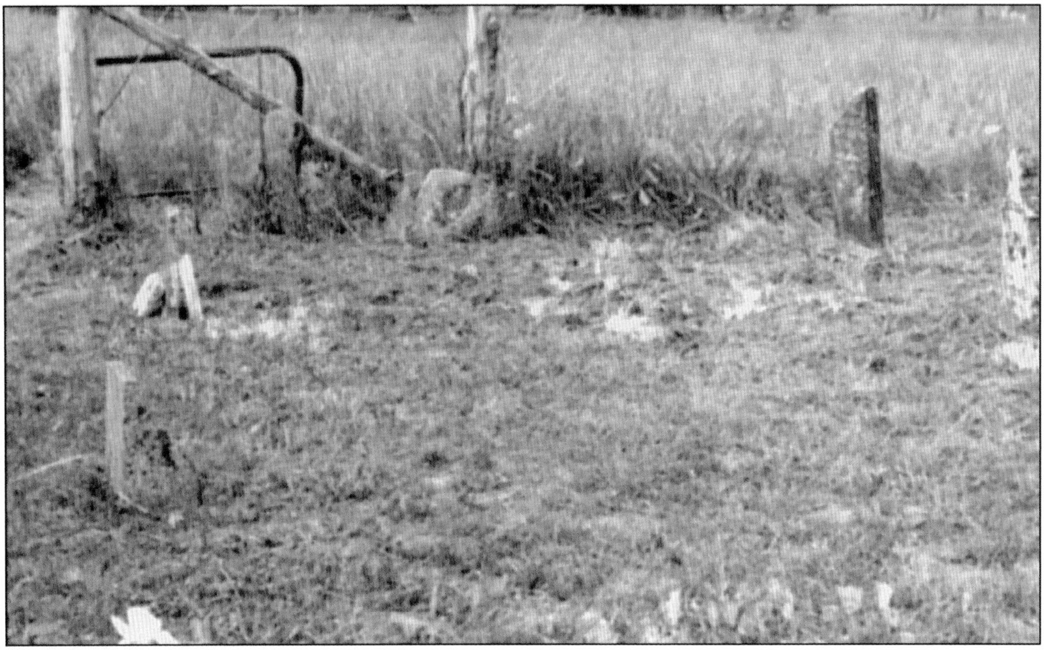

The Layton cemetery as it looks in 1987 on the Thomas and Julia Layton homestead.

6. Pheobe J. Layton. Born, October 13, 1846. Died, January 11, 1899. Thomas Foster Layton's second wife.

7. Thomas Foster Layton. Born, February 27, 1822. Died, July 20, 1899.

LAYTON SOUVENIRS

The "yard bell" Thomas and Julia brought to their Taney County homestead still stands, although the land now belongs to Mrs. Vernon Layton, who has several Layton souvenirs.

When Thomas Layton rode his horse over the beautiful hills near his home, he could hear the clanging of the bell as Julia Ann would call him home to dinner. The bell was used in communication between them. Perhaps, while the Civil War yet raged through this area near the Missouri-Arkansas line, Julia rang the bell when sending out messages of warning to notify the Confederate troops of information she had. Julia and here sister Cordelia Richards smuggled items through Union Army lines to supply Confederate troops in southern Missouri and northern Arkansas.

For many a soldier away from his home and family, Julia Ann filled a void, not only by helping with supplies, but also those who were injured. It has been said that soldiers may have died on the Layton homestead and were buried in unmarked graves by who ever found their bodies.

A black powder flask was found beneath the steps of the original Layton house while it was being torn down by Vernon Layton, who built a new home in its place. It could have belonged to Thomas Foster Layton, or one of his sons. The flask must have come from a fine store as it was elegant in design. It still contains black powder today.

One can imagine the fine muskets and guns the Laytons must have owned. It is a well known trait for Laytons to be fine marksmen. Thomas Layton must have carried the flask with him while hunting turkey and deer.

To the east of the house and down a slope runs a small creek which flows over the gravel road. This area contained a pear orchard years ago, but the trees gradually died out. An old rusty .22 revolver was found by Vernon Layton near a rock by this creek. Inscribed upon the rock were the words "BY FRITZ." The gun could either be an Iver Johnson or an H&R. The gun had been buried many years and as time passed, soil erosion left it exposed.

Sacramento Belle was born March 7, 1858, and died March 11, 1953, the daughter of Thomas and Julia Layton. Belle married Henry Glitsch—an attorney from Hesse Dornstabt, Germany. They were married on horseback. They had a son, Fritz, who was born in 1891.

Belle's second marriage was to Joseph H. McEvoy and they had a son. In April, 1891, Belle and her son Fritz visited the Layton homestead in Hollister from their home in Ansonia, Connecticut. Belle may have inscribed her son's name on the rock while here on the visit.

The inscription was hand chiseled. Little did Belle know at the time, if it were true in fact she did chisel those words, what curiosity they would create almost a century later. It will be a lasting memory of her as she walked before our steps. She was a grand lady, indeed.

Whether or not the gun is connected with the rock is speculation. Only the older generations of Layton's could answer that. It has also been suggested the gun may have been left behind from the Civil War.

A story was told by Floyd Layton about Belle. "One relative had been arrested in Illinois and accused of horse theft. When Belle was informed he had been cleared of all charges through the efforts of his attorney, Abraham Lincoln, it is said, 'She stomped her foot and stated she would rather have been hung as a horse thief than to have been defended by Abe Lincoln.'"

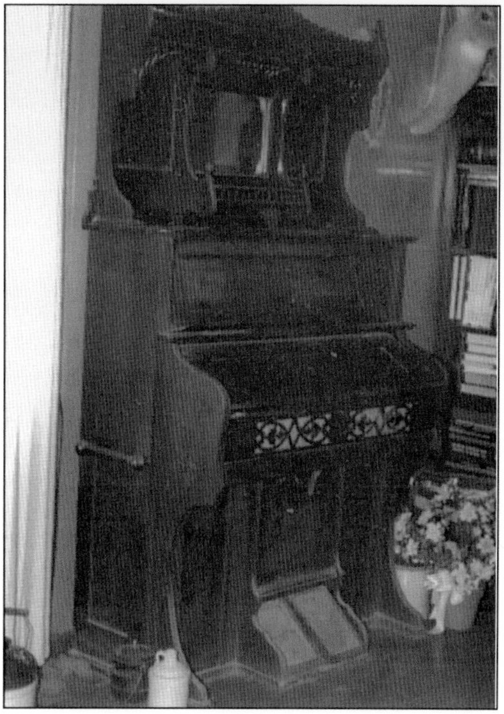

Thomas and Julia Layton's organ.

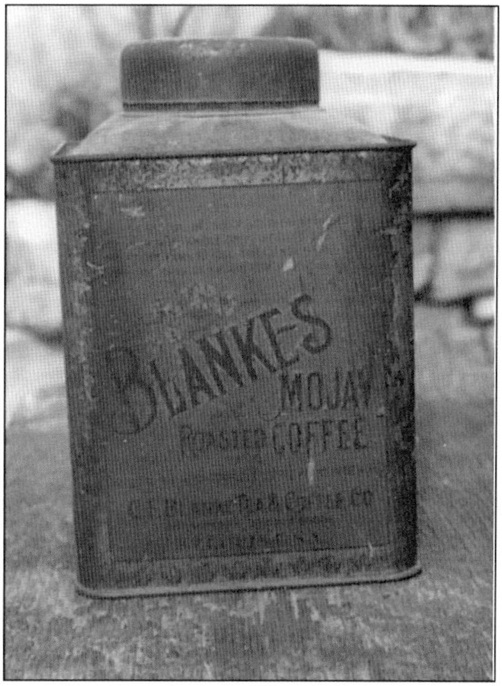

Maude Whorton Rittenhouse's coffee tin.

THE ORGAN, COFFEE GRINDER, AND COFFEE TIN

The old-time coffee tin (see photo) belonged to Maude Whorton Rittenhouse.

She lived in a rock house near the Whorton Cemetery by Turkey Creek in Hollister. She lost her life tragically when her home was destroyed by fire. A train was traveling the line of track nearby and the engineer was the first to notice the flames. The train stopped and they notified the nearest available help, but it was too late.

The organ (see photo) belonged to Thomas and Julia Layton who kept it in their home for many years, then passed it down to their son, Claude. Claude remained on the Layton homestead many years before he sold it to the Vernon Layton family. The organ was sold at a family sale and was taken a short distance down the road to the home of Price and Edna Layton Brittain. It remained there many years. After Price and Edna both passed away, the organ was once again sold at a family sale. Wanda and son, Tom Layton , bought it and returned it to its original home on the Layton homestead.

The coffee grinder belonged to Fronea Whorton Layton. Fronea and her children would walk the railroad tracks to Hollister from their farm carrying a basket of eggs and fresh churned butter to trade at the store for fresh coffee beans.

Alf Bolen: The Meanest Ozarker Of Them All

Bloody Alf Bolen was considered by many as the worst outlaw the Missouri Ozarks ever produced. He was a wanton killer, with at least 40 dead men to his credit.

He ranged across southern Missouri from the western border to the Mississippi River, but most of his crimes were confined to the counties of Stone, Christian, and Taney.

About the only rewarding thing that happened in his sordid life was when he met about the same kind of ghastly end that he had dished out to so many of his victims.

An example of the kind of torture he gloried in occurred in 1861. Uncle Billy Smith, 70, lived alone in a log cabin near Pinetop, in Taney County, almost on the Missouri-Arkansas border line.

Bolen and three companions rode out of the woods one evening, dismounted, and demanded food from Smith. The old man nervously prepared a meal of pork, cornbread, and beans. Bolen gulped the food down, wiped the drippings from his heavy black beard, then reached down and grabbed the old man by the shirt-front. "Now, I reckon, ye'd might as well tell us whar ye got yer money hid away, old codger," the outlaw growled. Uncle Billy told him that he had no money—that he had no way of making cash money. He said he was barely able to raise enough to eat. Bolen shook him until his toothless mouth fell open. "All ye old codgers has got a little savings hid around."

"I'll make him talk," Bolen grated, pulling a knife from his belt. He grabbed one of Smith's ears, sliced it off with one stroke, and shook it before the old man's horror-filled eyes.

"Now tell me whar yer money is—er I'll whack off the t'other!"

"I can't tell where something is that I ain't got," the old man pleaded.

Bolen caught the other ear between his thumb and finger. He twisted and cut at the same time. He flung the ear from him and leered at the hoarse scream of pain that welled from Smith's throat.

Merciful unconsciousness pitched the old man's head forward as he fainted. The two men dropped his limp body to the puncheon floor.

Bolen looked down at the senseless form, his eyes wild in his twisted face. He jerked a heavy pistol from the waist-band of his coarse pants. Then he struck again and again at the old man's head.

"He's dead, Alf," one of the men protested weakly.

It was several seconds before Bolen regained his composure, his tobacco-stained teeth no longer bared like an animal.

"Take him out and throw him down the hollar. We didn't get no money, but we can hole up in his cabin and live on his grub for a couple of weeks," he stated.

This account may be blood-thirsty, but it

is not exaggerated. Much of Bolen's career of crime followed this pattern. Near Forsyth is an outcropping of boulders still called Murder Rocks. There, he reportedly waylaid, robbed, and murdered at least two dozen travelers who had to pass the spot on their way to Ozark and Springfield.

He apparently had no conscience. He left few of his robbery victims alive. This senseless killing was not carried out because he was afraid they would talk. He was a mad-dog, filled with hatred. He killed to satisfy some sadistic urge buried in his hulking, illiterate body and soul.

He was able to go about this untamed wilderness preying on settlers with little fear of retribution because the southern tier of border counties became a no-man's-land during the Civil War. The natives were split equally in their sympathies. Bushwhackers such as Bolen were "northern" or "southern" as circumstances demanded. One day he would be a Yankee. The next he wore the gray coat of the Confederacy.

The danger of these marauders became so great that many settlers abandoned their claims and left the county. Whole villages, such as Blue Eye, on the Missouri-Arkansas line, became virtually abandoned until several years after the war had ended.

Although he is known by the name of Bolen, Alf's real name was Bolden, if it can be said that he had a name. He was actually a "woods colt."

He was born in the Stone County wilds in the winter of 1842 near the present village of Ponce de Leon. His father could have been almost anyone, and his mother, a widow named Matilda Bolden, always hated the manchild forced upon her. Perhaps that had much to do with the warping of young Alf. Then to add to his twisted thinking, his mother deserted him when he was eleven. One day she climbed on a wagon with an itinerant horse trader and left young Alf to shift for himself.

He stayed around the little one-room log cabin built near a creek that ended up in James River about five miles away. One day he wandered down the creek and across the river to the frontier home of Calvin and Mary Jane Cloud.

The Clouds felt sorry for him and offered their home and their care. He moved in and sullenly accepted their kindness but he always remained a strange and fathomless youngster.

When he was 17, he disappeared one day. The Clouds did not hear of him for months. When they did, his name was linked with the notorious Sam Hilderbrand gang that terrorized eastern Missouri. Hilderbrand taught young Alf all the tricks of the slaughterer's trade.

In the spring of 1862, Calvin Cloud walked out of his log barn one morning with a basketful of ear-corn, on his way to feed some hogs. He looked up and saw a group of hooded riders approaching. His wife was in their cabin, 50 yards from the barn.

The riders pulled their horses up when they reached Cloud. The farmer looked at the soiled flour sack hoods hiding the faces of the four riders, with the exception of holes through which he caught the glint of eyes. He asked what they wanted, saying that he had no money but would be glad to feed them if they were hungry.

One rider had no gun in sight. The others carried rifles. The gunless one said, "We don't want nothin' but yer gun. Jist give hit to us and we'll ride on."

"I ain't got a gun," Cloud said.

"Yer a black liar, Calvin, "the rider blurted. "Ye got a good gun, and I'm aimin' ter take hit."

It was then Calvin Cloud recognized the voice he had not heard for months. He said, "Alf Bolen, it ain't beholding of you to come here robbing, after all me and Mary Jane have done for you. If you're wanting something, you know you can have anything I've got. But get off that horse and take that mask off your face and ask for it like a man!"

Bolen cursed as he jerked the hood from his head. He reached out and grabbed the rifle from the hands of the nearest rider. He swiftly triggered the gun and watched Calvin

Cloud pitch forward with blood spurting from his chest.

Mary Jane Cloud came screaming from the cabin. Alf fired in her direction. She stumbled and fell, though the bullet missed her. Alf and his riders, evidently fearing that some neighbors who lived close by might come to investigate the shots, whirled their horses and rode away into the deep woods.

For nearly two more years Bolen continued to terrorize the countryside. He killed one man south of Reeds Spring, at White Rock bluff near Kimberling Bridge on the White River, strictly for revenge. The man, named McMonigle, had led a posse trying to capture or kill Alf. One day McMonigle walked out of his barn at the base of the bluff. A rifle shot rang out from the top of the bluff. McMonigle never knew what hit him. Alf Bolen rode away, satisfied that he had taught the hill folks not to come hunting for him.

A reward of $1000 was offered for Bolen, dead or alive. Detachments of soldiers rode almost continuously, seeking to kill or capture him. He evaded all their traps and efforts.

Company B, First Iowa Calvary was stationed at Ozark, in Christian County. Most of the 200 civilians who normally occupied the town had moved away. The courthouse had been burned along with many buildings in skirmishes between Federal and Confederate troops. First one side then the other chose to station itself there on the banks of the Finley.

Early in January, 1863, a troop of these soldiers captured a man named Jim Richards, a known cohort of Bolen's. Richards' home was near the Taney-Christian line, on Bull Creek between Forsyth and Highlandville.

Richards' wife, Myrtle, went to Ozark immediately, seeking the release of her husband. Sgt. Wellington Allen and Captain Arch Forrester talked to her. They offered Richards his release if his wife would decoy Alf Bolen into a trap, whereby he might be captured or killed. Richards and his wife readily agreed.

A burly private with a good fighting record was dressed in conventional mountaineer clothing. He accompanied Myrtle Richards back to her home, which was a one-room log cabin with a small lean-to kitchen at the back. Her 14-year-old son, who had remained at the cabin while she had gone to Ozark, was sent with a message to be given to Alf Bolen.

"He and some of his men are holed up between here and Forsyth," Mrs. Richards told the soldier. "I sent word for him to come here, at once, alone; that I had something important to tell about Jim being captured by the soldiers. I told my boy to stop and stay with a neighbor, after he contacts Bolen."

Snow was on the ground, hard frozen from the extreme cold. It was late evening, nearly dark when Myrtle Richards sighted Bolen coming through the woods toward the cabin, alone.

The soldier quickly stepped from sight into the lean-to kitchen, his rifle clamped tightly. Myrtle Richards heard the crunch of Bolen's boots on the snow. She opened the door and the big man stamped across the floor toward the warmth of the fire, his cold hands extended. He leaned his rifle against the fireplace mantle and rubbed his hands before the blaze.

"Must be awful urgent business to ask a feller to stir out in weather liken to this," Bolen growled. He squatted down, trying to rub some warmth into his feet through the stiff leather of his boots.

Mrs. Richards was pouring a cup of coffee. "Here, drink this," she said. "It'll warm you."

The soldier, from his place of concealment, tried to get his rifle lined with Bolen's back, which was sideways to him. But the angle from the doorway would not permit an accurate shot. He didn't dare shoot unless the bullet was sure. If he only wounded the outlaw, Bolen would kill Mrs. Richards for the betrayal.

He looked around for something he might use as a club. He saw an iron poker behind the kitchen stove. He stood his rifle against the wall and caught up the poker. He could now hear Bolen slurping at the hot coffee. He looked cautiously in and saw Bolen, still on one knee before the fire, the cup to his mouth.

Swiftly the soldier sprang from the doorway and brought the poker down on Bolen's head, protected only by a battered felt hat.

The outlaw crumpled without a sound, nearly falling into the fire. Taking no chances, the soldier brought the poker down again. Then he dragged the limp form away from the flames. He rolled the big man over and saw that he was dead.

The soldier told Mrs. Richards that there was no need to carry the heavy body through the snow to Ozark, since only the head was needed for identification. They chopped this off with an axe, placed it in a burlap sack, and spent most of the night walking to Ozark, taking turns at carrying the gruesome load.

Mary Jane Cloud was called to Ozark to identify the head. She rode horseback through the cold and snow from the place where Bolen had slain her husband, Calvin Cloud, near the present old McCall bridge across James River. She said the head belonged to Alf Bolen, the man she and her husband had helped to raise.

The head was then placed on a 10-foot pole and placed in the center of the encampment for all to view. People came from miles around to see the gruesome sight, the end of the Ozarks' butcher.

For several days it stood there. Then one night the pole fell over from a stiff wind. The head was dragged away by range hogs that roamed at will through the town and encampment.

Sgt. Wellington Allen and some troops accompanied Jim Richards and his wife back to their cabin in the forest. The headless body left there was removed and buried in an unmarked grave—a fitting end for the bloodiest man the Ozarks ever produced.

(Author's note: According to family history on the Layton side, it is recorded that the death of Alf Bolen occurred in the home of Julia Ann Foster Layton's sister. In the computer print-out her name is Cordelia Elizabeth. She was born January 10, 1837, and died in 1925 at Fulton, Missouri. Why the name Myrtle is used in this story is unknown. Quintus Richards was the son of Cordelia Foster Richards. Cordelia's husband was Rufus Richards: he was in the service and they lived on the Layton property. Julia Ann Foster Layton and her sister Cordelia ran the Union blockade at Forsyth several times. The Rufus and Cordelia Richards' home was visited by Bolen, and he was killed in there.)

John and Elizabeth Layton and Jim and Ada Swalley

Thomas Foster Layton had a brother named John, who was born in 1829 while his family still lived in Virginia. John married Elizabeth Jarrett on December 21, 1854, in Greene County where she lived at the time. She was born in 1835 in Knoxville, Tennessee. John died in June of 1880 and was buried near the School of the Ozarks. Elizabeth died September 1, 1917, in Oklahoma. They had 10 children.

John and Elizabeth left their home in Greene County as did his brother, Thomas Foster Layton and wife Julia Ann. John and Elizabeth homesteaded on land near where the School the Ozarks is today.

The youngest daughter of John and Elizabeth was Ada Layton. Ada married Jim Swalley and they were farmers raising corn, wheat, hay crops, horses, cattle, and hogs. They had four sons.

John and Elizabeth Layton are the author's great-great-grandparents, the parents of William David Layton (Dank). Cordie Reese Cobb's letter told of the death of Ralph Reese. It read:

Springfield, Mo.
Sept. 8, 1904 or 9

Mr. Charlie Layton

Dear Uncle Charlie,

I regret to tell you the sad news Brother Ralph is dead. The morning that he rode home with __________ was the last time he was out of the house. He took sick at half past 12 o'clock that day the 10th of August and died with Typhoid fever, was the ______ ___ or would have let you knowed. But one day he seemed to be getting better and the next he was worse. We buried him at Maple Park Cemetery tuesday evening at 4 o'clock. It nearly killed mama and me. But he said that he was going to heaven, he wasn't afraid to die. Bless his heart I know that he went to heaven. He died with the sweetest smile on his face. Well I will close as I want to write to Grandma. So goodbye.

Your niece
Cordie Reese Cobb

Historical Legacy

The annual Layton Reunion is held at Jack and Tommy's Clubhouse located at Highway 65 and 165 south of Hollister, Missouri. It is fitting that the reunion be held here at this site since John Layton, my great-grandfather, homesteaded this land which included the land where the School of the Ozarks College is located. He is buried near the Cedar Springs School site, less than a mile east of the reunion location.

In 1987, Ben Clemons, age 101 of Forsyth, and Ollie Layton, age 84 of Branson, represented the Taney County pioneer families as they reigned King and Queen over the festivities of the Fourth of July Sesquicentennial Celebration, hosted by the historical committee of the White River Historical Society.

Almost from Taney County's beginning, the fabric of the Layton family is woven into its

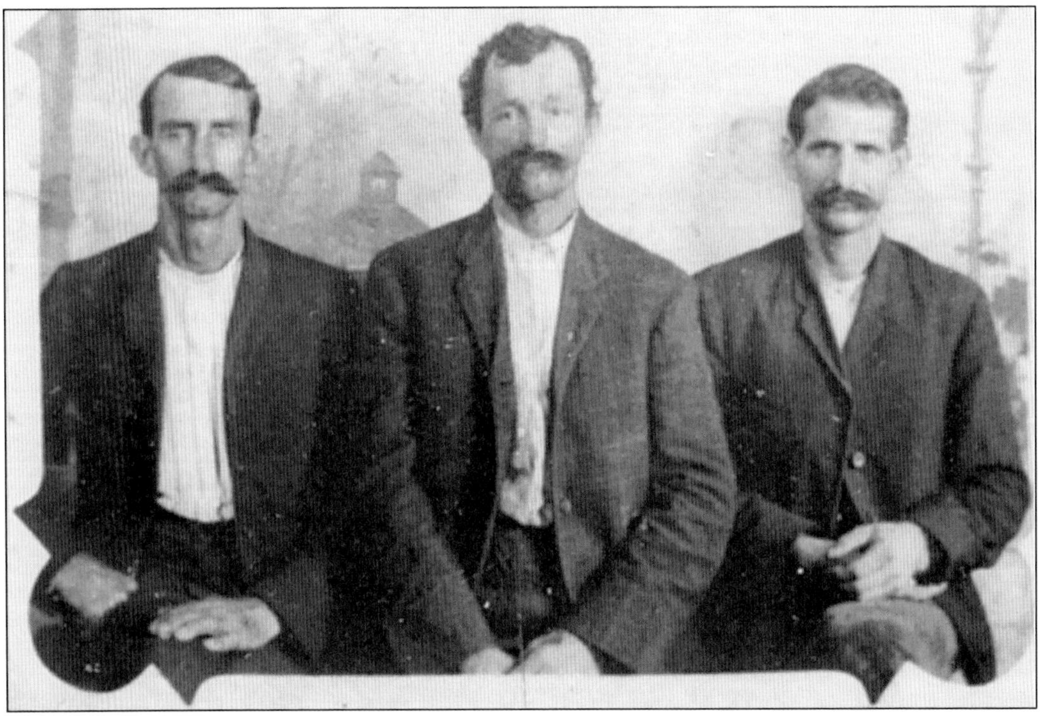

Charley Layton, also a son of John and Elizabeth Layton. He is pictured here (center) with two of his friends. Charley remained a bachelor all of his life. He lived with his widow sister Susan (Sis) Layton Reese in Springfield. He was born in 1856 and died June 28, 1906.

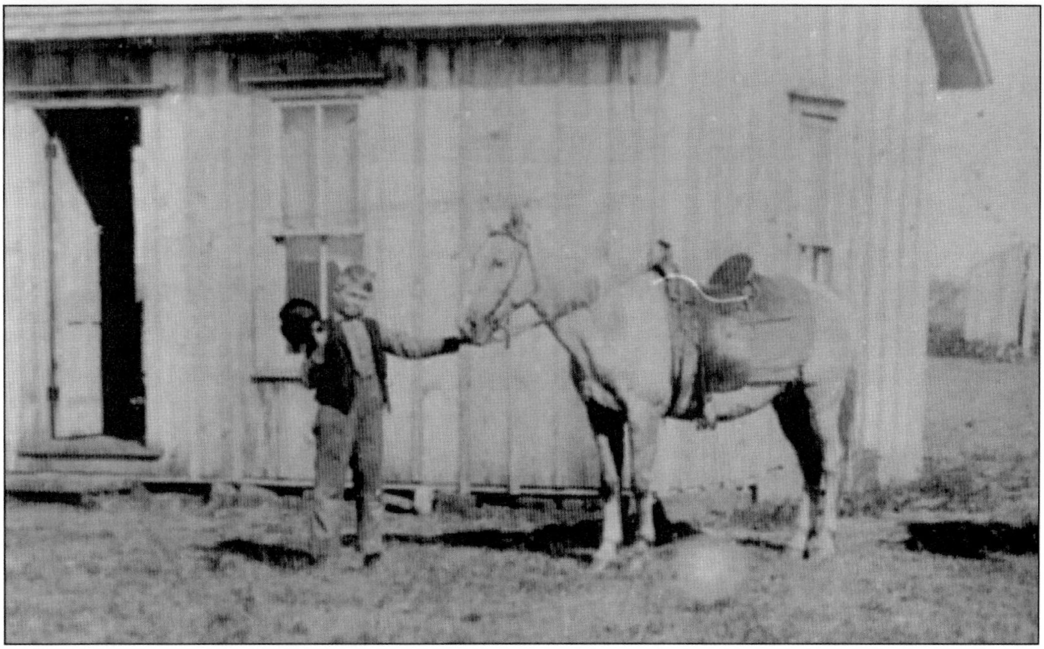

This little boy above is Fred Swalley, a relative of John and Elizabeth Layton. Below, Ralph Reese drives an old time hearse in the city of Springfield, which he drove for many years.

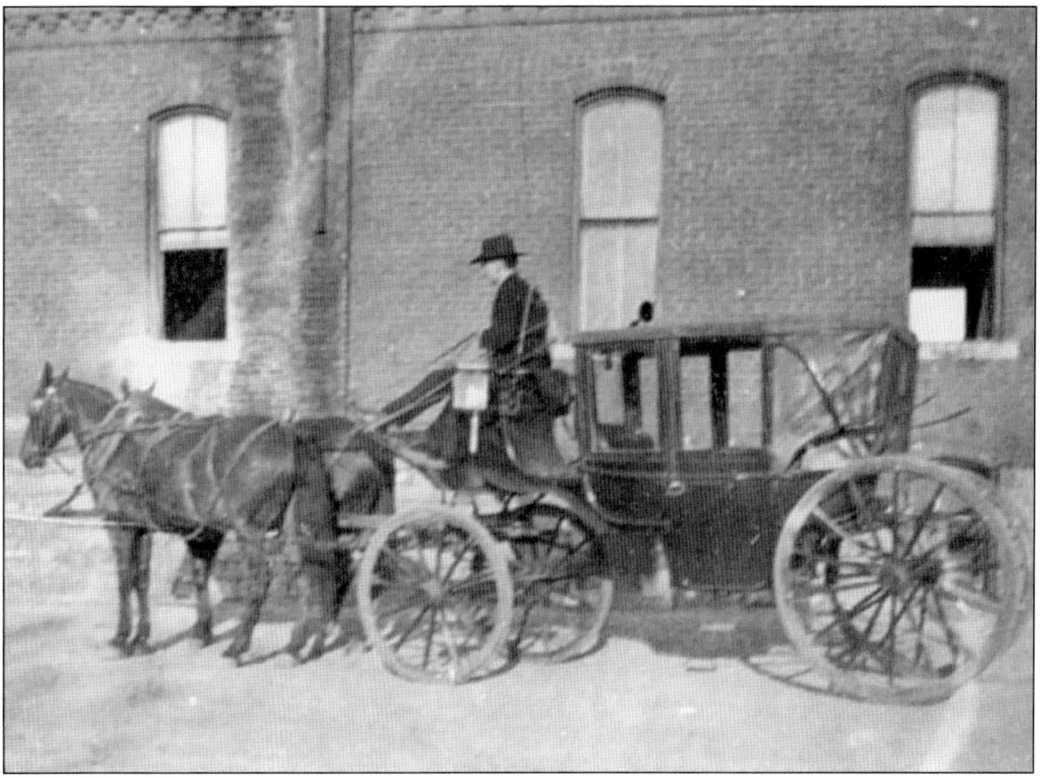

history. There were Layton's in Taney County in the 1840s, while the modern computer prints out pages of Layton history going back to pre-Revolutionary War days with the Laytons, Fosters, and Mitchells coming into Virginia from England and Scotland. The move to Taney County started when two brothers married two daughters of John and Susannah Mitchell Foster. John Layton married Susannah Foster, December 27, 1810, in Spotsylvania County near Fredericksburg, Virginia, and Charles married Sarah Foster at the same place August 2, 1813. Their children were all born and educated in Virginia.

These two brothers with their families, slaves, and other possessions moved to the plains of Springfield, Missouri, about 1840. Two of John and Susannah's sons, Dr. Augustas Layton, a medical doctor and businessman, and John Mitchell Layton, were in Taney County in the 1840s.

It has been said that Dr. Augustas Layton brought the first cookstove to Taney County. In a 1914 interview in the book "Stories of the Pioneers," by E.J. and L.S. Hoenshel, early settler Ann Jennings Wyatt states, "We all had log houses and fireplaces. I recollect the first cookstove I ever saw. It was a Charter Oak. Dr. Layton got it for his wife, and father sent for one soon afterwards."

In the appendix of Elmo Ingenthorn's "Land of the Taney," these Layton's are listed as office holders: John Layton held the dual office of sheriff and tax collector from 1848 to 1850, Albert S. Layton was coroner from 1878 until 1880, and Thomas Foster Layton was clerk from 1874 until 1876.

Kirbyville as we know it today was called Layton and the postmaster was Austin S. Layton, who served from December 11, 1860, to November 20, 1863, when the post office was discontinued during the Civil War. Today some have letters with the Layton postmark. From January 21, 1888, until September 24, 1889, there was a Layton Mill and post office located on the Springfield-Harrison Road near Murder Rock, now Highway JJ. After that, the mail was sent to Kirbyville. Miss Edna Layton opened a subscription school at Kirbyville in 1891. This was a school in which parents paid $1 or $2 per child per month.

The most entrepreneurial Layton in Taney County to date would be Thomas Foster Layton whose nearly perfect Abraham Lincoln-like penmanship remains on many records, business books, and ledgers. A letter Thomas Foster Layton wrote on November 13, 1849, from the gold fields of California was published in the 1980 Fall White River Historical Society Quarterly.

Thomas Foster Layton was in charge of 2 cattle drives with about 1500 cattle in each. One of the drives was in 1849 and the other in 1854. He planned to settle down with his wife, Julia Ann Foster Layton, and his children and run his cabinet-making shop, but the Civil War intervened. Layton was with General Price and went through the battles of Wilson's Creek and Pea Ridge.

After the war, he homesteaded land near Hollister that is still held in the Layton family. He built a Jeffersonian-like mansion with pillared verandas, grand lofts, carvings, and satin polished woodwork. He sawed the choice oak and pine at the nearby Layton Mill. The furniture came from Chicago. A few pieces are in the School of the Ozarks' Ralph Foster Museum. While some parts were saved, the 100-year-old mansion was replaced by a modern home in the late 1950s.

Thomas Foster Layton worked for the betterment of the country. He employed teachers, boarded them, and paid their salaries. His children attended the Clarke Academy at Berryville, Arkansas, and his daughter Virginia married Professor Clarke.

Layton was a lover of fine horses and at one time kept 72 brood mares on his farm. He kept black-as-jet saddle horses with a tiny star on their foreheads. Travelers from far and wide bargained for the Layton horses.

A story was told to me by Jim C. Johnson of Hollister about my father, Ben Layton. It happened about 1910. Jim's father, William W. Johnson, had developed Hollister into a beautiful English Village. The railroad went along with him and built the English depot, laid double track and landscaped the right-of-way through Hollister. Mr. Johnson said it was not unusual for as many as 18 Pullman cars and special trains to be sidetracked at Hollister.

There was a problem though. Stockmen nearby had always had free range for their cattle and hogs. They had no intention of rounding up their livestock. Tourists from Kansas City, St. Louis, and Memphis would step off the train in their stylish clothes, see clear, sparkling Turkey Creek and the untouched wooded hills. But hogs lay in the mudholes in the streets and cattle ate and trampled the flowers and shrubbery. City officials Rolland Kite and Bill Johnson searched for a lawman to handle the problem, but none could be found. Mr. Johnson finally advertised in a Kansas newspaper for a Dodge City type lawman. One arrived that fit the bill right down to his pistols. He was sworn in and sauntered down to the front porch of the local general store. After listening to the conversation he turned in his badge and caught the next train back to Kansas.

The problem continued until one day young Ben Layton rode into town on his horse and said he understood they needed a marshall. Looking him over they agreed he looked pretty young. Layton admitted being 17. Johnson asked, "How do you know you can do the job?" With a determined look Layton said, "If I tell them to put their cattle up, they'll put their cattle up. And I really need a job."

So they put the star on him, and he put the cattle up and there was no trouble, no shooting, and no fighting. Jim Johnson said that was the end of the trouble. Ben Layton later served as deputy sheriff of Taney County.

While working on his farm March 12, 1920, Ben saw and heard the devastating and killer tornado turn the mining town of Melva, Missouri, into a ghost town. He traveled the 3 miles as fast as his horse would go, without hesitation diving in and pulling small bodies from the icy swirling waters of Turkey Creek which raised Lake Taneycomo eight feet that day. When others arrived they found Ben comforting the living among those children who had started a day of play by Turkey Creek.

Layton's are listed in all our country's wars. Elmo Ingenthorn's book *Borderland Rebellion*, states that first Lieutenant John Mitchell Layton, a former sheriff of Taney County who was a Union scout and General Sweeney's principal guide, had a brother, Dr. A.S. Layton, a Confederate slave owner and the father of two sons, Leonidas and Licurgus, who served the cause of the South. Licurgus was killed in the early part of the war. The Layton Mill served as a camp for the Union Army.

Other wars came. During World War II, my brother Vernon, toughened and strengthened mentally and physically by hard work and hard times, became a Sergeant with the Second Marine Corps and survived the Japanese inferno of Tarawa. He was later wounded and received the Purple Heart for his part in the South Pacific battles of Saipan and Tinian. His younger brother, Harold, barely got into World War II, but was on the front during the Korean Conflict.

Springfieldian Floyd Layton's son, First Lieutenant Marine Corps pilot Ronald Dean Layton, is one of the 11 Layton names etched in the black marble Vietnam Memorial in Washington, D.C. He lost his life while on a mission in Vietnam.

It is planned that the Layton Reunion will continue. New faces and new pages will be added to their history while the old faces fade. The youth will be charged to carry on a proud family heritage.

By Pauline Barton
Branson, Missouri

Tribute To A Friend

Truly this woman in every storm of life
was oak and rock, but in the sunshine
she was vine and flower.

Nor in the darkness of the storm
did she doubt that clouds would break
and the sun would come again
to light her life.

With a faithful heart and purest hands
she faithfully discharged her daily work
in life with honest sweat of here face
she earned her daily bread.

By Alta Littig Irish

Written by Alta Littig Irish about her friend Fronea Whorton Layton.

William David and Safronea (Fronea) Catherine Whorton Layton

William (Dank) was the second son of John and Elizabeth Jarrett Layton. He was born March 14, 1857, and his wife Fronea was born January 25, 1867. They met at William's Uncle Thomas Layton's home near Hollister, and were married in February 1891. Their children were Ben, Randa, Edna, Lonnie and Ollie. Ollie, who is the only one living, contributed the following:

"Our father died with pneumonia, leaving mother with five children to rear on the little Turkey Creek farm just one mile up from Hollister. The Railroad crew surveyed the right-of-way, and took our home and all the outbuildings. Our father's good crop that year made 500 buckets of corn. When he died this was the amount left to mother and us children. He was a good farmer and enjoyed working in the fields. I have no recollection of him, and only know him through what my mother told me and various others.

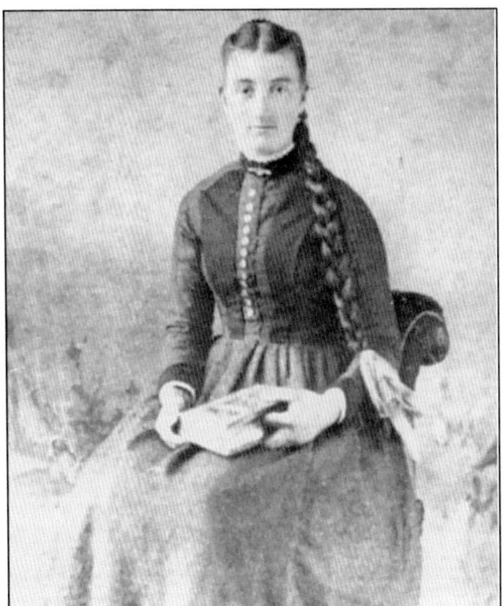

Safronea Catherine Whorton Layton, age 18.

"He had gone to Forsyth to pay the taxes on the farm in January when he died. He had taken cold and it developed into the pneumonia which took him. After this happened the Railroad paid $500 in restitution to mother for the damages. She took the money and bought 160 acres near Oak Grove church and school house. My two older brothers, Ben and Randa, were a big help to mother as well as her own brothers and sisters, and her parents, Mr. and Mrs. Randa Whorton.

"Our dear Uncle Jim and Aunt Almeda lived at Oak Grove near us. After us children were older, we all helped each other and worked together. Our dear neighbors Uncle Zepheras and Aunt Alice Rose lived close to us. Their two daughters Nellie and Pearl, and a boy Robert, were still at home with them.

"Uncle Mark Hensley and his family of eight daughters helped our mother on the farm. They helped her cut up the corn and set the fruit trees for an orchard that the total cost of planting equaled one penny. Those of us who lived in Oak Grove at this time enjoyed many good times together. Other neighbors were Aunt Maggie and Ben Welch; they were good to us children and helped mother raise us.

"Then there were the Branson's—Uncle Rube and his wife Mary—we all called her Aunt Tommie. Rube kept as many as 70 beehives at a time on his farm. 'Oh, the good honey!' I remember hearing him say. He was a good farmer, gardener, and a good neighbor and friend to us. All the children had to be careful when they went to the Branson's and near the beehives. There were times when some of us got stung.

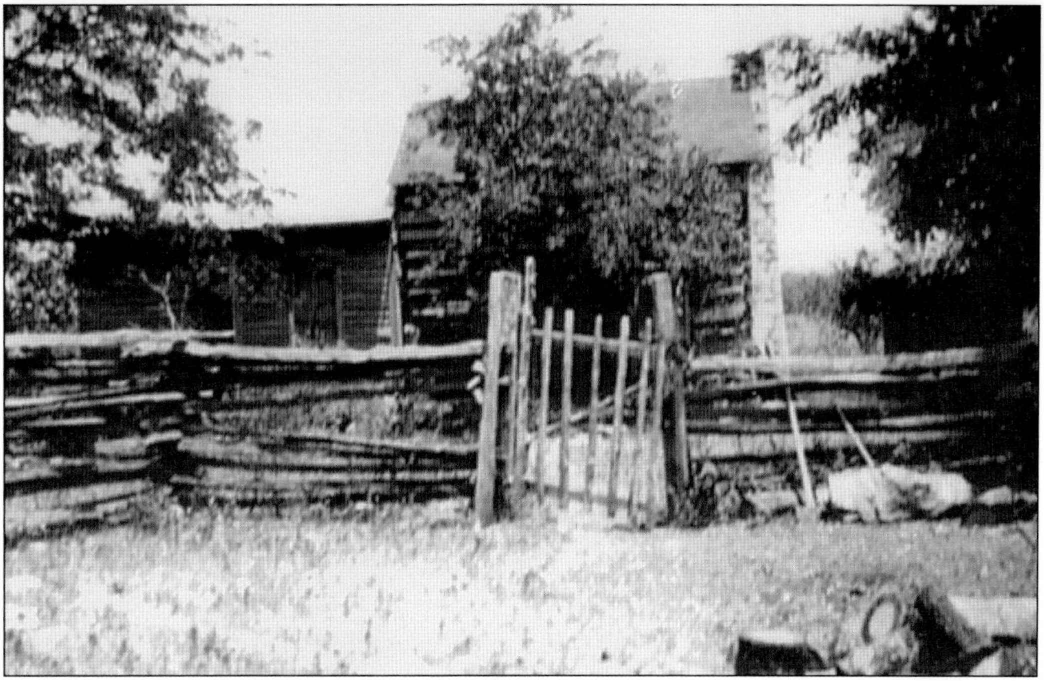

Fronea Layton's home at Oak Grove.

"The John Rose family and the Clarence Rose family were also neighbors to us in Oak Grove. We all went to church together on Sunday, and the children all went to school together there. It was a wonderful place to live and grow up in. Times were hard and it was tough on Mother to take care of us five children without our father. But there was no welfare, general relief, or food stamps for people in those days. Mother worked and fed us well. We never lacked for food nor shelter. We always had a place to sleep and a roof over our heads."

Fronea Whorton Layton Remembers

Fronea Layton was still living on her Oak Grove farm when she was 89 years old. She had moved there December 1905, and that was her home for the remainder of her life. She told the following history to her daughter Ollie, who wrote it down and submitted it to this author.

"I was 14 years old when I came to Taney County with my parents in February 1881. We had left our home on Whorton Creek in Madison County, Arkansas, and moved to what is now known as Taney County. We settled on the head of Turkey Creek. The creek got this name because the wild turkeys were so plentiful there. The pioneers at that time could have a turkey often to eat.

"The wild game was plentiful when I was a girl and the blue stem grass was tall and beautiful. All the early settlers had a flock of sheep, milk cows to furnish their milk and butter for home use. People butchered hogs for their meat and also cattle and sheep. The homesteads had orchards of apples, peaches, and pears. Some had cherry trees. These fruits were dried for winter use and were generally served with the meal. We had ham and vegetables.

"I've seen my father kill 15 hogs at one time. Then he would trade meat to work hands at spring time. We grew our grain, wheat for flour, and corn for meal. A threshing machine would travel from one farm to the next and thresh the wheat. My father would kill a lamb to feed the threshing crew and maybe the crew would spend the night at the farm home. They would sleep in the barn loft and were fed ham, eggs, and hot biscuits for breakfast. After the wheat was threshed, it was taken to the mill to be made into flour. The nearest mills to our home were Winkles Mill at Cedar Valley, and a mill at Kissee Mills.

"In the month of May butter was churned and put away in a jar with an inch of salt on top of the butter. Then it was put in the spring house for later use. We enjoyed the good homemade buttermilk that came from the stone churn after the butter was removed.

"Home gritters were made and used to grit a mess of meal. This was done when the corn was soft and new. We grew white hickory cane corn to make our hominy. I recall my mother making hominy. The corn was put in a large wash kettle with water, then some ash lye was added and this was put over a fire to boil.

"It was frequently tested to see if the skins were beginning to loose themselves from the kernels. When they were loose, the corn was removed from the lye water. It was put in baskets and we took it to the spring to wash it until the skins and the lye was removed. Then it was boiled again in fresh water for five minutes and drained again. The corn was boiled until the grains were swollen about three times their normal size which made them tender. This process usually required about an hour.

"Back in the early days when I was a child each family had an 'ash hopper.' The old-timers filled their ash hoppers with wood ashes and a small trough sat underneath the hopper. Water was poured into the hopper, and the lye water was saved this way to be used to make homemade soap. Some of it was used in the wash water to wash their clothing with.

"Each family had a small flock of sheep from which wool was sheared by hand in the Spring. The wool was carded into rolls and spun on the spinning wheel into yarn. I learned how to card wool and spin on the spinning wheel when I was eight years old.

"I wore linsy and made my own dresses. I wove one thread of blue, and one of red. This was made into a beautiful piece of material. I made a dress from this and there was enough to make my father a coat. I spun yarn, and knitted socks to sell. All material in those days was homemade. Cotton was grown and made into beautiful table linen, bed linen, and summer clothing. Homemade quilts were made from both wool and cotton.

"A cane crop was grown to make sorghum. Mother used sorghum as sweetener. Sugar was hard to come by so we had to use honey and sorghum. It was used for making ginger bread. Mother made eggnog by beating sorghum in a skillet, then she broke a few eggs and dropped into the heated sorghum. This was heated thoroughly. Sorghum was also used to sweeten pumpkins, and mother made a lot of "Jeff Davis" pies with ours.

"Most families had bees to supply the table with honey. Father had a pet bear and it broke loose one day and got on the table into the fresh bowl of honey. The bear would often disturb the hives while satisfying his sweet tooth.

"It has finally come to my remembrance that a man named Simpson made the spinning wheel for my mother. This was a good quality wheel, hardly ever threw the band. I had to get Father or Mother to put the board on for me, when it did throw the band—I was also a good hand at spinning fire. The wheel was made to go around real fast. With a little cotton and gun powder at the wheel, a spark of fire would fly off.

"This will give you an idea of what life was like when I was a girl. There is no comparison between my time and the time the people are living in today."

Remembering the Branson's

When the Layton family lived in their log house in Oak Grove, some of their close neighbors were Rube and Mary Branson. The old log barn that Rube used then still stands today although the original house burned down years ago.

Randa and Ethel Layton (the author's grandparents) knew the Branson's quite well after they got married and even while growing up. Randa and Rube worked together tending to cattle and livestock. One time Randa and Rube walked from their Oak Grove homes over to where the School of the Ozarks is now in search of a stray cow. When they found her they began to drive her home. She balked and ran away from them, but Rube and Randa caught up with her. Randa grabbed her by the horns and threw her down like steer wrestlers do in the rodeos. Rube would tease Randa about this, saying he should have taken up and traveled with the rodeos.

When Ethel Smith married Randa Layton in 1924, Rube gave them a large, hollow steer horn. Rube had got it from a man in Marionville, Missouri, years before this. Ethel used the horn to call Randa home. Even in their later years, she could pick it up, put it to her lips, and blow it, making it "toot." Randa would hear her "tootin'" the horn and know it was time to go home.

The Laytons and Bransons remained friends and neighbors for many years.

Ollie Layton Remembers Uncle Rube

"Into the mountain bound community in the early 1880s came a young man named Reuben S. Branson, with his wife, Mary, who was referred to as 'Aunt Tommie.' They moved here from Gasconade County. R.S. Branson purchased 7 acres of land from Thomas J. Berry, south of what is now the Branson Grade School. Rube moved his store there and sold merchandise to the pioneers.

"R.S. Branson was granted a Postmaster's commission and opened the Branson Post Office in his store, June 13, 1882. He was also a druggist, carpenter, school teacher, and an excellent gardener. Beautiful grapes and strawberries grew in his garden.

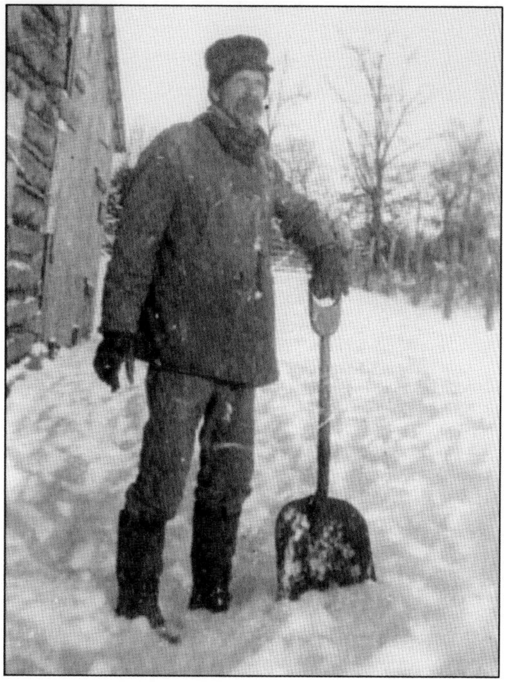

Uncle Rube Branson.

"I remember the time when he had 70 bee hives on his farm. Uncle Rube and Aunt Tommie would get up as early as 3:00 in the morning to save the first swarm of bees. These first ones were the ones that produced a hive full of honey, sometimes two, if it was a good year for honey.

"The Bransons were good friends to all, and good neighbors. They were good to help the people. The town of Branson, so meager was it in the beginning, was named after 'Uncle Rube' Branson."

Memoirs of Ollie Layton

By Ollie Layton, written July, 1987

"A few years ago I read about the Lake Taneycomo Dam at Forsyth being built. Oh, fond memories of our old home place. Each day some of the material was hauled from Branson to where the dam was being built. We lived on the road from Forsyth to Branson; also, the Springfield and Harrison road crossed there at our house. This was long before the automobile.

"Wilson Betts carried the mail from Forsyth to Branson. In the afternoon he passed by from Branson to Forsyth. Uncle G. C. Whorton got his mail at the box there, also the Devall family.

"William David Layton, my father, died with pneumonia fever January 1, 1903, leaving my mother with five children to care for. Lonnie and I were 10-week-old twins, my sister Edna was 3 and a half years old, Randa was 6, and Ben was 10. Mother kept faith with God. She was faithful and true and was a good manager. She just lived for us children. She prayed to God to spare us children's lives to her as long as she lived.

"I spent my life with mother. She left us June 2, 1958, at age 91 plus 4 months. She told me she didn't think she could live another hour when my father died.

"I'll tell you about our home here in the Oak Grove Community, east of Branson. The Railroad destroyed our home as all buildings were on the right-of-way. Mother asked the damage of $500. They didn't want to pay that price but finally did. Mother bought the farm here at that price.

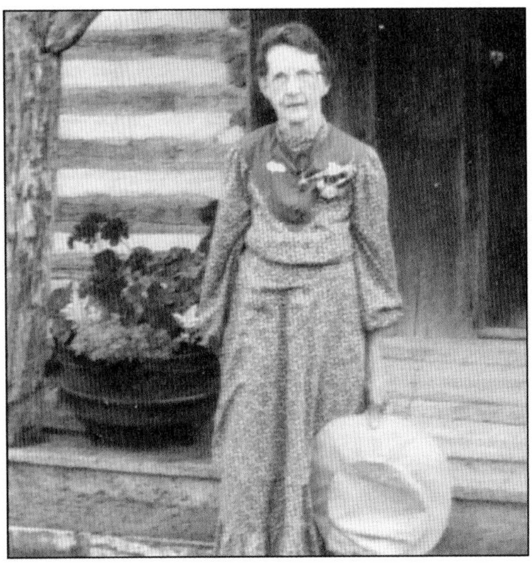

Ollie Layton.

"Mother moved here the last day of December 1905—a great blessing for my mother—one of the best places in the wide world for us children to live and to enjoy the beautiful old homestead. Mother nature was wonderful.

"The homesteaders had planted many seedling peach trees, some of the best peaches you ever ate. At that time all families had a home orchard. Mother put out two orchards. Uncle Mark Hensley set the first orchard. My brother Randa and I set the next trees in the year of 1918. The delicious apple trees grew large. They were beautiful when in full bloom and beautiful with a crop of big red apples.

"Oh, they were good. Mother kept busy making apple preserves. We put out a row of Alberta peach trees and one cherry tree. We had dewberries, blackberries, and gooseberries. We were blessed with fruit.

"Our mares, Daisy and Nick, plowed the ground for corn, wheat, and oats. Our mule, Sam, was a family mule. We all could ride Sam, and he plowed the ground, too. Barney was the colt. We loved Barney, and I played at his feet. He grew up for us to ride and work to the buggy. Ben rode a little mule, Beck, and she could pace. He would let me ride with him. Mother rode Daisy when she made trips back to Turkey Creek to see her father and mother, Mr. and Mrs. Randa C. Whorton. Daisy walked fast. Mother told me she had Arabian in her.

"Mother hitched Daisy and Nick to the Springfield wagon, and we'd drive out over the Springfield-Harrison road to Kirbyville to the Parnell store where they carried a good line of clothing and groceries.

"Kirbyville was a thriving little town and the first town even before Branson or Hollister. We had a good time going there.

"We had our cows to milk and made the best butter you ever ate. Oh, the good buttermilk, it was the best. We had our own hogs to kill. They made the best meat and sausages. Little children don't known what good meat is now days. All farmers had hogs and had their own meat.

"The school house, known as Oak Grove School, set on this tract of land. We were blessed with the school which was used as a Baptist church. Church was held Saturday night, Sunday school and church on Sunday morning and Sunday night. I can hear Aunt Alice Rose singing, "Sweet Hour Of Prayer" and "The Great Physician." Oh it was a happy place to live. How we enjoyed all the spring beauties. The dogwood trees were a sight to behold.

"Our Uncle G.C. Whorton lived 1 mile south on the Springfield-Harrison Road. He was just older than mother. They were blessed to live near each other. He helped us when we were small. He farmed the land and made hay.

"I am now 84 years old and have seen lots of changes. I love Taney County. It's a good place to live."

(Ollie Layton was Taney County's Sesquicentennial Queen.)

OLLIE LAYTON REMEMBERS EARLY TANEY COUNTY

"Many people moved to Taney County in the 1880s. Blue stem grass grew to the horses' shoulders. Deer and wild turkey were plentiful, and the White River was full of fish. A homestead law had been passed, a grant of up to 160 acres of land. The homesteader had to build a house, clear the land, plant it with crops, and be able to live off the land.

"Bales of cotton were hauled to Springfield by wagon and mules or horses before the Railroad was built. By 1887 Thomas Berry had built a cotton gin. Many farmers had cattle herds and they were driven by road to market in Springfield.

"Some owned as many as 150 head of 3- and 4-year-old steers. Even young turkeys were driven by flocks to the market. Young mules were in demand: there were many who bought mules to work on their farms and pull their wagons.

"Several years passed and the Railroad was built. The Missouri-Pacific had surveyed routes through western Taney County; mention was made of a railroad down Roark Creek, and up Turkey Creek. Branson route was the final choice for the Missouri-Pacific. With completion of the railroad, freight was shipped. The time of Freighters using their team and wagons was over.

"The first man to put a store in Hollister was a big fella named Rube Kirkum; he had a daughter named Willard. The store was a big, long frame building. He sold a lot of groceries. There was plenty of teamwork going on up and down the creek and the teamsters and everyone else bought there. When the store burned the Kirkums left. Tom Jennings had a new building put up and went on with the business. Then a bunch of buildings were moved from Kirbyville to the Branson and Hollister area. Rolland (Pete) Kite put in a drug store. My brother Ben worked for Pete awhile. He sold candy, tobacco, and ran the soda fountain.

"The tourists came to Hollister on the train. Soda pop was kind of a treat back in those days—use to come in a big, thick bottle with no caps but sort of a push down stopper. Mr. Shoemaker built a beautiful passenger depot. The people missed the passenger trains when they were taken off the railroad. There were the morning passengers and the afternoon passengers; the people liked to travel by train. Later, Elmer Jackson and George Vanzandt put in a large store. Those were the first merchants of Hollister. People who lived in Hollister enjoyed the quiet peaceful homes they were blessed with.

"The pencil factory in Branson employed 80 people. Edd Trout was the manager of the pencil factory. The factory was later moved to California. The people hated to see it go, since it brought jobs for the people, and teams of wagons would haul in lumber for the factory to make their product."

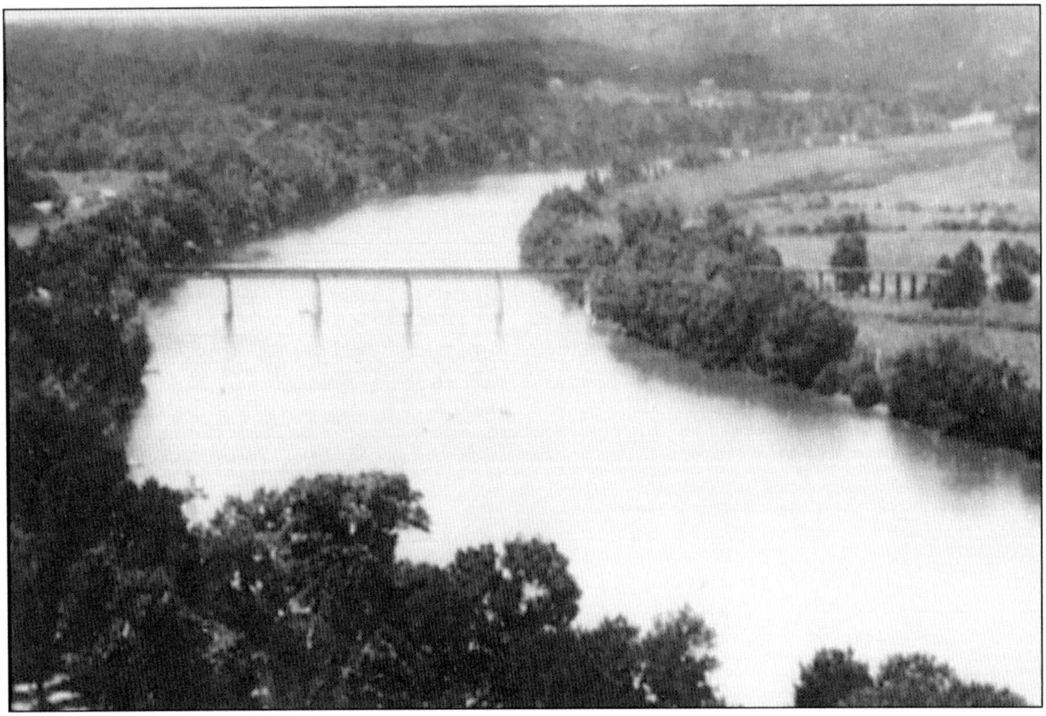

Photograph taken in the early 1900s. The bridge spans the White River before it was dammed.

Ollie Layton Remembers Dr. A.J. Storms

"Today as I passed Dr. Storms' homestead, many fond memories were brought back to my mind of my childhood days, especially one hog butchering day when I was there. Dr. Storms butchered hogs on New Years day, all day long. Many friends and neighbors gathered at his place to help him on this busy day.

"One man would kill the hogs while others did the scalding and scraping where large kettles of water were kept at a scalding degree. Then the water was put in a barrel and used as a scalding vat. Some of the men scalded the hogs nice and clean, then they were hung out on a tree limb and the entrails removed. Then several buckets of fresh water were thrown over them to cleanse them. Later the hog was placed on a table and cut up. These men had their wives with them to prepare the noon meal while they worked.

"The table was loaded with good food for the working men to eat. The liver, ribs and tenderloin were served. A tin boiler the ladies heated water in for the weekly wash was used to make coffee. I remember a big box of peppermint candy was on the table for the children.

"Dr. Storms paid the men who worked for him with meat. He sold hams, shoulders, and side meat. He rendered lard for days and days with the help of the men. Dr. Storms made soap and hung a sack of this lye soap in the first limbs of his apple orchard to keep the trees healthy and drive the insects away. This kept the body of the tree black and shiny. His beautiful orchard was in the field between his house and where Slay Holiday lives now. Dr. Storms also kept as many as 40 head of hogs in the fattening pens.

"Today the old homestead has a hog ranch there, and beautiful fat cattle [now owned by the School of the Ozarks]. I know Dr. Storms would be happy to know his homestead still produces meat to feed the people. Dr. Storms was a man who went to bed early and arose early to work in his fields to produce corn and wheat. In those years all farmers grew their wheat for flour, and corn for meal.

"Dr. Storms was a good doctor. I recall he was called to my Uncle John Rittenhouse's place one time when Uncle John was sick with pneumonia. They got another doctor to come also, and he said Uncle John would not live til morning and said for them to fix him a pallet and put him to bed. When my mother asked Dr. Storms what he thought he replied, "As long as there is life, there is hope." Dr. Storms sat up all night with Uncle John and ended staying a total of two weeks with him, only going home to do his chores. How faithful and sincere Dr. Storms was to my uncle. My uncle got well and outlived the doctor.

"Dr. Storms had a huge courage and vision, could do an amazing lot of good for an entire community. He was a good doctor and rode his horse many miles from home to doctor the sick. He gave people good advice on how to eat and live. He worked hard and was a good farmer, and was a good citizen.

"I can recall one time our dear Aunt Tommie Branson saying they sent their son Mack Branson over to get Dr. Storms when Uncle Rube was sick. Aunt Tommie said he doctored the entire family and the dog for $1. He sure believed in living and let live. He was kept busy doctoring the people far and near.

"One time back when Hollister was growing into a bigger town, Bill Johnson and Pete Kite wanted a bank. Bill didn't have money enough to put in a bank. He went out to see Dr. Storms, to see if he would back him, put some money in the bank. The doctor was a nice old man, and worth a lot of money. He helped Bill Johnson get a bank started. Dr. Storms became President of the new Hollister bank, had his picture enlarged and it hung over the door for years. The bank sure was needed, and Dr. Storms realized the existing need and gave it a helping hand."

A Recollection of Harve and Berthie Brittain

(The following story was told by Hazel Layton Cobb)

"One time back in the 1940s my cousin Charlene and I went on a camping trip down the Old Blackwell Ferry road in the Kirbyville and Mildred community. There were many of the older Brittain family members there, about 30 or 40 of us altogether. We took food and our bedding to spend the night down by the water.

"It was nigh 2:00 in the morning when it begin to rain, and what a downpour it was. We all got soaking wet, and it sure put an abrupt end to our sleeping out under the stars. So we all went to Harve and Berthie Brittain's home which was about a half a mile from our campsite.

"Berthie built a cozy, warm fire in the wood stove and we all huddled up close to it to dry and warm ourselves. She prepared us all a breakfast of homemade biscuits, home cured ham and sausage, jams, jellies, and home canned peaches. Her kindness made being in her home as much fun as being at the river would have been.

"Harve and Berthie were about the first people I knew of who had a radio; I can remember us listening to Slim Wilson sing. They lived in the older Brittain house and it had a large upstairs.

"After eating the big breakfast, Charlene and I decided to slip off upstairs and take a morning nap. Some of the men went back to the river and set a trot line and caught some big cat fish. The other Brittain boys were there: Price, Dewey, Hurley, as well as Harve. Older folks as well as young gathered together for this farewell party for some of the boys were going into the service.

"There was a minister there by the name of Dean Hall Jackson. It was always sad to see the young men go off to service. But they were good about playing pranks on us girls. The night it rained on us, Hurley Brittain had sneaked around and put a river

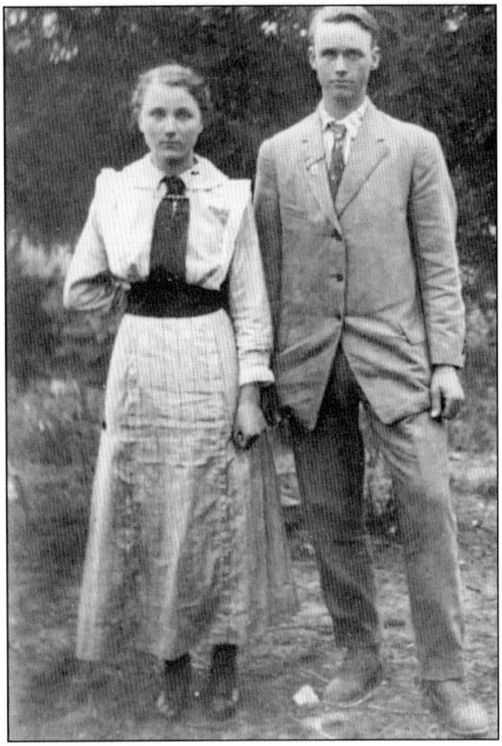

Milton Price Brittain and Sarah Edna Layton, 1915 at Oak Grove.

eel in my and Charlene's bed. We slipped in under the covers and felt that thing down there; we didn't waste any time getting out of the bed.

"That also brings back to my recollection another time a bunch of us were together. Austin and Jesse Brittain took me and Charlene out in the woods to hunt for snipes. Well, they showed us how to hold the bags open out in the middle of the dark woods. Then they took off and never came back.

"What good memories there are of these fine people. Berthie was kind and never had a cross word to say to anyone. As my cousin Charlene and I walked through the quiet little Brittain cemetery along the Black Well Ferry road a few days ago, many memories came back to both of us. To see Hurley's stone made me think of the times all would gather at Aunt Edna's for dinner. The cemetery is kept up so nicely by loved ones.

"There are so many of the older folks gone, but yet they live always in the hearts of those who loved them."

Remembering Milton Price and Edna Layton

Sarah Edna Layton was the oldest daughter of William and Fronea Layton. She was born June 10, 1899, near Turkey Creek in Hollister. She was four when her father died with pneumonia. This left her mother to care for the two older boys, and the ten-week-old twins, as well as Edna.

Her brothers Ben and Randa helped their mother care for the small children, washing their clothes on a slab rock down at the creek. They helped to feed and change them, doing what they could to help.

Edna was still too little to help much and consequently she spent considerable time out-of-doors playing in the warm summer sun. Summer days were barefoot days and many times she would play near the waters of Turkey Creek feeling the squish of velvety, cool mud ooze between her toes as she walked along the creek bank.

As she grew older she began to learn to do things as her mother did; learning how to care for the small children, Lonnie and Ollie. She learned to cook meals for the family on the wood cookstove. Her mother had a spinning wheel which Edna soon learned how to use, along with carding sheep's wool which would be used for their clothing.

In December of 1905, Fronea Layton bought the 160 acres of land in the Oak Grove community with the $500 she received from the railroad in damages. Edna and the other children attended school there at the Oak Grove church and schoolhouse.

As the years passed and Edna grew older, she would work by her mother's side in the fields hoeing corn during the heat of the day. In the evenings they would piece quilts together and knit socks for the family. Sometimes she would help her mother can and preserve vegetables and fruit from their orchard so they would have something to eat during the winter months. Ben and Randa always managed to keep meat on the table whether it be deer, wild turkey, squirrel, or rabbit.

When Edna was 16, she and Milton Price Brittain began a courtship. The Brittain family ancestors are also among those pioneers who were the first settlers of Taney County. Price was the son of Milton and Mary Brittain.

His grandparents were Mr. and Mrs. Milton Price Brittain, who were married January 25, 1843, in Henry County, Iowa. They moved to Warnersville (later Kirbyville) on the Springfield Harrison Road. The Brittains owned a store and built the home which was sold to Andrew Brown when the latter moved to the area. Andrew was the father of Thomas Lee Brown who was born in the house."

Price and Edna were married December 24, 1916. To them were born three sons: Austin, Jesse, and Virgil. They lived on a farm east of Hollister. Price was quite a hand with carpentry work, and built his family a new house. They were farmers, raised cattle, hay, crops, and livestock. Price and Edna purchased the organ at Claude Layton's sale when he sold the Thomas and Julia Layton homestead to Wanda and Vernon Layton. After moving the organ to its new home and owners, it remained there for many, many years.

The author's paternal great-grandfather, James David Cobb, lived down the Blackwell Ferry road near Mildred and Kirbyville. He had a sister named Leona who married Uncle Jim Crouch, (the Crouch descendants came from England). Leona and Jim had a daughter named Berthie, who married Harve Brittain (Price's brother).

Harve and Berthie lived in the log house near the old Brittain Cemetery along the Blackwell Ferry Road. Oscar Brittain's grandparents lived in it at one time. The author's paternal grandfather, Charlie Cobb of Forsyth, said he believed the log house was built by Tom and Annie Anderson. Charlie, who was born in 1895, has mentioned that when he was young, he use to spend the night in the old log cabin with the Brittain family. Charlie and Price Brittain knew each other when they were both young men. They spent many a Saturday night riding the hills of Kirbyville on horseback going to see their girl friends.

One of Edna's nieces, Hazel Layton Cobb, had the following to say about her Aunt Edna:

"Many years ago when all of us kids were growing up on the Oak Grove farm and around Turkey Creek, there were many days when we would walk the road to our Aunt Edna's house.

"Down the road we would stroll, go through each gate, and cross each creek. We made our way over each beautiful hill through the rough timber step by step. In the distance we could see a white house setting on a hill nestled among the trees with smoke rising from the chimney.

"The closer to the house we got, we could smell the fresh aroma from the dinner Aunt Edna was cooking. After walking for miles, this only made us children all the more hungry.

"In sight of the house and the gate we could hear the dogs bark as the folks inside would come to the door to greet us. 'Oh, look who's here,' Aunt Edna would say, wearing her big print apron made from feed sack material. She would greet us all with a hug and a welcome to come on in. 'Dinner is on,' she would say as we gathered around the table filled with a delicious meal and a white cake baked in her wood cookstove. She would have chicken and homemade dumplin's.

"I would always sit close to my cousin Austin, who was the oldest of the Brittain boys. The other two were Virgil and Jesse. My brother William would sit between them and Mom and Dad would sit near Price and Edna. The men and boys would talk about the livestock and hunting, maybe decide on a day to fish. There was always plenty of work that had to be tended to.

"After dinner Mom and Edna would sit on

the front porch and visit, swinging in the porch swing. Their talk would consist of the kids, the chickens, and they would plan a trip to Branson or Kirbyville to pick up a few things they needed and trade some eggs for coffee, salt, and other essential items.

"Our lives back in those days were hard but they were good times, and kinfolk helped each other and spent time together in both good and bad times. Aunt Edna left us November 15, 1986. Her little white house knows no more the sound of her voice, nor her footsteps. For she, too, has rounded the corner entering into another white house sitting high upon a hill. Perhaps she still wears her big print apron, made of pink and blue feed sack cloth.

"One fine day to come, each of us who knew and loved Aunt Edna will also round a corner and then shall hear Aunt Edna say, "Come on in, dinner is ready, we are all here at last."

"Price Brittain was born February 5, 1896, and died January 5, 1974. Price and Edna are both buried at the Branson Memorial Cemetery."

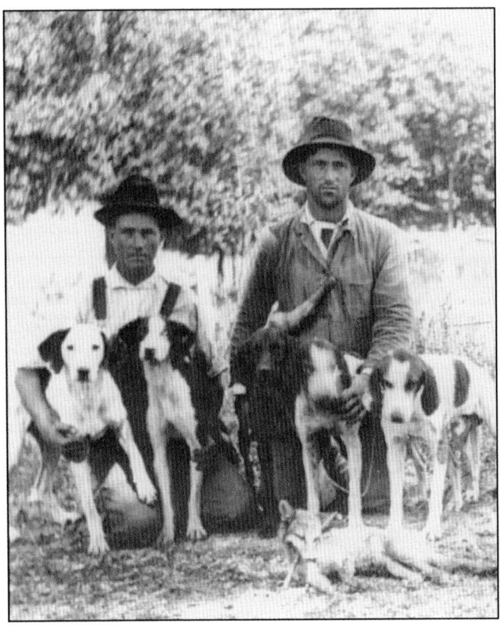

Ben and Randa Layton.

Ben and Randa Layton

Clinton Ben Layton was born November 22, 1882, and died March 19, 1978. He is buried at the Whorton Cemetery. Randa D. Layton was born September 27, 1896 and died April 1, 1987. He is buried at the Gobbler's Knob Cemetery.

Ben and Randa were the two oldest children of William and Fronea Layton. They were born on Turkey Creek on the old Bob Powers' place. They lived there until the railroad came and destroyed their home.

Ben was ten and Randa was six when their father died of pneumonia. This left quite a burden on their mother's shoulders with another young daughter and two ten-week-old twins.

When their father was alive, Ben spent much of his time by his side. This helped him later to carry on the responsibilities he would have to handle when his father died. He learned how to cut and saw wood and manage the livestock which helped his mother tremendously.

The Layton brothers had to accept and endure this hardship which fell upon the family. When word came to Randa that his father had passed away, he wouldn't accept that but replied, "No, my daddy isn't dead, he isn't dead."

Though they were yet boys, they knew how to hunt. The deer and wild turkey were plentiful and they knew how to lay down on the flat rocks near the water's edge of Turkey Creek and catch fish with their bare hands. They had to grow up quickly as they helped their mother with the other children. It wasn't unusual to see them at the creek helping her do the wash on the flat rocks as they used her homemade lye soap.

The railroad agreed to pay Fronea $500 in damages and with this money she moved the children to the farm in Oak Grove. To the east of their log house was one of the balds where the Bald Knobbers held their secret meetings. Many times Fronea watched from her front steps as bands of the night riders rode by en route to Forsyth for a hanging or a shootout.

The Layton brothers helped their mother plant the spring garden near the cabin and the field crops of wheat and corn were planted. They had to raise, as all the old timers, their own grain to feed the livestock. Ben learned to plow behind the mule named Barney while Randa led him down the rows breaking the soil with a single-point plow. Fronea would follow behind them, dropping kernels of corn. Then they would go back and cover each row over with dirt.

As the boys grew older, they became wise in the ways of the woods. They'd set a bunch of traps to catch possum, coon, fox, and any fur bearing animal they could. In those days, a good fur meant a few pennies. They never went hungry as the boys kept the table supplied with meat with their homegrown fruits and vegetables.

They would leave Oak Grove early in the morning with their hounds and hunt through Hollister then meet the train as it came through town. Then they'd go through Happy Hollar just south of Hollister and hunt through that area, and end up spending the night in the woods or in one of the caves.

They'd build a campfire and cook a rabbit or squirrel over the open flame for their supper. Their mother sent a small sack of sourdough biscuits with them, and the creek flowed nearby where they could get drinking water. They'd sit around the fire and tell stories they heard from the older folks, and talk about their future plans. If the moon was full they'd run the hounds into the night after coons before going to sleep.

The next morning they'd wake up and find a little frost on the seat of their britches, with only a few coals of the fire left. They'd get themselves woke up good, pick up their rifles, whistle for the hounds and continue on through the woods. They'd circle back around and come back through Hollister and meet the same train coming into town as they met on their way hunting the day before. It wasn't unusual for them to spend 24 hours or more in the woods at a time.

There were times when they encountered the most feared animal in the woods, a panther. They had experienced losing a good hound to their deadly claws and powerful jaws. Not only was the panther a threat, but they also had to beware of the wild hogs that roamed the hills freely. A man or a hound could easily lose its life with one slash from the hog's razor sharp tusks.

As they grew to be strong men, their love for the outdoors became a characteristic which remained with them throughout their lives. They made good money with their hunting and trapping skills for that day and time. The pelts were sold to a buyer in Springfield.

Randa went on to become a river guide working for Charlie Barnes and Jim Owens. Ben spent time in the law enforcement field and was well known for being a dog trader and hunter.

Way Down on Bullcreek

This author's grandfather, Randa Layton, told many stories about when his brother Ben and he were young men. They hunted and trapped all over the hills of Taney County, Missouri, and knew the country well. Randa told the following story about Ben.

"One time when Ben was Town Marshall of Hollister, he needed to go to the general store in Walnut Shade. There was some business he needed to tend to with Hap Kinckly, the man who ran the store. Ben had saddled his horse early in the morning and was soon on his way.

"Within a couple of hours Ben was there. As he slid down from the saddle he tied his horse to the hitching post in front of the store near the water trough. When he went inside he noticed two neighborhood men playing checkers on top of an empty barrel Hap had in the store for that purpose. In those days, the small general stores were one of the social gathering places for the community. They interrupted their game long enough to exchange "howdy's" with Ben, tell him who was winning, and asked how the hound business was.

"Hap was behind the counter weighing

sacks of coffee, flour, salt, and sugar. He also measured so many yards of pretty dress material for Mamie Dobbs who had brought her eggs and butter to trade for items she needed. Greetings were exchanged and Ben helped Mamie carry her store bought goods to her wagon. He laid them behind the spring seat then gave her a hand into the seat. They visited a few minutes before she left.

"Ben went back inside the store, picked up the coffee pot from the wood stove and poured himself a cup. Then he pulled a piece of paper from his vest pocket, handed it to Hap and told him to give it to the Freight man Carl Jenkins the next time he was there.

"Before they finished their conversation a boy came runnin' in excited and out of breath. Between gasps of air he said, "Hap, ya gotta come quick! There's a fight down at the creek and Roy Blansitt is a-fixin' to kill old man Henry!"

"Ben set his coffee cup down while he asked the boy how far down the creek it was. He told Ben to go about half a mile and they were on the gravel bar. Ben hurried out the door, jumped on his horse, and took off in a dead run.

"When he got in sight of the fight he heard the awfullest commotion a-goin' on. Roy had the end of a gun barrel stuck smack dab in the middle of Henry's belly, and Henry was sure a-sweatin' it. His eyes were bugged out, his mouth hanging open and tobacco juice goin' everywhere.

"Before Ben could dismount, Roy pulled the hammer back on the revolver and fired. A cloud of smoke boiled from the end of the gun, then a dead silence followed. The strangest thing happened, Henry was still standing. However, his legs were shakin' so bad, the teeth in his head rattled.

"Ben jerked the gun from Blansitt, broke it open, and saw that the bullet hadn't disengaged from the chamber, and the firing pin was only half way down. He asked Roy why he wanted to kill Henry. Roy answered him, "I tell ya the truth Ben, he deserves it, he surely does. Why, I caught him red handed stealing two of my best laying hens, ye know, the ones that lay them brown eggs before breakfast."

Ben turned to Henry and asked him what he had to say for himself. He kind of dropped his head and wiped his mouth with his shirt sleeve. "I tell ye the gospel truth Ben, I wasn't stealing them chickens of Roy. No sirree! Why, I found them way on down the road from Roy's place. I was tryin to be a good neighbor. I was just going to return them all safe and sound!"

"The three of them discussed this back and forth until they got it settled. Ben didn't arrest either one of them, but warned them not to let it happen again. Ben kept Roy's gun and took it to a gunsmith in Branson to have it checked.

"Ben helped Henry mount his mule since he was still shaken up over what had happened. Ben mounted his horse and the two rode back to Hap's store. For several weeks after this, Roy had a good time bragging about it and told everyone what a fighter he was from 'way down on Bull Creek.'"

Remembering Aunt Rosa Kaneaster Layton

"Back in my childhood days when we lived on the old Pleake place near Hollister, we lived close to the Ben Layton family. Ben was my dad's oldest brother and the first to marry. His wife Rosa was very talented for back in those days. She could make the best homemade lemon pies from scratch and wonderful biscuits.

"I spent a lot of time with her and she taught me many things in my teenage years. How I did love to go over and spend an afternoon with dear Aunt Rosa. She was alone a lot with Ben gone. He was busy on his farm, or working with the law enforcement of Taney County. He dealt a lot in livestock as well as traded and trained hounds to hunt.

"Aunt Rosa talked of her childhood days and many other things. She could chop wood just like a man, she cooked on a wood cook stove and heated their home with wood. She washed their clothes on a washboard doing it the old time way, even draw the water from the well. I would help her wring out Ben and the boys' overalls and hang them on the line. She would speak of the many things she learned as a child while we worked.

"Ben and Rosa had six children: Mildred, Vernon, Lucille, Pauline, Harold, and Lee. As of now in the year of 1989 there are only two left. I remember the family so well, such good cousins to have. We shared many good and hard times together. Lee was my age.

"Today I still visit with Pauline Layton Barton, she has always lived in the Branson area. Her mother Rosa has been gone now a number of years. She spent the last eight years of her life in a nursing home. When we lost her, we really lost a lot.

"She was a kind lady and could sew so neat, and how her hands worked hard to mend overalls for the men folks. She made neat little stitches. She raised a good family, all her children turned out to be good natured. Her son Vernon was in the Marines. He and I would write to each other. I still have in my scrapbook a Christmas card he sent me in 1944. It just says, 'Merry Christmas,' your cousin Vernon.

"We lost Vernon in a tractor accident on his farm in March of 1977. It was such a tragedy and so sad for the family to have lost such a fine man. My own family was notified by telephone so my husband Junior, my dad Randal Layton, my brother Bill Layton, and myself all went down there to his home. The same old home place where in my childhood days I would visit with Aunt Rosa and her children. The same old large trees still stood in the yard and as the March wind blew through them it seemed to sound like the singing of sad songs. It was in the springtime and the flowers were beginning to bloom once again.

"I remember when I was small my mother (Ethel Smith Layton) had a sister named Ola and her husband Bill Lowry lived on the old Layton place. We would go there to visit my Uncle Bill Lowry's sister Lena, and her mother. Lena was such a neat person. Each morning when she got up she would powder her face and put rouge on, which is called blush today. She wore a little white apron every day. She was so tidy, never wanted a speck of dirt on her.

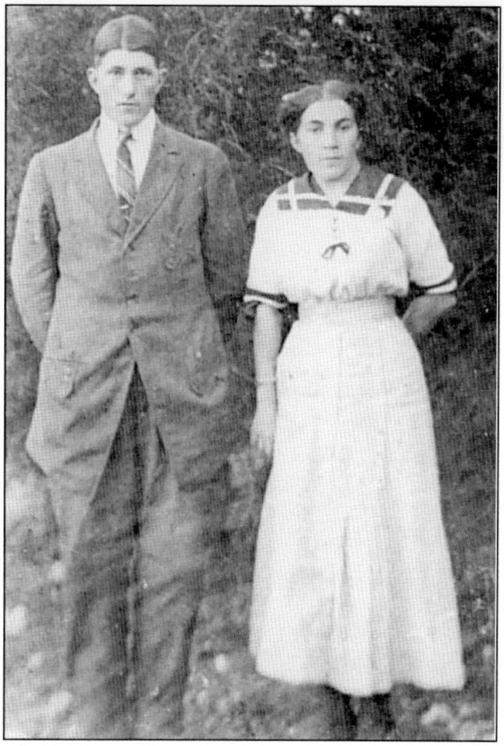

Ben and Rosa Kaneaster Layton, married January 9, 1914.

"So at the old Layton homestead I've seen a lot of family members live there. Many have come and gone through the years but the homestead has always remained in the Layton family. Vernon's widow, Wanda Dickens Layton, and her son Tom live there today. You can still feel welcome to go there, it will always be the family homestead. The old trees still stand and the old cellar from which our dear Aunts carried their canned jars of fruits and vegetables. Many of them worked hard to have food to feed their families, or as we say, "when the snow flies this winter."

"I sure remember how good the canned peaches and sweet pickles Aunt Rosa canned tasted. My mother and I often went to visit Rosa on a Sunday and also when Aunt Ola lived there. Some times they would come to our home.

"We use to gather for dinners and many of the kinfolk would come. Mildred would come in from Oklahoma and bring her babies. The house would be filled with good food and a large crowd always showed up. Those were the good days, the days I remember Aunt Rosa."

Written by Hazel Layton Cobb

Randa D. and Ethel Mary Smith Layton

The author's maternal grandfather, Randa D. Layton, was born September 27, 1896, on the old Bob Powers' place along Turkey Creek near Hollister, Missouri. He was the second child born to William and Fronea Layton.

During his lifetime Randa spoke continuously about the early days of Taney County. He always claimed his first recollection was when he was three years old about a man named George Lewallen. Randa said he and his father were at George's home. The men were doing some repair work on his barn. It got late in the evening and George told Randa and William to spend the night there with him. So that's what they did.

They went inside George's small cabin home, ate supper and fixed Randa a pallet on the floor near the fireplace. Randa laid down and fell asleep while George and William sat up and talked a while before they too decided to sleep.

George had the lantern very dim and being cross-eyed anyway, this caused him problems with his vision. He saw Randa on the pallet and thought it was his dog. It had slipped his mind that's where he laid Randa down to sleep. George walked over and kicked him a couple of times trying to get that hound dog up. Randa woke up and asked him why he was kicking him. That was his first recollection.

Randa grew up learning the things in life he would need to know from his uncles and his grandpa Whorton like hunting, fishing, trapping, and working on the farm tending to the livestock and the crops. He cared not for the things of this world and always lived a slow life which allowed him to live 91 years.

Randa was one of the last of the old-time river guides. He started guiding for Charlie Barnes out of Cotter, Arkansas, when he was young, for $2 a day. Then he later guided for the legendary Jim Owens of the Owen Boat line out of Branson, Missouri. He spent time on the river with such personalities as Gene Autry and Smiley Burnett.

There were also the years he traveled from Kansas to South Dakota as well as through Missouri with the wheat harvest crew. He would leave his wife and family behind while he made the harvest earning money to make their living.

Randa always lived the way his ancestors did before him remaining old-fashioned and one of the last of the true "Ozarkian Old-Timers." He made many boat paddles, axe handles, and homemade hunting knives.

Randa and Ethel Smith were married February 6, 1924. Ethel was the daughter of Tom and Mary Smith of Kirbyville. She grew up with a nickname of Pete. The author visited with Cecil McClary in February of 1989 and he explained how Ethel got the nickname of Pete.

"When Ethel was real small, her dad had an old white mule they called Pete. One day Ethel was with some of the other children in the barn lot. When she saw old Pete she got excited and started hollerin' 'Petsie, Petsie.' And from that day on her father called her Pete, and that's how she got the nickname."

Ethel was born December 7, 1901, at Moore's Ferry near Kirbyville. She, too, grew up on a farm with her brothers and sisters sharing in the hardships of that era of history. Ethel was a good gardener, farmer, hunter, as well as a housewife. For many years she wrote for the Branson newspaper while they lived on the little farm at Oak Grove.

Both Randa and Ethel remained old-fashioned, worked hard, believed in God and their families, as well as their native homeland of Taney County. Three children were born to them: William, Hazel, and Virginia June, who died shortly after her birth. They were all born in the little house down in the field at Oak Grove, not far from Fronea Layton's log cabin.

Ethel used to talk about her dear friend Velma Lowry. They grew up together riding their horses and squirrel huntin'. Ethel knew Douglas Mahnkey as they, too, grew up together and played in the catalpa tree house. Their mothers were good friends.

Randa and Ethel were both believers in the use of old time herbs and remedies. For many years she made a pleasant tasting cough syrup from hickory bark. She would always have a little pot of goldenseal tea sitting on their wood cookstove. It tasted terrible but they claimed it was "good fer what e'er ailed ya." Randa would find it growing wild in the woods in the fall of the year and dig up the bright yellow roots. He would also say, "What's bitter to the mouth is sweet to the belly."

They also kept a good grade of whiskey around the house for a cold remedy which would consist of hot water, a little lemon juice, a dab of butter, a shake of ginger and a little whiskey. Taken at bed time it was a very effective medicine to help clear up congestion and sweat out a fever.

Randa used to mention from time to time about the courtship between Ethel and himself many years before when they were young. He could hardly wait to hear the sound of her little mare's hooves coming up the road, and how they would ride side by side on their horses down the dusty roads of yesterday. He'd say that little mare could foxtrot so pretty it was just like music to the ear.

Randa passed away April 1, 1987, and Ethel on February 3, 1987. They were both laid to rest in the Gobbler's Knob Cemetery near Hollister, resting peacefully near the tract of land the first Laytons homesteaded in the 1850s. It is also close to the little creek Randa spoke of fondly when he and his brother Ben would swim and fish the waters of Turkey Creek.

They sleep quietly in the land that was always home to them, as well as so many family and friends. Gobbler's Knob has long been a part of Taney County's history with so many of the old timers buried there. It sets within listening distance of the train as it makes its way through Hollister and passes the Whorton Cemetery. So many of those buried in both cemeteries at one time played a major role in the birth and establishment of Taney County, Missouri.

Lonnie Layton

The following was told by Ollie Layton, twin sister of Lonnie Layton:

"My brother Lonnie loved horses, and he had some beautiful horses. He was a farmer and was content where he lived. He went to the wheat harvest when he was young with his brothers Ben and Randa.

"One time he took bad sick and the doctor told him he would have to get

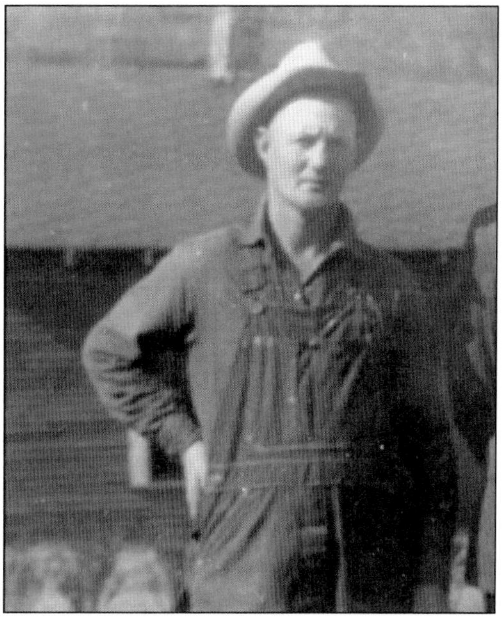

Lonnie Layton.

some treatments. So he and his son Bobby went to Kansas City. He worked in the mail department at the Post Office while there with our cousin Albert Whorton.

"Lonnie was a hard worker and enjoyed his cattle. He was good to people and a good neighbor and the people thought a lot of him. One time when he took bad sick there was 16 different people come to see him one day. He came up here one day and told Mama he was going to live with us as long as he lived. The doctor didn't know what was wrong with him but he had liver trouble.

"They had a sale down here one time when Ben, and Randa didn't want him to have it. He had bought some nice white-face heifers and I told him to keep them, they would help him raise his children. He sold his milk cows and his big fat sows; that's when Troy Compton told me Lonnie could fatten hogs quicker than any one he knew.

"Lonnie didn't fish much but he hunted with his brothers and they'd kill skunks, coons, and possums. Our Uncle Jepp Whorton was quite a fur trader and buyer.

"Lonnie was a good manager and worked for the phone company for many years. He helped run the phone wire across this place. He was born October 13, 1902, and died January 1, 1961. His wife Josephine Bull Layton was born November 3, 1897, and died March 22, 1938. Lonnie and Josie had two children, Bobby and Charlene. They had six grandchildren."

In a conversation the author had with Donald Whorton, Don said that when Lonnie was little, his brother Ben would hold him on his lap and cry. Ben was afraid Lonnie would never grow to be big enough to look after and take care of himself.

Oak Grove

The Oak Grove community is located off T Highway, what local people refer to as the Long Beach road, east of Branson. The original church and school house was lost to fire in the early 1900s. The author's grandpa, Randa Layton, has told the story of how it happened.

"A local man, Fletch Kaneaster, was caretaker of the church house. He filled the stove too full of wood one Sunday after everyone had left to go home. It blew up, and the stove pipe fell loose from the ceiling when it exploded. By the time some of the neighbors realized the church was in flames, it was too late. So all they could do was stand sadly by and watch their little country church turn to ashes."

Not long after the fire, folks in the area got together and went about the task of rebuilding. This time they built it out of stone. Some of the last teachers to teach at Oak Grove before it consolidated with Branson Public Schools were Helen Fancher Awberry and Jane Kenner, both from Arkansas. Others were Bess Wither, Ira Rittenhouse, and Jimmie Davis, who was the last one to teach there. Lonnie and Josie Layton lived next to the school house and the teachers boarded with them.

There were many children who walked to school no matter what the weather was like. They would hang their wet coats and hats near the pot bellied stove on a cedar rack as they huddled to warm themselves. At recess or break the children would play outside on the bald to the east of the building where the Bald Knobbers held their secret meetings in the dark shadows of the night. Some names of the children were Hodge, Rose, Cornealson, Kaneaster, Brown, Layton, Whorton, and others.

In the years of life when the one room church house was in use, it was home for many social events in the community. There were many pie suppers held on Saturday nights that gave the young folks a place to go. The young girls in their mid-teens would bake a pie, and they'd all be put out on a table for display. The young boys, with their hair slicked back and their cleanest overalls on, would pick out a pie baked by one of the girls they liked. When the bidding started, the boy would run the price up until he got it. Then the girl who baked it would help him eat it.

That's how many of the young folks in those days did their romancing. When it came time to go home, usually the boy would politely ask the girl if he could walk her home. If she said "yes," they would walk down the road on foot; or, if the boy had a horse, they'd ride double-back.

But that was all many years ago. Many Saturday nights have passed since the last pie supper church service. But there are still a few left who grew up around there who remember those days.

Ollie Layton Remembers Uncle Harrison Collins

"At the home of Uncle Harrison Collins, friends and neighbors gathered on the Fourth of July for all day church service and a basket dinner. Uncle Harrison Collins was a Baptist minister and rode a beautiful horse to other communities to preach God's word. He lived close to God receiving spiritual food from heaven. He spread God's holy word to the people everywhere he went so they would hear and learn of God's good way of life, and live for God.

"He lived in the Mountain Grove area near Oak Grove community line. He was a good singer. He had a nephew named after him. He visited here and worked for Ben Hensley. He taught a singing school at Oak Grove. His home was near Huntsville, Arkansas. He and his wife were loved by many friends.

"Uncle Harrison Collins had two brothers, Saul and Esau. Saul was a preacher and a singer like Harrison was. Esau chose to walk a different path in life. Saul was a bald headed man and didn't have a tooth in his head, but he could sing the old time songs.

"One time Hazel and Charlene Layton were walking the road en route to Hazel's home in the field when they passed the Oak Grove church. Charlene said to Hazel as they passed by, 'I don't hear a thing, why it's just as if someone has died.'

"When they were past the church a little ways Elly Whorton motioned from the door for them to come to her. Elly told them that Saul Collins had just fallen over dead while he was preaching. Charlene was startled to hear that. She told Hazel later, 'I wonder why I said what I did when we passed by there?'

"Hazel and Charlene went on down the road and stopped at the first place they knew had an automobile for someone to get word to the funeral home in Branson."

Remembering Oak Grove

"I was born 1928 in the little house my dad Randa Layton, built at Oak Grove. That's where I grew up as a child. My dad's brother Lonnie and his wife Josie had a daughter, Charlene. Although we are first cousins, we are more like sisters. When Josie passed away, my mother Ethel Smith Layton took Charlene in under her wing.

"Charlene and I played together every day with our dolls and a play house. We had old broken dishes and old pans we made our mud pies in. We'd spend hours mixing up those mud pies and getting it on ourselves. It sure was a simple way to have fun. I wonder how many little girls make mud pies today?

"Charlene and I had a little place away from the house where we buried the cats, kittens, and puppies when they died. How we would sing and carry on those grave side services. Mom always said she could hear us clear back to the house.

"Charlene was a year younger than I. Our other cousins were Harold, Lee, Vernon, Pauline, Mildred, Ben and Rosa's children. They lost Wilma Lucille in 1930 to a hunting accident. Charlene's brother was Bobby, who was always into some kind of orneriness. When he was in trouble with his dad Lonnie, to avoid a whipping he would go and stand among the bee hives. The bees wouldn't bother him, but they would Lonnie. Then there was a time when Bobby walked by the wood stove and threw the cat in. The cat jumped out and left the country.

"There were also Price and Edna Brittain's three boys: Jesse, Virgil, and Austin. I had a brother Bill, and we lost a sister, Virginia June, shortly after she was born. We had many aunts and uncles that lived near and far. We never knew our grandpa William Layton, but I knew grandpa Tom Smith. He was an old time freighter in Taney County with his own freight crew. He died when I was 13. I also knew my grandma Layton and Smith.

"Grandma Fronea Whorton Layton lived in a log house up the path from our home in the field. Her house was built near the time of the Civil War, and was an old house when she moved in it. It is near the bald where the Bald Knobbers held their meetings during the time they roamed the hills. Grandma lived on one side of our place and Charlene on the other.

"At grandma's house, she always had a warm fire in the fireplace that we would sit close to and warm ourselves. All the kinfolk used to gather there for evening meals or maybe an ice cream supper. There would always be lots of company at her home. Charlene and I would go there so we could visit with relatives we didn't see often. There would be Laytons, Whortons, and Bollingers come up from Arkansas. Their ages would range from babies to the older ones.

"Grandma use to raise turkeys on her place. She had one old gobbler—I'll never forget him. Why, he'd see me coming up the path and come meet me half way just to chase me back down toward home.

"Grandma had lots of good fruit trees. There were delicious apple and cherry and she shared with all of us. Out of the 12 grandchildren she had, there would usually be one or two staying with her. Cousins Lee and Austin spent as much time there as they did at home.

"Dad worked hard on the 40 acres of land his mother gave him. I can remember watching him dig the well, it was all done by hand. Then one by one, he built the little out-buildings. I can still see him as he would go to the timber, cut the trees down, then cut logs by hand and drag each one up behind the horse. It took him all winter to build one of them. Then he would fill the cracks with mud. One building had a loft in it. Charlene and I spent a lot of time playing there. On moonlight nights a bunch of us kids would get in the loft and watch the night sky with the twinkling stars and we'd talk. We did enjoy those simple pleasures unknown to most children today.

"Charlene and I had our dolls to play with although we didn't have many. But what we had, we appreciated it. We never got bored with our few dolls. I had three dolls all the years I was growing up. One was named old Blackdraught. Charlene had a rag doll named Pearl. My last one was Ollie Mae, and I managed to keep her to the time I had my own children, and they got to play with her.

"A lot of times we children would get together and play games like "the fox and the hound," "hide and go seek," and others. We spent a lot of time out-of-doors and in the warm summer months Turkey Creek was a good place for us to play. In those days, children improvised their own amusement. Some would hide in the tree tops and I could never find them.

"Dad always kept a gentle horse around for we kids to ride. We loved to ride Old Shorty and Ribbon; they were both gentle and we loved them. Dad would plow the garden and the fields with the horses and at times he had mules to work with.

"I can remember one time my brother Bill, and cousins Harold and Vernon pulled an ornery stunt. They took an old tomcat that belonged to one of our Aunts, and put him in a gunny sack, then tied it shut and hung it from a tree limb. Then they took some sticks and began to beat the poor kitty. Seems like Aunt Ollie caught sight of this and hollered at the boys to let the cat loose. They opened the sack, the cat jumped out, and was never seen at Oak Grove again.

"Times were hard in those days and in the hills of Taney County many a barefooted kid could be found. Summer would be hot and dry thus making the water supply scarce. Many times we would have to haul water in from somewhere else. That made every drop of it precious and we were careful not to waste any. We didn't have running hot and cold water like there is today. Nor did we have refrigerators, or electricity. We never gave it a thought since it was what we were used to.

"We had our cows for milk, butter, and cream. Homemade buttermilk was a treat. My mother would make cottage cheese. We had chickens, hogs, and beef for meat. Plus, my dad and Bill would hunt for squirrel, deer, rabbit and wild turkey. One of my favorite memories are the days we butchered hogs. We'd scrape them clean, then hang them in a tree and dad would cut the meat up. The aroma of fresh dressed pork smelled so good. My mother would cook the pork chops, which we called tenderloins, in a cast iron skillet. The meat had the best taste, not like meat in the grocery stores today. There's nothing like meat cooked on a wood cookstove.

"Mom made homemade lye soap in an iron kettle and it took her all day to make a batch. When finished, she would pour it in a pan and cut it into square cakes. We had enough soap to last all winter. We washed our clothes and bedding on a washboard. We had to carry the water from the well house to where mom washed. We'd hang the clothes on a line or along the fences. It took all day to do a week's washin'. Mom used a sad-iron to iron with. There is no comparison in the ways we did things back then with now. We have nice washers and dryers today and electric irons.

"One time we lived in Hollister for four years near my cousin Pauline. We spent a lot of time together. She couldn't peddle a bicycle, so when we rode I peddled and she sat on the handle bars.

"To look back, it seems as if it was a day or so ago when we rode in Uncle Jim's ox-drawn wagon, or when we went to school at Oak Grove. The little church building is quiet today, with only silence and cobwebs to fill it. No more does it know the sound of a child's laughter, or the prayers of a faithful servant.

"One can close their eyes and catch a glimpse of life as it was in Oak Grove years ago. The house my brother William and I were born in still stands. It is in need of repair, and is weather beaten with it's age showing. The beautiful flowers my mother planted along the path leading from the house and around the yard are still there. They continue to bloom each spring as if nothing ever changed. The lone pine tree my dad set out years ago still stands. It has continued to grow strong as the winds of time and change pass by.

"In Oak Grove life was simple and our families worked hard. People combined their strength as they struggled to survive in those hard times."

Written by Hazel Layton Cobb

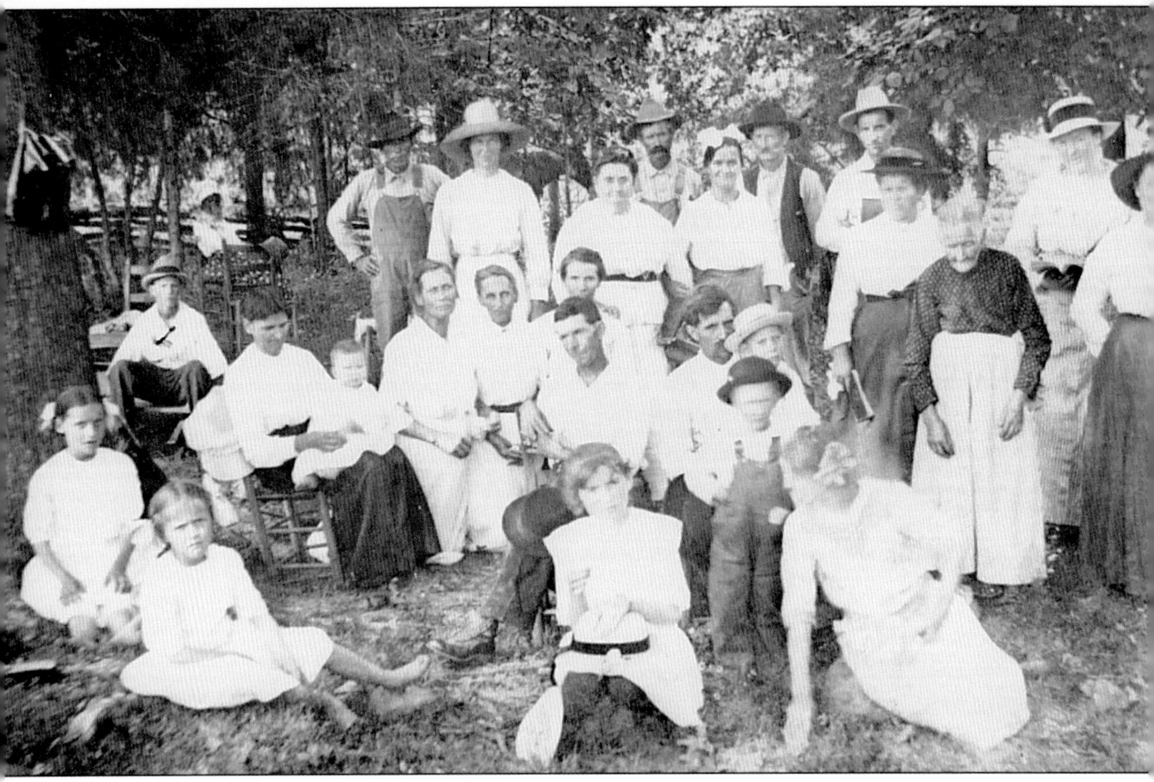

Pictured is a get together on the Fourth of July at the home of Uncle Harrison Collins in Huntsville, Arkansas. One woman in the photo is still holding onto the songbook from which they were all singing the old time hymns of yesterday. The actual identity of their names may not coincide correctly with the picture sequence, but it was as close as Aunt Ollie Layton could remember.

Right to left: Almeda Whorton, Kate Branson, Grandma Collins, ____Howard, Delbert Whorton, Tommy Branson, Sara Snapp, Joe and Jesse Snapp, Ed Branson, Sara Thompson, Artie Snapp, Cora Howard (she is holding a baby who is William Howard, he became a doctor), Edith Ruby Howard, Ethel Nezzie Howard, Lonnie Layton, Jeanette Collins, Bill Snapp, Loua Haggard, Alice Rose, Ethel Harris, Esau Collins, and Rube Mitchell.

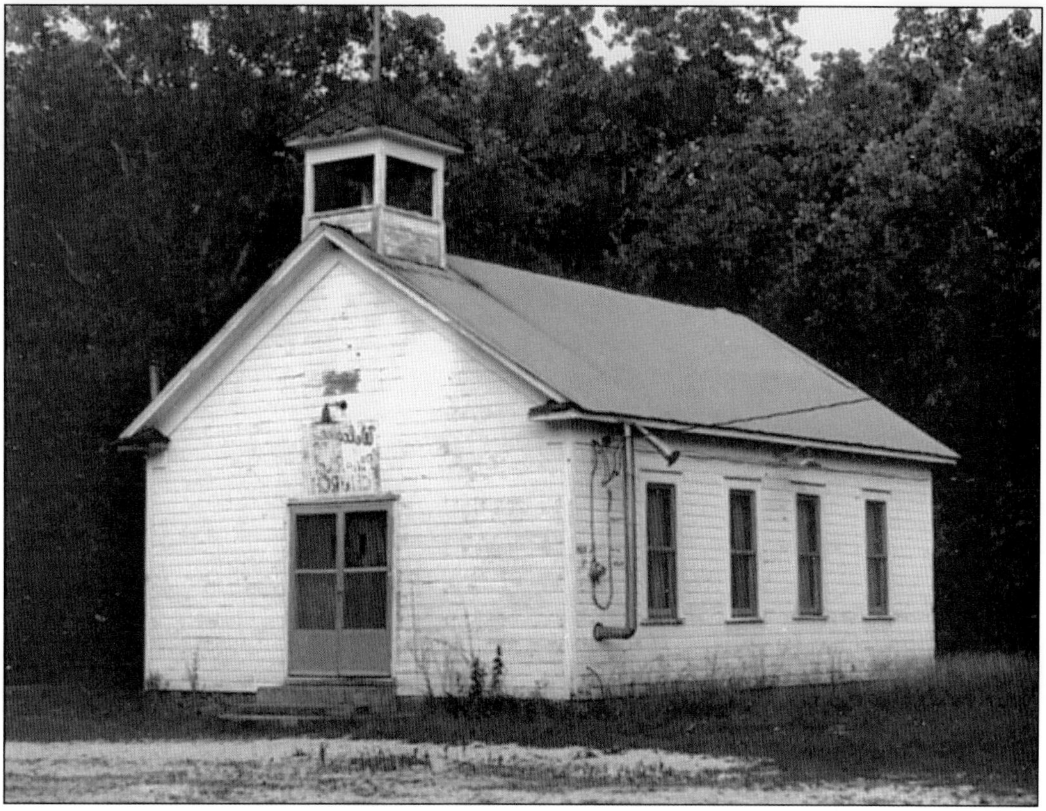

Pine Ridge church house, Highway H, near Chadwick.

PART SIX

HISTORICAL COLLECTION OF ASSOCIATED ARTICLES

Ecclesiastes 12:13-14 *Let us hear the conclusion of the whole matter: Fear God, and keep His commandments, for this is the whole duty of man.*

For God shall bring every work into judgement, with every secret thing, whether it be good, or whether it be evil.

Home Papers Means!

From the files of the Taney County Republican and written by former editor and publisher, W.E. Freeland, comes thoughts of the hills and the companionship of their people.

Not for some far-off heaven's higher bliss,
Not for some destiny that waits for me,
But for the simple loveliness of this;
Close to the throbbing hillside's fragrant breast,
I love Thee with a beauty-broken heart.

Lines from "A Hill Prayer":

"Home is the dearest spot on earth, and memories of home associations cling to the heart as long as life endures. Taney County is home to those who live here. News about Taney County claims first interest of those who live here.

With beauty comes strength and patient love. The hills compel patience.

This paper is dedicated to the people of the hills. It tells what happens here. Many personal items will be a source of happiness or of solace in after years. You want to read these items, to keep many in your scrapbook. These will be an unfailing treasure from which you will draw comfort.

You wilt be disappointed if you do not keep in touch with home news regularly with the Taney County Republican."

"The spirit of the hills, was close to him."

Goodbye to the Kirbyville-Mincy

It is sad indeed to see this column no more printed in the Taney County paper. For it was a column that many long-time residents of Taney County could keep up on news about their many friends and family members.

Augusta Whorton Johnson's "Kirbyville-Mincy News" has just become another page in the past of Taney County's history. Like so many of the old timers, this column too, has vanished. Times have changed and it is sad to see the uniqueness of the old Taney County ways become more commercialized. Foreigners from other states and big cities attempt to get the public to accept new ideas of capitalizing on the area, while crowding out those individuals whose heritage is the very root of the community.

It is sad, indeed, to witness how the greed for making money can spoil the plain and simple, down-to-earth way of life which made this area so special in it's beginning. At the rate it is expanding, one wouldn't venture to say where and how it will all end.

Saying goodbye to the Kirbyville-Mincy News column brings the end to an era in Taney County's history. That is why the author chose to include the article "Home Paper Means!" written by Taney County Republican former editor and publisher, W. E. Freeland, April of 1981. I believe he said it better than any attempt the author had in mind to get this point across to the public.

The Haunted Village

This was submitted to the "Kirbyville-Mincy News," which Augusta Whorton Johnson wrote for many years in the Taney County Newspaper. The date is unknown. Jessie Yarnell Cox wrote the following poem about Kirbyville, her old home place, and sent it to Augusta to put in her news.

They call it the Haunted Village
This once thriving little town
Which now appears to be sleeping
So many who knew it are gone.
We were once a part of the busy life
Of Kirbyville, my old hometown.
Haunted indeed, with memories
Of days when you and I
Were young, gay, and carefree.
In happy days gone by
Sad, sweet memories linger
Around its' houses and trees
Its' dusty streets where trod the foot,
Of those most dear to me.
Dear ones, whose Shadowy Presence

Seems to linger round it still
Round this little village,
Nestled in the Ozark hills,
And a feeling of sadness steals over me
While memory backward flies.
When change brings me to this village
So fraught with memories.
I said "goodbye" to my old home town
With its' memories sad and sweet.
O, time, turn back! Let me live again,
In this quiet and peaceful retreat!
Let me dream again as I used to do.
When life was at springtide,
And dreams came true.

Written by Jesse Yarnell Cox

Printed beneath the poem was the following:

"The first time I saw Kirbyville was on my 11th birthday and the last time was October 1971 on my 92nd birthday." Jesse.

"She went over the old trails at Gobbler's Knob and Happy Hollow. Her first teacher was Andrew Brown (Winnie Stottles' father). And he was one of the best, a wonderful teacher. The old home in Happy Hollow, the big oak tree under which we played "Happy is the Miller Boy" and "Skip to my Lou," was gone, not even the stump left. But so many, many memories." Augusta Johnson.

The Old Trails

South of Hollister is the steel bridge that was built in the early 1900s. The trains today still cross over Turkey Creek near the Whorton Cemetery where many of Taney County's first pioneers are buried.

Many of these pioneers, at one time, walked the railroad tracks between their homes and Hollister carrying baskets of eggs and home churned butter to trade for needed items at the general store.

Many fond memories were made as they walked through Happy Hollow where children played in the refreshing waters of Turkey Creek, or hid in the tree tops which surrounded the creek. Happy Hollow and Turkey Creek were always an element in the lives of the Laytons, Whortons, Rittenhouses, and many other families. The creek acquired its name because wild turkeys were plentiful and the people who lived there could often have a turkey to eat.

The other end of Happy Hollow continues southeast of the steel bridge making its way between the beautiful hills. Happy Hollow ends at what is known as "Murder Rocks," or "Alf Bolen Rocks," (see photo). The photograph shows the path between the two large boulders on Highway J. There is no telling how old and how far into history these boulders go. But they are near what used to be called the old "Springfield-Harrison Road," which was the main route of travel many years ago.

The way these two boulders are situated with the space between them apparently made an ideal hiding place. One can only guess how many times Alf Bolen waited there for his next victim to travel the road not knowing at these boulders, death awaited.

There is a story that many years ago there was a baby's grave with a stone marker near Murder Rocks. Someone remembered to decorate it with flowers every year. No one suspected anything other than a baby had been buried there. But later, someone returned and dug up the grave. The hole left resembled the perfect shape of an iron pot. The truth to the story was, instead of a baby being in the grave, an outlaw had buried a large pot of stolen money there in hopes of returning someday for his treasure.

Another old area is the tranquil plot of ground known as Gobbler's Knob Cemetery. Similar to the Whorton Cemetery or the Vanzandt Cemetery, it too goes back into the early history of Taney County. Many of the area's first pioneers are at rest within its quiet boundaries. Uncle Sol Linzy is buried there. He was the Postmaster at Kirbyville in the 1800s. This author's great-great-grandparents, Peter and Nancy Smith, are there but the location of their graves is unknown.

This author's great Aunt Ollie Layton has

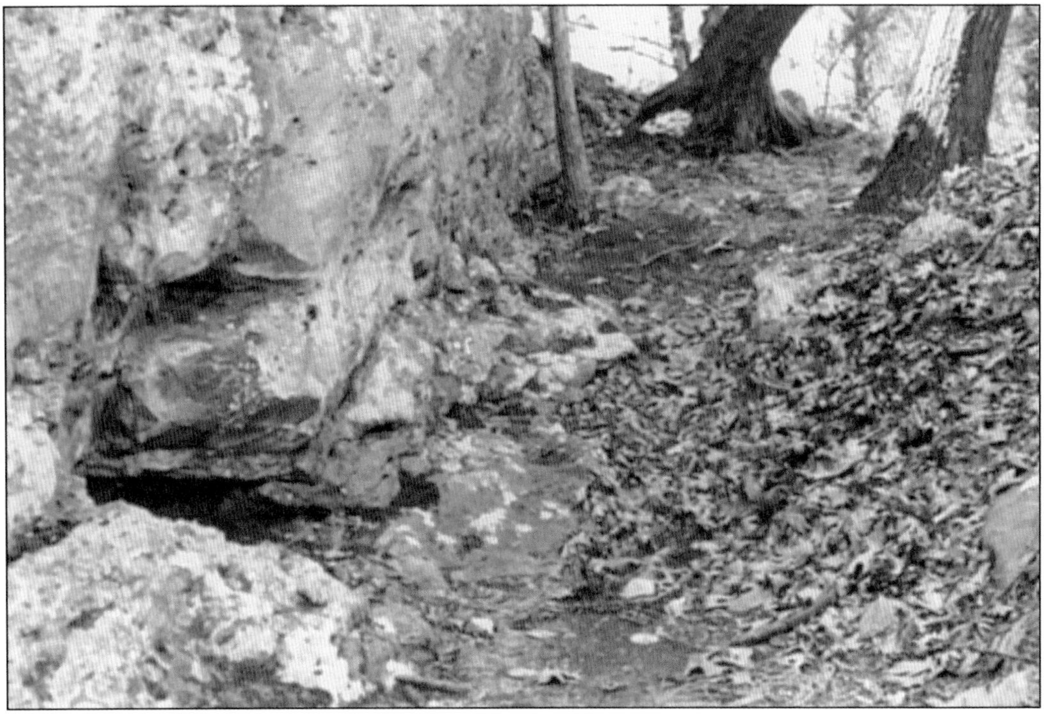

The path between two boulders at Murder Rock.

spoken of her parents attending church and Sunday school at Gobbler's Knob many years ago. Once, there was a Baptist minister named U.G. Johnson who held a revival there. He had lived in Taney County all his life. He wrote a letter to his brother who lived in one of the western states and asked him to come to the revival and help him with it. But before the brother received the letter, God had already revealed it to him to go and help U.G., so he came to Gobbler's Knob.

They had a baptism at the creek and several of the kinfolk were baptized. U.G. was overwhelmed with the Spirit, as he had to lie on the ground awhile. The congregation had left the church service and walked from Gobbler's Knob to Roark Creek near where Skaggs Hospital is today. Some of the Whorton family were baptized that day.

U.G. Johnson was well known as a faithful minister and worked hard to get the people interested in living for the Lord. He held office at the Forsyth Courthouse for many years.

This Is My Birthday

This is my birthday, I am still right here
The devil has been chasing me for eighty-five years.
He crippled my hands, he crippled my legs
But he has never been able to make me beg.
He gave to my body both sickness and pain
But the effect that he wanted he could never gain.

He gave me sorrow, he gave me grief,
But the One that is keeping me he giveth relief.
Yes, this is my birthday, I am just eighty-five
It finds me alone without any mate.
No one to comfort me, no one to guide.
The good Lord only is on my side.
But He is sufficient, for He is all power.
He is amply able to keep me each hour.

He has promised to keep me if I only prove true,
To guard me and guide me all the way through.
He is omnipresent, He knows my heart.
He has created and kept me from the very start.
He guards me in thought, He guards me in mind.

His ways and his dealings are always so kind.
I know that I am a cripple, not able to do
But I know that He is able to take me on through.

He giveth me clothing, He giveth me bread,
He has promised to keep me, even after I am dead.
He has promised to call me and awake me to life,
In a world that is sinless, also without strife.
He will give me a body that is perfect and strong
A mind that is perfect, no thoughts that are wrong.
So, I must be faithful, kind hearted and true
And ever be striving to follow Him through.
I do love to trust Him, He giveth me grace
Which will ever be with me to the end of the race.

(This was written by U.G. Johnson and submitted to the Taney County paper by his daughter Mrs. Ed Arnold. He wrote it when he was staying with them.)

Vows That Were Secret

The first meeting of what would become the Bald Knobbers was held in the back of a side room (used as a warehouse) of Jim Everett's store in Forsyth, in 1885. Jim was dead then and his murder was one reason why the good citizens of the community had rallied.

James M. Everett and his brother Barton Yellville Everett operated a general store that was important as a base of supplies for the hills. Jim and another partner also operated a saloon up the street a few doors from the store. The store was a frame building two stories high, with the one-story side room.

Like all the establishments of that kind in the hills, its merchandise ranged from pins to plow points. There was a section of shelves filled with bolts of calico and muslin. Barrels of sugar, crackers, pickles, and coarse salt stood at convenient locations. Snappy varicolored buggy whips dangled from a small wheel-shaped holder attached to the ceiling. Kegs of nails sat under the counter and near by, a heap of horseshoes. Bright tin buckets, stone and cedar churns, and white crockery tempted the housewives to make purchases.

It was to this store the hill people had come for help during a terrific drought of 1882. Their crops had burned in the fields. Even the timber had died on some of the hillsides. The people were without food, but Jim Everett cheerfully extended them credit. He sent freight wagons across the hills and hauled in bacon, beans, corn, and other provisions, which he let men take for their families on the promise they would pay when they could. Naturally, this made many loyal friendships for the merchant.

Then on the afternoon of September 23, 1883, Jim Everett and a rough young hillsman, Al Layton, were playing pigeonhole in the back of Everett's saloon. The game, which was scored on a table resembling pool, was friendly enough. The two men left the game and came up to the rough bar, where each took a drink. Then Layton walked outside.

There was considerable activity in Forsyth that afternoon. At a horse race up the road from the town there had almost been a fight. Some rough youths had attacked the county's prosecuting attorney, and his friends rescued him barely in time. Consequently, there was an undercurrent of excitement.

Everett had a large group of men employed building a millrace on Bull Creek. About the time Layton began to feel good from his drinks of liquor, the workmen came off the job toward the saloon.

Layton created a disturbance. Everett stepped outside to see what the trouble was and took hold of him. That started a sort of wrestling match that ended up in a room just off the saloon. Layton was on top of Everett and wouldn't let him up.

Hearing the trouble, Yell Everett rushed to the assistance of his brother. He was carrying a long gun.

"What's the matter?" he demanded.

"Al's mad, and he doesn't know what about," replied Jim.

"Let him up," urged Yell, and Layton was finally persuaded to get up. Everett also started to rise. As he did so, Layton grabbed his revolver, fired once, and killed Jim Everett. He jumped behind a door, shot once at Yell Everett, hitting him in the arm, then made a dash from the saloon. He jumped on his horse and galloped out of Forsyth. Later he was arrested, tried, and released.

People were incensed. Many of them still owed money, and most of them owed loyalty to Jim Everett. They said this was another instance in which the courts had failed to punish a Taney County killer. All through that winter, men talked in little groups about trying to take the law into their own hands. Often they met behind closed doors in solemn conference. Almost a year wore along, and still men were asking what good citizens should do to insure law and order.

The above incident involving Al Layton was one event that eventually led to the formation of the organization of citizens which would later be known as the Bald Knobbers. Al Layton was a distant cousin of the author's clan of Laytons.

Ozark Bald Knobbers

Dodge City and Tucson may have been tough and wild in their day, but they had nothing on the Missouri Ozarks in the 1880s. And it all started when a man named Nat Kinney came to the hill country looking for peace.

At least that's what he said he was looking for when he bought a farm near Kirbyville, only a few miles from Branson. He was a giant of a man, weighing nearly 300 pounds, and standing 6 feet, 7 inches in his sock feet. In addition, he wore two six-guns strapped to his hips, and he let it be known that the guns bore four notches. He had fought in the Civil War, ranged over the Wild West, broke several heads in Springfield where he had owned a saloon, and was now ready to settle down and lead a tranquil life.

To prove his intention, he started a Sunday school and church service at the country schoolhouse known as Oak Grove. He placed his Bible on a homemade pulpit and laid a pistol on either side. And he started telling the Ozark hill folks that something should be done to change the lawless ways of the country, and he was willing to show them how it could be done.

He was right, in one sense of the word. And he had records to prove it. More than 30 known murders had been committed in Taney County since the close of the war, and not one killer had been sent to the pen in Jefferson City. In addition to the murders, there were other crimes that ranged from robbery to rape. Peaceful folks just weren't safe with all this lawless element roaming about in the woods.

Kinney was a powerful talker, especially with his giant size and two guns to back him. So a lot of citizens told him he had a good point, and they would go along with him. What was his plan?

Kinney knew about the vigilantes of the West. He had run afoul of a few of them, nearly being hanged once for killing a man. He figured a vigilante committee, with himself as the leader, was just what the hills needed. And it would be good for his own well-being too, since this way he would always be on the right end of a rope.

For the sake of privacy, the organization met atop a bald mountain near Kinney's home. Here there was plenty of room and no outsider could attend without being noticed. They decided, because of their meeting place, that the organization would be known as the Bald Knobbers. It was not long before the membership amounted to several hundred.

There followed a period of terror for many Ozarkians. The Bald Knobbers lashed their horses and rode through the night, their crude floursack masks blowing in the wind, their horses' hoofs beating out a warning of punishment to all who incited their wrath. They were now the law of the hills, Nat Kinney their judge. They would receive punishment to suit his taste. By whip, by rope, by bullets—beware!

But the hillsmen on the other side of the fence were no weaklings. And certainly not all outlaws. As many of the better element condemned the organization as condoned it. The county grew into two mighty factions: the Bald Knobbers and the Anti-Bald Knobbers. The greatest hill feud in mountain history was in the making.

This was the spark needed to touch off the powder keg. Every night bands of men roamed the hills and the fires of burning homes lighted the Ozark skies. Screams of men under the whip echoed like banshee cries, wafted far by the night winds. Women, raped by masked riders, cried brokenly and pleaded for mercy. Children not understanding, begged and whimpered, and were knocked from the paths of the crashing boots by merciless hands as vengeance demanded vengeance.

In the bloody months that followed, no one was sure of who was doing what. The Knobbers laid the crimes at the door of their enemies. The Anti-Knobbers blamed the men under Kinney. The outlaw element had an open field. Any crime they wanted to commit could be laid at the doors of the Knobbers or Anti-Knobbers, and no one was the wiser. It was hell.

One of the most outspoken opponents of Kinney and the Bald Knobbers was young Andrew Coggburn. Coggburn had reason for his bitterness. He had been badly beaten by the night riders when he openly called Kinney "the old blue gobbler," adding that Kinney always strutted about like a swelled up turkey.

The whip didn't quell young Coggburn as it did most victims, however. He grew more outspoken and wrote a challenging song that went in part:

There is one big black rascal whose name I will expose,
His name is Nat N. Kinney and he wears his federal clothes,
He tried to boss the people and make them do his will,
There's some that do not fear him, but others mind him still.

After this song a meeting between the two men was inevitable. it came early in March, 1886. Kinney still preached at the Oak Grove school, and one evening as he marched up the path to the building, he saw young Coggburn standing with a group of men.

Their eyes met, and hands hung close to gun butts. Suddenly, there was movement, and shattering gunfire rocked the little building. When the smoke cleared, the Old Blue Gobbler stood unharmed, and young Coggburn lay dying in the dust.

That was the beginning of the end—the last straw. The Anti-Knobbers sent out the word, "Get him! Nat Kinney has got to die!"

The end came August 21, 1888. Kinney was alone in a Forsyth store he had recently acquired through a lawsuit from a man named Berry. Folks in the street heard the crash of gunfire in the building. A moment later a young man named Billy Miles appeared in the doorway with the announcement that he had "got the Old Blue Gobbler, for sure this time!" When they went inside they found Kinney stretched out, four bullets in his body, dead.

The Bald Knobbers claimed their leader was the victim of a cowardly murderer. Billy Miles claimed self-defense. He was arrested as a matter of routine and quickly acquitted. And the town celebrated, many folks shouting with joy in the streets, acclaiming Billy Miles a hero.

Some said the shooting would be avenged. But nothing ever happened. Kinney was buried in an over-sized, unmarked grave in Swan Creek Cemetery, and the peace that Nat Kinney came to find settled at last over the Ozark Hills.

DEATH OF NAT KINNEY

"Nathaniel N. Kinney moved from Springfield to Taney County in 1883. He served the Union cause in the War of the Rebellion as a private in Company L, 6th Regiment of West Virginia Infantry Volunteers." He enlisted at West Union, West Virginia, December 28, 1863, at the age of 20 years. His enlistment record noted that Kinney "has gray eyes, light hair, fair complexion, and is 6 feet, 7 inches high. "

Nathaniel and his wife, Maggie L., purchased 146 acres near the old Oak Grove school house, on the right bank of the White River (Lake Taneycomo now covers part of this land.)

In 1883, this area was suffering in the aftermath of the Civil War. Kinney observed the situation and made a public statement about the reign of terror: "Over 30 men have been shot in Taney County since the war," he said, "and not one of the murderers has been punished . . . The county is over $42,000 in debt, and doesn't have a plank to show for it."

On September 23, 1883, Al Layton shot and killed Jim Everett. He was acquitted in January, 1885. That night, 13 men met in the side room of the Jim Everett store in Forsyth. Nathaniel Kinney, Col. A.S. Prather, J.K. McHaffie, G.E. Branson, and James A. DeLong were some of those present.

Layton's acquittal brought matters to a head. This group elected Nat Kinney as Captain of their "law and order league." Kinney had served as special agent for the Santa Fe Railroad, which gave him plenty of experience in dealing with rough situations. He was a natural leader. The men met on the bald knobs north of Kirbyville and were called "Bald Knobbers."

The Captain and his men meant well and did some good in curbing the lawlessness. One night they took Frank and Tubal Taylor from Taney County jail and hanged them on a giant oak tree northwest of Forsyth. The Taylors had shot and wounded John T. Dickenson and his wife at the Dickens' store.

Feelings were bitter against the Knobbers. Kinney shot and killed Andy Coggburn at Oak Grove Church House. The opposition also organized. Gov. Marmaduke sent the Missouri Adjutant General to Forsyth to investigate the situation with the idea of sending in the state militia.

Gen. J.C. Jamison called a meeting for March 10, 1886, and Capt. Kinney summoned the Bald Knobbers to Forsyth. Five hundred hillmen rode into town, unmasked and unafraid. They agreed to disband. Col. A.S. Prather wrote the resolution which officially ended the Bald Knobber organization. In August, 1888, Capt. Kinney was invoicing merchandise in the James Berry store in Forsyth in a bankruptcy case when he was shot and killed.

The Captain and his wife are buried in the cemetery directly across Swan Creek from old Forsyth. John H. Ray, a young man at the time, attended the Captain's funeral. Some 50 years later he carved their names on stones to mark the final resting place of the brave Captain and his wife. In October, 1977, a soldier's marker was placed at Kinney's grave. Had not John Ray marked the grave site so long ago the burial place would have been unknown."

The author's great-grandmother, Mary Elizabeth Coggburn Smith, attended the funeral of Nat Kinney. According to an interview with Cecil McClary of Kirbyville, he had this to say about Mary Smith's feelings toward the death of Kinney: "Mary Smith walked up to the edge of Kinney's grave and threw in a small box of matches, saying, 'just in case old Satan ain't got any matches to start a fire for this old devil, I'm a gonna make sure that he does have some."

Last of the Bald Knobbers
(The wild 1880s around Sparta and Ozark, Missouri)

(Note: The story of the Bald Knobbers in Taney County appeared in the 1961 Ozark Guide Yearbook. The reign of Bald Knobber terror ended there on August 21, 1888, with the death of the night-riders' leader, Capt. Nat Kinney. It did not end in neighboring Christian County for several months, however. This is the story....)

Terrified George Greene tried to force more speed from his aged legs as he stumbled along a wilderness trail toward the cabin home of his neighbor, James Edens.

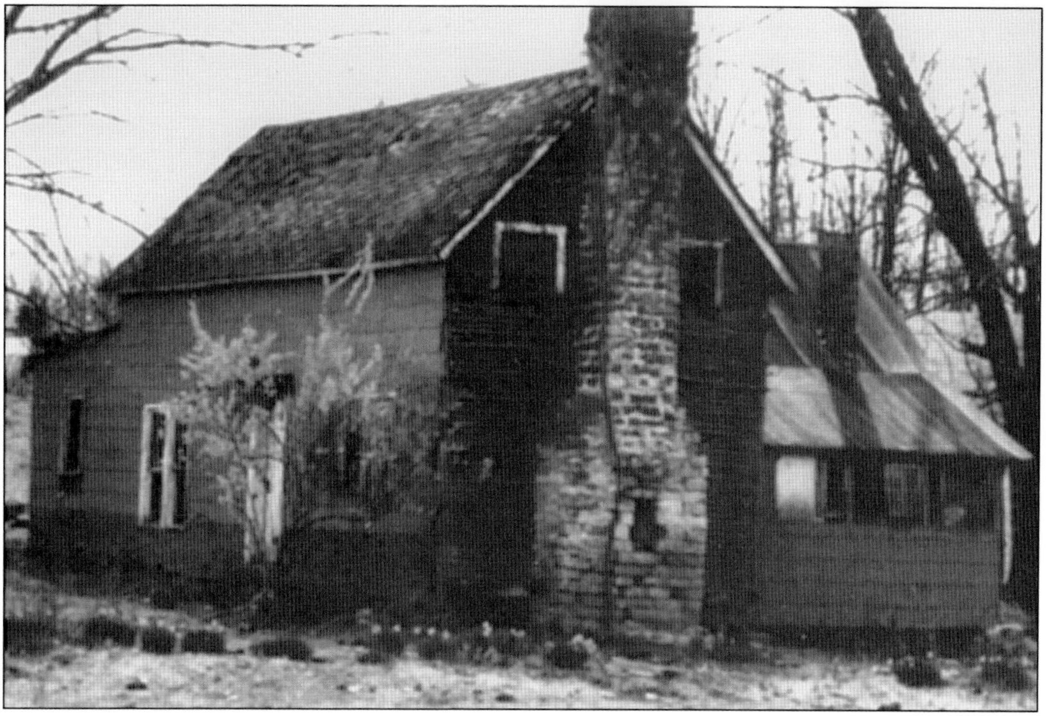

House located near Murder Rocks where Alf Bolden was killed. The house was also a stage Depot. This homestead is known as "the Jackson place."

It was midnight, March 11, 1888, and winter winds whipped across the rolling Ozark hills of Christian County, Missouri.

A few moments earlier he had been jerked out of bed by screams of pain and terror, punctuated by gun-blasts coming from the direction of the Edens' farm home. He paused a moment to catch his breath, and to listen.

The bedlam of angry cries and roaring gunfire had ceased. But above his heavy breathing and the sledge-hammer pounding of his heart, George Greene could hear the pitiful cries of his two small grandchildren. A rasping sob broke from his lips as he started running again.

His feet were like lead weights as they pounded across the cabin yard. He came to a gasping halt in the open doorway with its splintered door hanging crazily by one hinge. The 16-foot square room, lighted by yellow flames in a fireplace, presented a bloody, gruesome sight. An exclamation of horror burst from his burning throat. Dead, broken, and bleeding bodies seemed to be scattered over every inch of the cabin floor!

Then the old man settled his thoughts as best he could and remembered that eight persons had been staying the night here—Mr. and Mrs. James Edens, their son William and his wife Emma, their daughter Melvina and her husband Charley Greene (George Greene's son) and their two small children. Now the only sign of life among all these persons was the pathetic wailing of the Greene children and the low moaning sound which bubbled from the throat of their unconscious mother, Melvina.

Hysterical sobs shook the old man's body as he went from one victim to the other. He discovered the following:

Charley Greene was dead with a bullet in his brain; young William Edens had been slain; likewise, Old James Edens had a bullet wound in his throat and his skull had been split; evidently by a blow from a crimson-stained axe lying nearby; Mrs. James Edens was bloody and unconscious from innumerable blows on her face and head; Emma Edens lay senseless where she had been struck down; Melvina Greene, with one finger nearly shot off, was in a shocked stupor; and the two children, little more than babies, were scratched and bleeding, though their hurts appeared not to be serious.

It was then that George Greene saw the weird, fantastic mask—a sort of hood—clutched in his daughter-in-law's right hand. He stared at the horns and the grotesque markings. He looked at a shotgun lying on the floor, and realized that since neither his son nor the Edens had owned such a weapon it must have been dropped by one of the monstrous killers.

"It's them damned Bald Knobbers, again," he ground out between sobs. "I've got to get word to Sheriff Johnson..."

The following day Sheriff Zack Johnson, Prosecuting Attorney Almus Harrington, and Coroner J. P. Ralston arrived at the scene of the crime from Ozark, seat of Christian County. They learned that the women and children had been removed to a neighbor's home. They examined the blood-spattered cabin and the men's bodies.

George Greene pointed to the shotgun and Sheriff Johnson picked it up, studying it. He did not recognize it, but decided that it was a valuable piece of evidence. The owner of this gun might be able to explain the mystery surrounding this awful crime.

Johnson and Harrington then went with Greene to the neighbor's place where they questioned Melvina Greene. They found it hard to control their emotions at the gruesome tale she told.

"William, Emma, and Charley and I live on little farms near Papa and Mamma," she begin brokenly. "We had gone over to visit them that evening, and decided to stay all night. Charley and I slept with the babies on one bed, and my parents slept in the other one. William and Emma made a pallet on the floor by the fireplace.

"About midnight we were awakened by a loud noise—men shouting and cursing and firing guns. Then something was thrown through the front window, and they began hammering at the door, demanding that we let them in.

"We barely had time to get out of bed when they broke the door down. A dozen or so masked men sprang into the room and started shooting." Her voice broke as the awful memories flooded back. She sobbed for a moment, then gulped and went on.

"Poor Charley and William never had a chance. But Papa grabbed his pistol off the fireplace mantle and shot one of the men in the leg before they hit him with an axe. The man he shot stumbled over against me. I grabbed at his mask and pulled it off his face. He fell to the floor yelling, "Get me out of here, boys! They've broke my leg!"

"Two of the men carried him outside, and that's all I know. Something hit me on the head, and when I came to they were gone and..." her voice trailed off and she covered her face with her hands, trying to shut out the horrible picture.

After a while the Sheriff asked, "Did you recognize the man you unmasked?"

Melvina shook her head. "No," she wailed. "I couldn't see him very well in the dim light—but he was young, not much more than a boy!"

"How do you know that?"

"He had no beard or mustache. All men in this country wear them as soon as they can grow them. This boy's face was smooth as a girl's."

"Did anything else happen that would cause you to believe you knew any of the other men—their voices, their actions?"

"No," she answered. "I only know that they were Bald Knobbers."

"But why would even the Bald Knobbers want to murder you people?" Johnson asked, trying to find a motive for the crime. He knew that the Greenes and the Edens were hard working, respectable people. There seemed no reason for this cowardly attack, though he had to admit of late that the mysterious night-riding vigilante organization called Bald Knobbers had been committing many outrages in Christian County that were bringing protests from many quarters.

Men had been whipped with switches and driven from the country by this masked citizen's organization which meted out punishment under the pretense of upholding law and order. And it had only been a few short months since the band had hanged two young men suspected of having a hand in a neighborhood killing.

"What did the Bald Knobbers have against you people?" Sheriff Johnson asked.

Melvina Greene didn't know, nor did the other Edens women. They could offer no reason for the attack.

The two officers left, satisfied that they could learn no more from the dead men's wives. As they walked back to the murder cabin they examined the Bald Knobber mask that Melvina Greene had given them. This was their first close-up glimpse of one of the hideous creations, and they saw that it was, indeed, a Devil's mask, with its horns and fantastic markings.

"This is the slip we've been waiting for," Prosecutor Harrington ground out, eying the mask. "For more than two years now these outlaws who call themselves Bald Knobbers have been growing bolder and bolder. They are harassing innocent folk more and more. And this brutal murder proves that they will stop at nothing.

"During all this time they've kept their identities secret. This has been accomplished not only through caution, but by instilling fear in the people. They threaten anyone with death who exposes them to the law.

"But we have something to go on now. This mask is the number one clue. Then, too, we know that the wearer of this mask is a kid with James Edens' bullet in his leg. And last, but not least, there is a shotgun. We've got to trace it to its owner."

It sounded simple the way Harrington put it, but Zack Johnson knew it was far from that. He took his viewpoint because he knew that they must go about the country questioning people—and any person they chose to question might very well be a member of the Bald Knobber gang they were trying to convict. Who, then, could they believe? How would they be able to sort the truth from lies? It appeared hopeless even before they started, Johnson had to admit.

Then was this monstrous crime to go unsolved, as had to many others? Would the night-riders continue to meet on one of the barren-topped bald knob mountains which dot the Ozarks, and from which the outlaws had drawn their name? These gladed, barren tops are referred to in the hills as bald knobs. The outlaws chose them as meeting places because they could not be approached by the law or outsiders without detection by the gang.

At first the name Bald Knobbers had been applied by persons outside the organization, but it was later accepted as the organization's official trademark. A bundle of switches left at a man's door, a burned house, a destroyed whiskey still could be identified as the work of the riders with the devil masks, for they always left notes signed: "THE BALD KNOBBERS."

Arriving at the Edens' cabin, Johnson and Harrington found that the coroner had removed the bodies. They searched about the premises but found nothing more to add to their case.

Johnson said: "Let's go to Sparta. We'll try to learn if there's anyone in the country with a bullet in his leg, and we'll do some tracing on the shotgun."

An hour later the two officers had interviewed the only doctor in Sparta. The doctor shook his head and told them that he had not treated anyone with a gunshot wound.

When they were on the street again, Harrington said, "That doesn't mean anything. There's a possibility that the wound wasn't as serious as Mrs. Greene thought. Or the Knobbers may have treated him and are now hiding him in the hills."

"Yes," Johnson nodded, "and that doctor may be one of the Knobbers for all we know."

They continued asking questions about town, singling out persons whom they knew to be opposed to the night-riders. At last they talked to an old man who repaired watches, sewing machines and guns. The Sheriff showed the shotgun and asked the old man if he had ever seen it before.

'Wal, I can't be sure," the repairman said thoughtfully. "Seems to me I ought to know it. Yeah, I recollect now! A young fellow named Bud Ray brought that gun in two–three months ago and wanted to swap it for a rifle of mine. Yeah, that's it! I remember this funny crack in the stock shaped like an S. But I didn't swap with him. He wouldn't give enough boot."

The officers managed to hide their excitement till they were out of the shop. Then Johnson said, "I know Bud Ray, and he fits the description of the kid Melvina Greene unmasked! He's also something of a braggart and has hinted to several persons that he is a Knobber. If he'll just turn up with a bullet in his leg, we've got our man! Let's go!"

"Let's leave the horses and cut back through the brush on foot," Johnson suggested. "I'd like to take a look at Ray's place without him knowing we're there. I have a feeling that if he is actually a Knobber, or was lying about the gun, he'll be leaving out of there in a few minutes."

Harrington agreed, and they threaded their way back through thickets of oak and sumac. When they reached sight of Ray's cabin, Harrington caught Johnson's arm excitedly, and wheezed, "Look there!

Bud Ray was feverishly saddling a horse in front of the cabin, and his actions showed only too plainly the excitement which was working inside him!

The officers watched till he had the horse saddled. Then Ray went into his cabin and returned a few minutes later with a bundle in his hand. He glanced furtively about, then prepared to mount.

Johnson suddenly lunged out of the brush into the clearing. Harrington bounded close on his heels.

"Hold it, Ray!" the Sheriff commanded, running forward, the evidence shotgun in one hand, his own revolver in the other.

Bud Ray turned, a startled, frightened expression on his young face. His hands clamped the package tightly, then he edged in between him and the horse.

"What have you got there?" Johnson asked sharply.

"Nothing," Ray mumbled, gulping loudly.

The Sheriff stepped quickly forward and jerked the package from the youth's trembling fingers. He ripped off the covering and shook out some folds of black cloth. His eyes lighted at the sight of the padded horns and grotesque markings. He heard Harrington exclaim:

"It's a Bald Knobber mask!"

"It's not mine! " Bud Ray cried quickly. "I found it. I don't know anything about the Knobbers! I didn't have anything to do with the Edens' killing—-"

"You're going to jail, just the same," Johnson cut in, snapping a pair of handcuffs on the youth's trembling arms.

"You may change your mind about this Knobber business when the respectable people of this country start tearing down the jail so they can hang you from the nearest tree!"

"You won't let them hang me, will you?" Ray cried as they started for Ozark.

That evening, when Bud Ray was locked safely in jail, Johnson told Harrington, "We've got to make that young man talk. If we could throw a scare into him that is greater than his fear of the Knobbers, he may name all the members of his gang. Not only that, but we can name the Edens' slayers. If we could only think of something..."

"It threw a scare into him when you told him the people might tear down the jail to hang him," Harrington said.

"That's it!" Johnson exclaimed. "I'll make him think they're going to hang him. I'll round up a group of men I can trust. I'll have them come to the jail, pretending they're a mob that wants to hang Ray. If he thinks his end has come he may break loose..."

It was shortly after dark, two days later, when

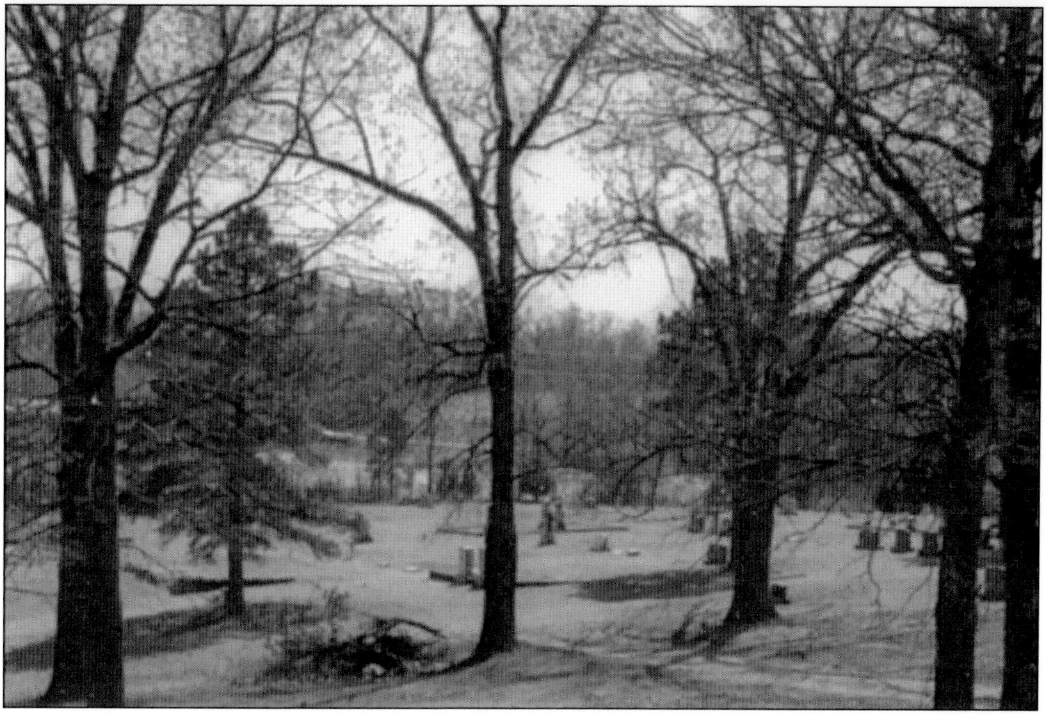

Gobbler's Knob Cemetery. "Their spirits are enfolded in the arms of Jesus . . . Their bodies are lying among the hills they loved."

Sheriff Johnson went to Bud Ray's cell. From the barred window the youth could see the shadowy group of men gathering near the jail. He could hear the low mumblings, and now and then he could make out unmistakable words that said, ". . . hang him . . .," ". . . stretch up the dirty Knobber. . .," and ". . . it's time to show these devil riders that they ain't runnin' this country..."

Bud Ray looked from the window to the Sheriff. His eyes were wide with fear, and he wrung his hands in desperation.

Johnson stepped close to the bars and said, "Ray, I hate to see it happen to you. Those men are out for revenge. Now the only thing I know that will save you is for you to come clean. You name the leader of the band and the members, and who actually killed the Edens and Charley Greene. When I tell that mob all those men's names, they're going to forget about hanging you. What do you say?"

The youth wiped at the cold sweat-beads on his forehead, but said nothing.

Sheriff Johnson went on, "Above that, I'll get you out of here. I'll take you to the Springfield jail. You'll be safe there, not only from a mob, but from your own gang."

This last was evidently the thing Bud Ray was wishing most for —protection from the Bald Knobbers, if he talked. He said, brokenly, "All right, I'll tell you everything. I am a Knobber—but I don't hold with this murdering."

He went on to name "Bull Creek Dave" Walker as the gang leader. Walker was a prominent farmer and churchgoer of that section. Bud Ray named Walker's right-hand man as being Deacon John Matthews, of the Baptist Church where Walker attended. Wiley Matthews, brother of the Deacon, was also named as a prominent member.

"We met the night of the killing," Ray continued, "on a bald knob near Chadwick. We were going to initiate a new member.

After we'd done that, they begin talking about the Edens and Charley Green, and how they had been shooting off their mouths about the Knobbers. Someone said that a few days ago Charley Greene shot a mad dog, and told everyone that he'd killed a Bald Knobber without his mask!

"Well, the majority decided that we should call on the Edens and teach them a lesson ... and you know what happened..."

Under questioning, he went ahead to name 25 men in the mob, but said that only a few had gone in the cabin. He named "Bull Creek Dave" Walker's son, Bill, as the youth who had been shot in the leg and unmasked. He also said that the shotgun belonged to Bill Walker, for it was he whom Ray had traded it to for a rifle.

Following this confession, Bud Ray was taken to the Springfield jail. Shortly after that, Sheriff Johnson swore in about 20 deputies, who, heavily armed, started bringing in the men named by Ray.

In a few days more than 25 men had been arrested. They were confined under heavy guard in the Odd Fellows lodge room over the general store in Ozark. This was necessary since the small jail would not hold half the accused men.

Among these were "Bull Creek Dave" Walker, Deacon John Matthews, and Wiley Matthews. The only missing person was young Bill Walker. Somehow, he had made good his escape.

Now, with wholesale arrests, the Knobbers began squealing on each other. Accusations flew thick and fast.

Sheriff Johnson and Prosecutor Harrington grew convinced that the men directly responsible for the crime in the Edens' cabin were Dave Walker and his son Bill, and John and Wiley Matthews.

A grand jury in Ozark then opened a serious investigation, returning indictments against many of the men. The charges ranged from unlawful assembly to first-degree murder. This latter charge was filed against the four Walkers and Matthews.

Most of the accused wanted to go on trial at once, but their lawyers thought differently. The men were taken to the Springfield jail, which was large enough to hold them all, and Sheriff Johnson started about the business of bringing in young Bill Walker.

He learned from a young man, Joe Newton, that Bill Walker had been in love with Newton's sister. Newton confided that his sister had only recently received a letter from young Bill, saying he was hiding out in a hill section of Arkansas.

With promise of reward, Newton was persuaded to go to Walker's hideout, where he was to try and talk him into coming to West Plains, Missouri, where he would be able to board a train that would carry him safely out of the country, probably to Mexico.

Young Bill Walker, evidently trusting Joe Newton, believed the story, and followed his sweetheart's brother into West Plains where Sheriff Jack Johnson was waiting. Walker was arrested, and a few days later joined his father and the others awaiting trial.

In March, a year after the Edens massacre, the trials began. Young Bill Walker was first tried for the murder of Charley Greene. The chief witnesses against him were three Knobbers who turned state's evidence to save their own skins. It was proven that the shotgun found in the cabin belonged to young Walker and Melvina. Greene identified him as the man she unmasked. Too, he still carried a scar on his leg where James Edens' bullet had ripped into it.

The defense attorney tried to impress the jury with the youth's tender age—he was only 17—but it was of no avail. Young Bill Walker was found guilty of first-degree murder and sentenced to death.

Wiley Matthews, 25 years old, was next up. And at the end of three days he was sentenced to hang along with young Walker.

Deacon John Matthews, 40, was next on trial. He, too, was found guilty of murder, with a sentence of death.

When "Bull Creek Dave," the acknowledged leader of the Knobbers, came on trial for his life, he testified that he had not gone into the Edens' cabin, and had not fired a shot. The prosecution did not offer any evidence that he had killed anyone with his own hands, but contended that he was guilty as the others because he was their leader and was therefore responsible for their acts. The jury found him guilty of murder, and sentenced him to hang by the neck until dead.

Since four men had been tried and each had been given the death sentence, the remaining Knobbers quickly entered pleas of guilty to the charges against them and were given sentences varying from a few months in jail to 25 years in the state penitentiary.

The lawyers of the condemned men appealed to the Supreme Court, but it was in vain. The Supreme Court judges upheld the decisions reached in the little courthouse at Ozark, Missouri. They also offered this opinion:

"The general scheme of this band embraced within it the destruction of property and the evidence shows that they left for the very purpose of visiting the Edens' home. They were armed, masked, and in every way conducted themselves as evil-disposed persons, bent on mischief and the perpetration of crime. "

And in the case of Dave Walker, the Court's opinion was:

"We deem it unnecessary to again enter upon a review of the facts, to which the trial court confined the evidence bearing upon, and connecting the defendant with this unprovoked and barbarous murder, or open a discussion of the law which the court fully and carefully laid down in appropriate instructions to the jury based upon these facts, holding that if the defendant was a member of the lawless band who perpetrated it, and of which the evidence tends to show that he was the leader, and master spirit, he could be guilty of no less a crime than murder in the first degree, and could have no grounds of justification to stand upon."

The morning after the prisoners were notified of this decision, Sheriff Zack Johnson found a hole in the wall of the jail. Deacon John Matthews and Wiley Matthews were missing. The Walkers, however, had been locked in different cells so were unable to escape.

A posse was quickly formed, and a reward offered for the capture of the two men. The following day a farmer captured and returned John Matthews to Ozark; but Wiley Matthews made good his escape and was never seen again.

On May 10, 1889, the three condemned men were handcuffed and led upon a scaffold. Black hoods were placed over their heads and the ropes were fitted about their necks.

This was Sheriff Zack Johnson's first hanging, and he admitted that he was almost as sick as the condemned men. He had built the scaffold with three nooses and one large trap door so all the men would be hanged with one drop. He wanted to get it over with as quickly as possible.

When he pulled the lever and the men fell through, a mighty groan went up from the crowd of spectators jamming the town. Women began to scream, and the men shouted, prayed, and cursed.

Sheriff Johnson looked down through the open trap and saw with horror that the ropes were too long. The men's feet were on the ground, and their necks had not been broken. They were now beating and threshing about, strangling to death!

He grabbed Deacon John Matthew's rope and managed to swing him off the ground where he was left to choke to death. Then he grabbed Dave Walker's rope and managed to swing him high enough till his feet were free.

The crowd moaned with horror. Brave men fainted along with their wives and children.

Then Johnson grabbed the rope supporting young Bill Walker. He sobbed as he tried to pull Walker into the air. He jerked hard, and an awful groan went up from the crowd. The noose had slipped off Walker's head, taking the black hood with it!

The youth fell to the ground, threshing about, his eyes wild with pain. Blood spurted from his lips as he cried, "Oh, God, get it over! Get it over! Won't someone shoot me so I can be out of this misery? "

Tears and perspiration blinded the half-mad Sheriff. With the aid of two deputies he managed to shove young Bill Walker up through the trap door, where the rope was again fitted about his twisted neck.

Johnson jerked at the lever again, and the youth went through for the second time.

Again the crowd screamed and Johnson looked down to see that the rope had stretched until it was again too long. He grabbed it, but this time his strength was spent. The Sheriff couldn't raise the youth higher, so he was left there, and after 16 long minutes, was choked to death.

So ended the Bald Knobber reign of terror in the Ozark hills. And it seemed to many who had seen the hangings that fate had willed that the accused Knobbers' death be as agonizing and terrible as the crimes they had imposed on the helpless Edens.

NEW YORK SUN *TELLS STORY OF BALD KNOBBERS*

(These are the sensational headlines of a story in the New York Sun date-lined December 10, 1888, from Ozark, Christian County, Missouri. Written by a reporter who was an eye witness to many of the instances cited, and with an objectivity seldom attained by any local reporter, who was neither "fer" nor "agin" either side, this is a story that can be told now that tempers and feelings are cooled off and we can look back in retrospect on some of the history in our Ozark area.)

Introduction:

For the first time since the organization of this country there is a probability of a legal hanging within its limits. Four men are now in the county jail who have after a long trial, been found guilty of murder in the first degree. Their cases were taken to the Supreme Court for final adjudication and the sentences of two of them have been affirmed. The other two sentences will be affirmed, for the cases are precisely alike. Then, unless the governor interferes, the men will be hanged. The date set for the first execution is December 28.

These four men who are now staring death in the face were the leaders of the Christian County branch of the widely known Bald Knobbers of the Ozark Mountains. Their names are David Walker, William Walker (father and son), John Matthews, and Wiley Matthews (uncle and nephew). The crime for which they were convicted was the murder of Charles Greene and William Edens. This act was so atrocious that a long-suffering community arose and invoked the aid of the civil law, and the Bald Knobbers organization disappeared. Whether it was destroyed remains to be seen.

But before this was done, 13 other men had lost their lives through trouble growing out of this organization. Three men and three women had been wounded with bullets, and two women and an unknown number of men had been unmercifully whipped. From brooding over the trouble in which her husband had been involved, one wife of a Bald Knobber went crazy, and after fatally crushing the skulls of two of her children with a hammer, she cut her own throat with her husband's razor, and died within two minutes.

Nor is this history one of bloodshed only, for the Knobber chief lost his life through his connection with a mountain romance, in which his chief lieutenant was the hero, while the lieutenant of the Christian County branch was lured into the road that leads to death on the gallows by his sweetheart. Of the homes that have been destroyed, and of the wives and children that have been reduced to pitiful want and misery, no account can be written. Their number is legion, their condition beyond description.

In the presence of this story the tales of the deeds of the White Caps in Indiana, and of the Hatfield-McCoy feud in the wilds of the Big Sandy dwindle into insignificance.

The Lone Grave

The Baldknobber J.A. Matthews' grave is located in a secluded area of the forest east of Chadwick. Beside him are two of his young children. Matthews and two other men were the last to be hung on the square in Ozark, Missouri for the murders committed in the story "Last Of The Baldknobbers."

After the three men were hung, John Matthews' wife took him home for burial in the back of a wagon and team. The trip may have taken two days.

The stone of John Matthews reads:

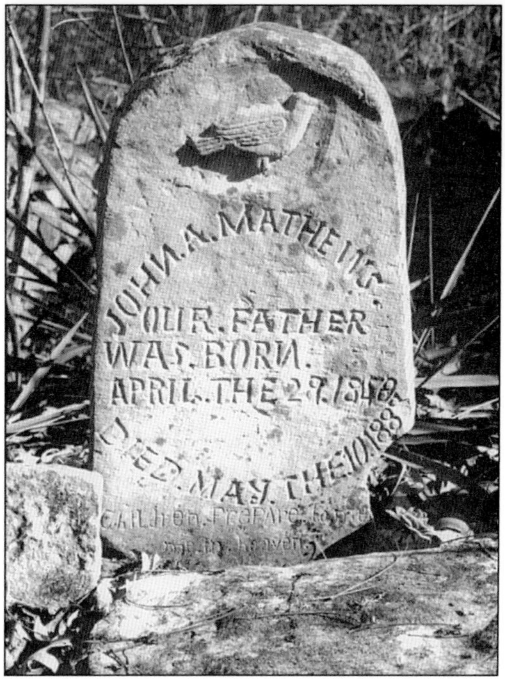

JOHN A. MATTHEWS
OUR FATHER WAS BORN
APRIL THE 29,1848
DIED MAY THE 10, 1888

Inscribed at the bottom of the stone:

CHILDREN PREPARE TO MEET ME IN HEAVEN.

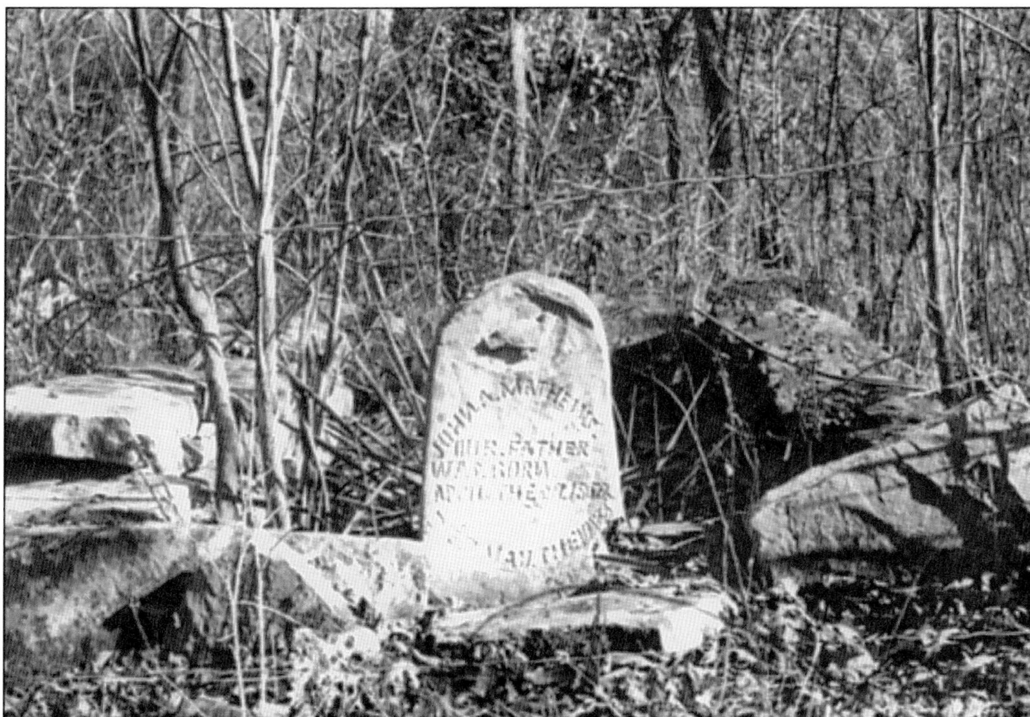

Conclusion

As *Fallen Leaves, Volume I* ends, the continuation of its legacy will be in Volume II which will be available to the public in the future, "Lord willin'." There is overwhelming amount of history to be revealed which deals with many members of long time Taney County residents. Such old family names as Haworth, Cobb, Breedon, Bedford, Pruitt, Pickett, McClary, Edwards, and more history of the Laytons, Whortons, Rittenhouses, and Brittains.

It would be difficult to list individually the names of those people from which information and photographs for this book were obtained. But I wish to thank the many relatives and friends who so graciously took the time to share their stories with me so they could be recorded and preserved for generations to come. Especially my grandparents Randa and Ethel Layton, who are no longer here, but who are the two people who encouraged me to be a writer

Vickie Layton Cobb

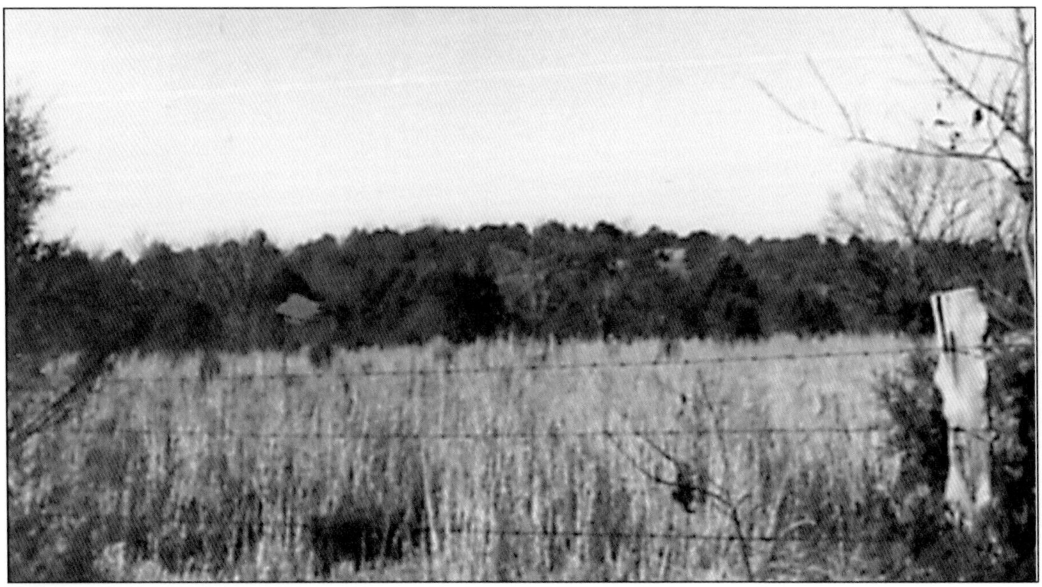

The small hill above the barbed wire fence and beyond the field is the Bald Knob were the Bald Knobbers held their first secret meeting.

Fallen Leaves

Fallen leaves gently fall
from all of God's trees.
Their beauty and splendor disappear
but not even death can claim their memory.

Their lives resemble the passing of a quiet,
peaceful, flowing country stream
Their spirits vanish into a hidden realm
the living know only in their dreams.

Although their earthly life has ended
another is born to take its place.
And that new life too, has its own
tears to cry and trials to face.

The ever changing cycle of life
is a deep spiritual mystery.
Every leaf that falleth from the tree of life
falls into the unknown hand of eternity

Vickie Layton Cobb

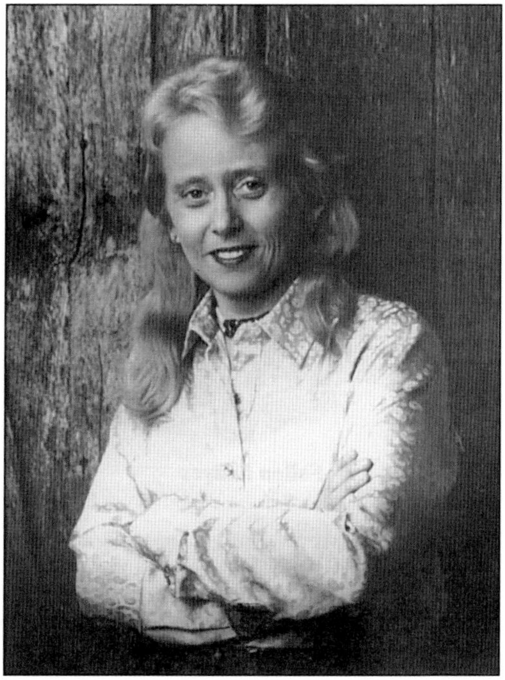

Vickie Layton Cobb.

BIBLIOGRAPHY

The American Heritage Picture History Of The Civil War. The American Heritage Publishing Company, Inc., 1960. pg. 532.

Castleman, Harvey N., *The Bald Knobbers*. Haldeman-Julius Publications: Girard, Kansas, 1944.

Chance, Emerald. "Last Of The Bald Knobbers," *Ozark Guide Yearbook*,"1966. Editor Publisher: Gerald H. Pipes, Reeds Spring, Mo., page 78–81.

————., "New York Sun Tells Story Of Bald Knobbers," page 81.

The Civil War Almanac. Bison Books Corp., 1982. pg 57, 58, 88, 120, 357, 359–360, 395.

Edom, Cliff and Vi. "Brittains, Early Settlers In Kirbyville," *Twice Told Tales And An Ozark Photo Album*, Kelly Press Inc.: Columbia, MO, 1983. pg. 165.

Freeland, W. E. "Home Paper Means," *Taney County Republican*, Thursday, April 30, 1981, Section A, page 3.

Hartman, Viola. "The Layton's," (three segments), Published in *Branson Beacon And Leader*, October 1976.

Mahnkey, Douglas. "Death of Nat Kinney," *Taney County Republican*, November 10, 1977.

Old Time Songs and Poems, "Lay Flowers Lovingly," Tower Press Inc., Spring 1974, 1971. pg. 18.

————, "Welcome Brave Soldiers, Welcome." pg. 18.

Pipes, Gerald H. " Alf Bolen, The Meanest Ozarker Of 'Em All, " Reprinted in *Ozarks Guide Yearbook*," 1966.

————"Ozark Bald Knobbers," from "Fabulous Barefoot Horizons," *Ozark Guide Yearbook*, 1966. Reeds Spring, Mo., page 13, 76-77.

Upton, Lucille Morris. "The Bald Knobbers," *Vows That Were Secret*, Chapter 4, pgs. 50-51, Original @ Caxton Printers LTD 1939, Assignment Upton 1950.

Wills, Lena. Published in *The Springfield Sunday News And Leader*, "Your Family Tree,"*Ozark Genealogy*, April 1971.